GEORGE ADAM SMITH'S
WORKS ON THE PROPHETS

JEREMIAH
BEING THE BAIRD LECTURE FOR 1922

JEREMIAH

BEING THE BAIRD LECTURE FOR 1922

BY

GEORGE ADAM SMITH

Kt., D.D., LL.D., Litt.D., F.B.A.

Principal of the University of Aberdeen

FOURTH EDITION, REVISED AND ENLARGED

HARPER & BROTHERS Publishers

NEW YORK AND LONDON

to

THE UNION

OF

THE SCOTTISH CHURCHES

PREFACE TO THE FOURTH EDITION

PREFACE TO THE FOURTH EDITION, REVISED AND ENLARGED.

BECAUSE the First Edition of this volume was published so recently as 1923 it has not required such full revision or so many changes as did my four volumes on the Books of Isaiah and of the Twelve Prophets which first appeared so far back as 1888-1898. I have, however, carefully reviewed my translations of Jeremiah's metrical oracles, slightly improving their form, I have added a Bibliography, pp. xiii-xv, and, because of the remarkable increase between 1923 and 1928 of works of research into the text and meaning of the Book of Jeremiah, I have given as a supplement to this volume a large number of Additional Notes, pp. 385-400.

In view of those and of some earlier works, I have once more considered the conclusions which I reached in 1923 on two prominent questions. But notwithstanding what Douglas, Wilke and others have ably argued to the contrary, I remain convinced of the soundness of the opinion of most critics from Eichhorn to Skinner that it is the Scythians whom Jeremiah, in the lyrics in Chapters IV-VI, describes or anticipates as *the Foe from the North,* and that any features in his description of this Foe which are unsuitable to the Scythians are due to the additions which, it is recorded, were made to his earlier oracles when he dictated these to Baruch in 604 B.C., and *the Foe from the North* ordained by God to punish His people was clearly seen by him to be the Chaldeans instead of the Scythians.   Again, with all deference to Volz, Welch and others, I do not think that the Babylonian tablet discovered by Gadd in the British Museum obliges us to substitute 612 for 608 as the year of King Josiah's death, as I have explained on p. 383, though 612 is as possible as 608.   Some changes in my opinions, due to Volz and others, are also stated in the Additional Notes.

GEORGE ADAM SMITH.

CHANONRY LODGE,
    OLD ABERDEEN,
        28th April, 1929.

FROM THE PREFACE TO THE
FIRST EDITION

THE purpose and the scope of this volume are set forth in the beginning of Lecture I. Lecture II. explains the various metrical forms in which I understand Jeremiah to have delivered the most of his prophecies, and which I have endeavoured, however imperfectly, to reproduce in English. Here it is necessary only to emphasise the variety of these forms, the irregularities which are found in them, and the occasional passage of the Prophet from verse to prose and from prose to verse, after the manner of some other bards or rhapsodists of his race. The reader will keep in mind that what appear as metrical irregularities on the printed page would not be felt to be so when sung or chanted ; just as is the case with the folk-songs of Palestine to-day. I am well aware that metres so primitive and by our canons so irregular have been more rhythmically rendered by the stately prose of our English Versions ; yet it is our duty reverently to seek for the original forms and melodies of what we believe to be the Oracles of God. The only other point connected with the metrical translations offered, which need be mentioned here, is that I have rendered the name of the God of Israel as it is by the Greek and our own Versions—The Lord —which is more suitable to English verse than is either Yahweh or Jehovah.

The text of the Lectures and the footnotes show how much I owe to those who have already written on Jeremiah, as also in what details I differ from one or another of them.

I have very much expanded and added to what were only six Lectures of an hour each when delivered under the auspices of the Baird Trust in Glasgow in 1922.

GEORGE ADAM SMITH.

CHANONRY LODGE,
OLD ABERDEEN,
18th October, 1923.

CONTENTS.

BIBLIOGRAPHY.

In addition to the earlier commentaries of Eichhorn, Hitzig, Ewald, Graf and Keil and the general Introductions to the O.T. by Driver, Cornill, McFadyen, G. B. Gray and Sellin, the following volumes and articles on the Book of Jeremiah may be noted:—

T. K. Cheyne—Jeremiah, his Life and Times, Men of the Bible Series. 1888.

G. C. Workman—The Text of Jeremiah. 1889.

C. J. Ball and W. H. Bennett—The Book of Jeremiah in the Expositor's Bible. 1890 and 1895.

A. W. Streane—The Double Text of Jeremiah. 1896.

A. B. Davidson—Jeremiah, Hasting's Dict. of the Bible. 1899.

N. Schmidt—Jeremiah, and Jeremiah (Book), Enc. Bibl. 1901.

B. Duhm—Das Buch Jeremia erklärt, Kurzer Hand-Commentar z. A.T. 1901.

C. H. Cornill—Die metrischen Stücke des Buches Jeremia reconstruiert, 1901; Das Buch Jeremia, 1905; Die literarhistorische Methode u. Jeremia, Z.A.T.W., 1907.

W. Erbt—Jeremia u. seine Zeit. 1902.

G. Douglas—The Book of Jeremiah. 1903.

Rose E. Selfe—The Work of the Prophets, ch. VII. 1904.

A. Ramsay—Studies in Jeremiah. 1905.

C. von Orelli—Der Prophet Jeremia, Kurzgefasster Kommentar. 3rd ed. 1905.

O. Kieser—Das Jeremiabuch im Lichte der neuesten Kritik, Theol. Stud. u. Krit. 1905.

G. Jacoby—Komposition d. Buches Jer. in the same for 1906.

S. R. Driver—The Book of the Prophet Jeremiah, a Revised Translation with Introduction, etc. 1906.

E. A. Edghill—An Enquiry into the Evidential Value of Prophecy. 1906.

W. E. Addis—Hebrew Religion to the Establishment of Judaism under Ezra. 1906.

E. Bruston—Le Prophète Jérémie et son Temps, 1906; Jérémie fut-il Prophète pour les Nations? Z.A.T.W. 1907.

F. Giesebrecht—Das Buch Jeremia in Nowack's Hand-Kommentar z. A.T., 2nd ed. 1907.

J. R. Gillies—Jeremiah, the Man and his Message. 1907.

A. S. Peake—Jeremiah and Lamentations, The Century Bible, 2 vols. 1910, 1911.

F. H. Woods and F. E. Powell—The Hebrew Prophets for English Readers, vol. ii. 1910.

A. Westphal—The Law and the Prophets, trans. by C. Du Pontet, pp. 307 ff., Jeremiah and the Reforms of Josiah. 1910.

E. Rayroux—Jérémie, L'époque, Le livre, L'homme, Le prophète. 1911. Not seen.

E. Klamroth—Die Jüdischen Exulanten in Babylonien, Beiträge z. Wissenschaft vom A.T., Heft. 10. 1912.

F. Wilke—Das Skythenproblem in Jeremiabuch, Beiträge z. Wissenschaft des A.T., Heft 13. 1913.

A. F. Puukko—Jeremias Stellung zum Deuteronomium, Ibid. 1913.

A. W. Streane—The Book of Jeremiah, Cambridge Bible, new ed. 1913.

J. M. Powis Smith—The Prophet and His Problems. 1914.

P. Riessler—Der Prophet Jeremias. 1914. Not seen.

A. C. Knudson—The Beacon Lights of Prophecy, ch. X., Jeremiah the Prophet of Personal Piety. 1914.

A. R. Gordon—The Prophets of the Old Testament. 1916.

W. Baumgartner—Die Klagegedichte des Jeremia, Beiheft 32, Z.A.T.W. 1917.

J. E. McFadyen—Jeremiah in Modern Speech, 1919; The Approach to the O.T., pp. 26 f., 229. 1926.

L. Elliott Binns—The Book of the Prophet Jeremiah, The Westminster Commentaries. 1919.

T. H. Robinson—Structure of the Book of Jeremiah, Exp., 1920; Prophecy and the Prophets in Ancient Israel, with Bibliography by A. S. Peake, 1923 (not seen) ; Baruch's Roll, Z.A.T.W. 1924.

P. Volz—Studien z. Text des Jeremia, Beiträge z. Wissenschaft des A.T., 1920; Der Prophet Jeremia, Kommentar z. A.T., ed. by Sellin, 1922.

K. Budde—Ueber das erste Kapitel des Buches Jeremia, J.B.L., Vol. xl. 1921.

H. Schmidt—Das Datum der Ereignisse von Jer. 27 und 28, Z.A.T.W. 1921.

F. C. Burkitt—The Code Found in the Temple, J.B.L., xl. 1921.

H. A. Kent—The Forgiveness of Sins in the O.T., Exp. xxi. 1921.

A. C. Welch—Call and Commission of Jeremiah, Jeremiah and the Essence of Religion, Jeremiah and Religious Reform, Exp. xxi, 1921 ; Jeremiah's Temple Address, Exp. xxii, 1921 ; When was the Worship of Israel Centralised at the Temple? The Death of Josiah, Z.A.T.W. 1925.

W. R. Thomson—The Burden of the Lord.

J. Skinner—Prophecy and Religion, Studies in the Life of Jeremiah. 1922.

J. W. Rothstein—Das Buch Jeremia in Kautzsch's Die Heilige Schrift des A.T. 4th ed. 1922.

F. Horst—Die Anfänge des Propheten Jeremia, Z.A.T.W., 94 ff. 1923.

H. Schmidt—Die Grossen Propheten, Die Schriften des A.T. in Auswahl. 2nd ed. 1923. Not seen.

D. Houston—The Achievement of Israel, a Study in Revelation applied to Life, ch. X., Jeremiah the Individualist. 1923.

G. Ricciotti—Il Libro di Geremia. 1923. Not seen.

E. Nestle—Das Buch Jeremia, griechisch u. hebräisch. 1924.

J. Moffatt—The Old Testament, A New Translation. No date.

W. F. Lofthouse—Jeremiah and the New Covenant, Student Christian Movement. 1925.

H. Wheeler Robinson—The Cross of Jeremiah, Student Christian Movement. 1925.

H. Gressmann—Neue Hilfsmittel z. Verständniss Jeremias, Z.A.T.W. 1925.

W. J. Farley—The Progress of Prophecy in its Historical Development. 1925. Not seen.

A. P. Kelso—The Religious Consciousness of Jeremiah, A.J.S.L., xli. 1925.

H. H. Rowley—The Text and Interpretation of Jer. xi. 18–xxi. 6. A.J.S.L., xlii. 1926.

H. Elvet Lewis—The Book of the Prophet Jeremiah. No date.

L. Gautier—Etudes sur la Religion d'Israel, 104-129, Apropos des Récabites, and 214-246, Le Prophète Jérémie. 1927. But these two papers were first delivered in 1900 and 1914 respectively.

B. M. Pickering—Jeremiah, pp. 486-514 of A New Commentary on Holy Scripture, ed. by Gore, Goudge and Guillaume. 1928.

A. C. Welch—Jeremiah, His Time and His Work. 1928.

P. Volz—Der Prophet Jeremia, Kommentar z. A.T., ed. by Sellin. 2nd ed. 1928.

ABBREVIATIONS.

A.J.S.L.   =American Journal of Semitic Languages and
                   Literature.
A.T.   =Alte Testament.
Enc. Bibl.   =Encyclopædia Biblica.
Exp.   =Expositor.
Hasting's D. B.=Hasting's Dictionary of the Bible.
Hist. Geog. or H.G.H.L.=Historical Geography of the Holy
                   Land.
J.B.L.   =Journal of Biblical Literature.
K.A.T.³   =Die Keilinschriften und das A.T. 3rd ed.
LXX.   =The Septuagint or Greek Version of the O.T.
S.B.O.T.   =Haupt's Sacred Books of the Old Testament
                   (Polychrome Bible).
Syr.   =Syriac Version of the O.T.
Targ.   =Targum.
Vulg.   =Vulgate.
Z.A.T.W.   =Zeitschrift für Alttestamentliche Wissenschaft.

PRELIMINARY.

First of all, I thank the Baird Trustees for their graceful appointment to this Lecture of a member of what is still, though please God not for long, another Church than their own. I am very grateful for the privilege which they grant me of returning to Glasgow with the accomplishment of a work the materials for which were largely gathered during the years of my professorship in the city. The value of the opportunity is enhanced by all that has since befallen our nation and the world. The Great War invested the experience of the Prophet, who is the subject of this Lecture, with a fresh and poignant relevance to our own problems and duties. Like ourselves, Jeremiah lived through the clash not only of empires but of opposite ethical ideals, through the struggles and panics of small peoples, through long and terrible fighting, famine, and slaughter of the youth of the nations, with all the anxieties to faith and the problems of Providence, which such things naturally raise. Passionate for peace, he was called to proclaim the inevitableness of war, in opposition to the popular prophets of a

I

false peace; but later he had to counsel his people to submit to their foes and to accept their captivity, thus facing the hardest conflict a man can who loves his own—between patriotism and common sense, between his people's gallant efforts for freedom and the stern facts of the world, between national traditions and pieties on the one side and on the other what he believed to be the Will of God.   These are issues which the successive generations of our race are called almost ceaselessly to face; and the teaching and example of the great Prophet, who dealt with them through such strenuous debates both with his fellow-men and with his God, and who brought out of these debates spiritual results of such significance for the individual and for the nation, cannot be without value for ourselves.

LECTURE I.

THE MAN AND THE BOOK.

IN this and the following lectures I attempt an account and estimate of the Prophet Jeremiah, of his life and teaching, and of the Book which contains them—but especially of the man himself, his personality and his tempers (there were more than one), his religious experience and its achievements, with the various high styles of their expression; as well as his influence on the subsequent religion of his people.

It has often been asserted that in Jeremiah's ministry more than in any other of the Old Covenant the personality of the Prophet was under God the dominant factor, and one has even said that 'his predecessors were the originators of great truths, which he transmuted into spiritual life.'[1] To avoid exaggeration here, we must keep in mind how large a part personality played in their teaching also, and from how deep in their lives their messages sprang. Even Amos was no mere *voice crying in the wilderness*. The discipline of the desert, the clear eye for ordinary facts and

[1] A. B. Davidson.

(3)

the sharp ear for sudden alarms which it breeds,
along with the desert shepherd's horror of the
extravagance and cruelties of civilisation — all
these reveal to us the Man behind the Book, who
had lived his truth before he uttered it.   Hosea,
again, tells the story of his outraged love as
the beginning of the Word of the Lord by him.   And
it was the strength of Isaiah's character, which,
unaided by other human factors, carried Judah,
with the faith she enshrined, through the first
great crisis of her history.   Yet recognise, as we
justly may, the personalities of these prophets in
the nerve, the colour, the accent, and even the
substance of their messages, we must feel the
still greater significance of Jeremiah's temperament and other personal qualities both for his
own teaching and for the teaching of those who
came after him.   Thanks to his loyal scribe,
Baruch, we know more of the circumstances of
his career, and thanks to his own frankness, we
know more of his psychology than we do in the
case of any of his predecessors.   He has, too,
poured out his soul to us by the most personal
of all channels ; the charm, passion and poignancy
of his verse lifting him high among the poets of
Israel.

So far as our materials enable us to judge no
other prophet was more introspective or concerned about himself ; and though it might be
said that he carried this concern to a fault, yet

fault or none, the fact is that no prophet started so deeply from himself as Jeremiah did. His circumstances flung him in upon his feelings and convictions ; he was constantly searching, doubting, confessing, and pleading for, himself. He asserted more strenuously than any except Job his individuality as against God, and he stood in more lonely opposition to his people.

√Jeremiah was called to prophesy about the time that the religion of Israel was re-codified in Deuteronomy—the finest system of national religion which the world has seen, but only and exclusively national — and he was still comparatively young when that system collapsed for the time and the religion itself seemed about to perish with it. ‹ He lived to see the Law fail, the Nation dispersed, and the National Altar shattered; but he gathered their fire into his bosom and carried it not only unquenched but with a purer flame towards its everlasting future. We may say without exaggeration that what was henceforth finest in the religion of Israel had, however ancient its sources, been recast in the furnace of his spirit. With him the human unit in religion which had hitherto been mainly the nation was on the way to become the individual. Personal piety in later Israel largely grew out of his spiritual struggles.[1]

[1] A. B. Davidson. 'Without Jeremiah,' says Wellhausen, 'the Psalms could not have been composed.'

His forerunners, it is true, had insisted that religion was an affair not of national institutions nor of outward observance, but of the people's heart—by which heart they and their hearers must have understood the individual hearts composing it. But, in urging upon his generation repentance, faith and conversion to God, Jeremiah's language is more thorough and personal than that used by any previous prophet. The individual, as he leaves Jeremiah's hands, is more clearly the direct object of the Divine Interest and Grace, and the instrument of the Divine Will. The single soul is searched, defined and charged as never before in Israel.

But this sculpture of the individual out of the mass of the nation, this articulation of his immediate relation to God apart from Law, Temple and Race, achieved as it was by Jeremiah only through intense mental and physical agonies, opened to him the problem of the sufferings of the righteous. In his experience the individual realised his Self only to find that Self—its rights, the truths given it and its best service for God— baffled by the stupidity and injustice of those for whom it laboured and agonised. The mists of pain and failure bewildered the Prophet and to the last his work seemed in vain. Whether or not he himself was conscious of the solution of the problem, others reached it through him. There are grounds for believing that the Figure of the Suffering Servant of the Lord, raised by the Great Prophet of the Exile, and the idea of the atoning and redemptive value of His sufferings were, in part at least, the results of meditation upon the spiritual loneliness on the one side, and upon the passionate identification of himself with the sorrows of his sinful people on the other, of this the likest to Christ of all the prophets.[1]

For our knowledge of this great life—there was none greater under the Old Covenant—we are dependent on that Book of our Scriptures, the Hebrew text of which bears the simple title ' Jeremiah.'

The influence of the life and therefore the full stature of the man who lived it, stretches, as I have hinted, to the latest bounds of Hebrew history, and many writings and deeds were worshipfully assigned to him. Thus the Greek Version of the Old Testament ascribes Lamentations to Jeremiah, but the poems themselves do not claim to be, and obviously are not, from himself. He is twice quoted in II. Chronicles and once in Ezra, but these quotations may be reasonably interpreted as referring to prophecies contained in our book, which were therefore

[1] Cp. e.g. Jer. xi. 19, with Is. liii. 7 ; and see Grotius, 'An notata ad Vetus Testamentum,' on Is. lii-liii; Cornill, 'Das Buch Jeremia erklärt,' pp. 11-12 ; John Skinner, 'Prophecy and Religion,' p. 351.

extant before the date of the Chronicler.[1] Ecclesi-
asticus XLIX. 6-7 reflects passages of our Book,
and of Lamentations, as though equally Jeremiah's, and Daniel IX. 2 refers to Jeremiah XXV.
12. A paragraph in the Second Book of Maccabees, Ch. II. 1-8, contains, besides echoes of
our Book of Jeremiah, references to other activities
of the Prophet of which the sources and the value
are unknown to us. But all these references, as
well as the series of apocryphal and apocalyptic
works to which the name either of Jeremiah himself or of Baruch, his scribe, has been attached,[2]
only reveal the length of the shadow which the
Prophet's figure cast down the ages, and con-

----

[1] II. Chron. xxxvi. 21 (with a reference to Lev. xxvi. 34, 35)
and 22, 23, the latter repeated in Ezra i. 1-2. Duhm, indeed,
but on insufficient grounds, thinks the former citation, because
of its reference to Leviticus, cannot be from our Book of Jeremiah but is from a Midrash unknown to us ; yet the chronicler's
was the very spirit to associate a Levitical provision with Jer.
xxix. 10 ; cp. xxv. 9-12. The other quotation Duhm refers to
some part of Is. xl. ff. (xliv. 28 ?) as though this had at one time
been attributed to Jeremiah.

[2] In the Apocrypha proper, (1) 'Baruch' to which is attached
(2) 'The Epistle of Jeremy' warning the Jews of Babylon in
general and conventional terms against idolatry. Apocalyptic
writings, (3) 'Apocalypse of Baruch,' (4) (5) and (6) three other
'Apocalypses of Baruch,' (7) 'The Rest of the Words of
Baruch,' or 'Paralipomena Jeremiæ,' (8) 'Prophecy of Jeremiah.' For particulars of these see 'Encyclopædia Biblica,'
arts. 'Apocalyptic Literature' (R. H. Charles), and 'Apocrypha
(M. R. James).

tribute no verifiable facts to our knowledge of his career or of his spiritual experience.

For the actual life of Jeremiah, for the man as he was to himself and his contemporaries, for his origin, character, temper, struggles, growth and modes of expression, we have practically no materials beyond the Canonical Book to which his name is prefixed.[1]

Roughly classified the contents of the Book (after the extended title in Ch. I. 1-3) are as follows :—

1. A Prologue, Ch. I. 4-19, in which the Prophet tells the story of his call and describes the range of his mission as including both his own people and foreign nations. The year of his call was 627-6 B.C.

2. A large number of Oracles, dialogues between the Prophet and the Deity and symbolic actions by the Prophet issuing in Oracles, mostly introduced as by Jeremiah himself, but sometimes reported of him by another. Most of the Oracles are in verse ; the style of the rest is not distinguishable by us from prose. They deal almost

---

[1] Following Hitzig, C. J. Ball ('The Prophecies of Jeremiah' in 'The Expositor's Bible,' 1890, pp. 10 ff.) refers Pss. xxiii, xxvi-xxviii to Jeremiah, and it is possible that in particular the personal experiences in Ps. xxvii are reflections of those of the prophet. But such experiences were so common in the history of the prophets and saints of Israel as to render the reference precarious.

exclusively with the Prophet's own people though there are some references to neighbouring tribes. The bulk of this class of the contents is found within Chs. II-XXV, which contain all the earlier oracles, i.e. those uttered by Jeremiah before the death of King Josiah in 608, but also several of his prophecies under Jehoiakim and even Ṣedekiah. More of the latter are found within Chs. XXVII-XXXV: all these, except XXVIII and part of XXXII, which are introduced by the Prophet himself, are reported by another.

3. A separate group of Oracles on Foreign Nations, Chs. XLVI-LI, reported to us as Jeremiah's.

4. A number of narratives of episodes in the Prophet's life from 608 onwards under Jehoiakim and Ṣedekiah to the end in Egypt, soon after 586; apparently by a contemporary and eyewitness who on good grounds is generally taken to be Baruch the Scribe: Chs. XXVI, XXXVI-XLV; but to the same source may be due much of Chs. XXVII-XXXV (see under 2).

5. Obvious expansions and additions throughout all the foregoing; and a historical appendix in Ch. LII, mainly an excerpt from II. Kings XXIV-XXV.

On the face of it, then, the Book is a compilation from several sources; and perhaps we ought to translate the opening clause of its title not as in our versions 'The Words of Jeremiah,' but

'The History of Jeremiah,' as has been legiti-
mately done by some scholars since Kimchi

What were the nuclei of this compilation?
How did they originate? What proofs do they
give of their value as historical documents? How
did they come together? And what changes, if
any, did they suffer before the compilation closed
and the Book received its present form?

These questions must be answered, so far as
possible, before we can give an account of the
Prophet's life or an estimate of himself and his
teaching. The rest of this lecture is an attempt
to answer them—but in the opposite order to that
in which I have just stated them. We shall work
backward from the two ultimate forms in which
the Book has come down to us. For these forms
are two.

Besides the Hebrew text, from which the
Authorised and Revised English Versions have
been made, we possess a form of the Book in
Greek, which is part of the Greek Version of the
Old Testament known as the Septuagint. This
is virtually another edition of the same work.
The Hebrew text belongs to the Second or
Prophetical Canon of the Jewish Scriptures, which
was not closed till about 200 B.C., or more than
350 years after Jeremiah's death. The Greek
Version was completed about the same time, and
possibly earlier.

These two editions of the Book hold by far the

greatest part of their contents in common, yet
they differ considerably in the amount and in
the arrangement of their contents, and somewhat
less in the dates and personal references which
they apply to various passages. We have thus
before us two largely independent witnesses who
agree in the bulk of their testimony, and otherwise
correct and supplement each other.

In size the Greek Book of Jeremiah is but
seven-eighths of the Hebrew,[1] but conversely it
contains some hundred words that the Hebrew
lacks. Part of this small Greek surplus is due to
the translators' expansion or paraphrase of briefer
Hebrew originals, or consists of glosses that
they found in the Hebrew MSS. from which they
translated, or added of themselves; the rest is
made up of what are probably original phrases
but omitted from the Hebrew by the carelessness
of copyists; yet none of these differences is of
importance save where the Greek corrects an
irregularity in the Hebrew metre, or yields sense
when the Hebrew fails to dc so.[2]

More instructive is the greater number of
phrases and passages found in the Hebrew Book,
and consequently in óur English Versions, but absent from the Greek. Some, it is true, are merely

---

[1] It has been calculated that the Greek has 2700 words fewer
than the Hebrew, i.e. about 120 verses or from four to five
average chapters.

[2] E.g. ii. 19, 29 ; iii. 1 ; v. 4a ; viii. 16, 21 ; xxxii. 12, etc.

formal—additions to a personal name of the title *king* or *prophet* or of the names of a father and grandfather, or the more frequent use of the divine title *of Hosts* with the personal Name of the Deity or of the phrase *Rede of the Lord*.[1] Also the Greek omits words which in the Hebrew are obviously mistakes of a copyist.[2] Again, a number of what are transparent glosses or marginal notes on the Hebrew text are lacking in the Greek, because the translator of the latter did not find them on the Hebrew manuscript from which he translated.[3] Some titles to sections of the Book, or portions of titles, absent from the Greek but found in our Hebrew text, are also later editorial additions.[4] Greater importance, however, attaches to those phrases that cannot be mere glosses and to the longer passages, wanting in the Greek but found in the Hebrew, many of which upon internal evidence must be regarded as late intrusions into the latter.[5] And occasionally a word or phrase

[1] *nĕʾum Yahweh: utterance* or *oracle of Yahweh.*

[2] E.g. the words *at his mouth*, xxxvi. 17 ; xxxviii. 16.

[3] E.g. *Jerusalem* in viii. 5, and in xxxvi. 22 *the ninth month.*

[4] E.g. ii. 1-2 ; xxv. 1*b* ; xxvii. 1 ; xlvii. 1 ; l. 1.

[5] E.g. viii. 10*aβ*-12 ; x. 6-8 ; xi. 7, 8 ; xvii. 1-4 (perhaps omitted by the Greek, because partly given already in xv. 13, 14) ; xxv. 18 *and a curse as at this day;* xxvii. 1, 7, 12*b*, 13, 14*a*, 17, 18*b*, clauses in 19, 20, the whole of 21, and 22*b* ; xxix. 14, 16-20 ; xxx. 10, 11 (=xlvi. 27 f.), 15*a*, 22 ; xxxiii. 14-26 ; xxxix. 4-13 ; xlvi. 26 ; xlvii. 1 (except *to the Philistines*) ; xlviii. 45-47 ; lii, 28-30.

in the Hebrew, which spoils the rhythm or is
irrelevant to the sense, is not found in the
Greek.[1]

Finally, there is one great difference of arrangement. The group of Oracles on Foreign
Nations which appear in the Hebrew as Chs.
XLVI-LI are in the Greek placed between verses
13 and 15[2] of Ch. XXV, and are ranged in a
different order—an obvious proof that at one
time different editors felt free to deal with the
arrangement of the compilation as well as to add
to its contents.[3]

[1] E.g. i. 10, 17, 18 ; ii. 17, 19 ; vii. 28*b* ; xii. 3 ; xiv. 4, etc.
[2] Verse 14 is not found in the Greek.
[3] In his Schweich Lectures on 'The Septuagint and Jewish
Worship' (for the British Academy, 1921) Mr. St. John
Thackeray presents clear evidence from the different vocabu-
laries in the Greek Version that this Version was the work of
two translators, the division between whom is at Ch. xxix.
verse 7. The dividing line cuts across the Greek arrangement
of the chapters, which sets the Oracles on Foreign Nations in
the centre of the Book. This shows that it was not the translators who placed them there, but that the translators found the
arrangement in the Hebrew MS. from which they translated.
Further, he thinks that the division of the Book into two parts
was not made by the translators, but already existed in their
Hebrew exemplar. For this the Hebrew text gives two evidences: (1) the titles of the Oracles, (2) the colophons appended to two of them. The titles are some long, some short.
In the Hebrew order the Oracles with long titles are mixed up
with those with short, but in the Greek order the six with long
titles come together first and are followed by the five with short.
There are two colophons—one to the Moab Oracle, the other to

Modern critics differ as to the comparative value of these two editions of the Book of Jeremiah, and there are strong advocates on either side.[1] But the prevailing opinion, and, to my view, the right one, is that no general judgment is possible, and that each case of difference between the two witnesses must be decided by itself.[2] With this, however, we have nothing at present to do. What concerns us now is the fact that the Greek is not the translation of the canonical Hebrew text, but that the two Books,

the Babylon Oracle ; but the Moab Oracle stands last in the Greek order and the Babylon Oracle last in the Hebrew order.

From all this two conclusions are drawn : (1) when the titles were inserted the chapters were arranged as in the Greek, which, therefore, was the original arrangement ; (2) they afford Hebrew evidence for a break or interruption in the middle of the Oracles—the longer titles cease about the end of Part I of the Greek Version, which therefore follows a division of the Book into two parts that already existed in the Hebrew original from which it was made. The Hebrew editor who amplified the titles had apparently only Part I before him.

[1] E.g. Graf ('Der Prophet J. erklärt,' 1862), George Douglas ('The Book of Jeremiah,' 1903) for the Hebrew ; and Workman ('The Text of Jeremiah,' 1888) for the Greek. For a judicial comparison of the two editions, resulting much in favour of the Greek, see W. R. Smith, 'The O.T. in the Jewish Church,' Lectures IV and V.

[2] 'The Hebrew is qualitatively superior to the Greek, but quantitatively the Greek is nearer the original. This judgment is general, admitting many exceptions, and each passage has to be considered by itself.'—A. B. Davidson. Cp. Duhm, 'Das Buch Jer.,' p. xxii.

while sharing a common basis of wide extent,
represent two different lines of compilation and
editorial development which continued till at least
200 B.C.   Between them they are the proof that,
while our Bible was still being compiled, some
measure of historical criticism and of editorial
activity was at work on the material—and this
not only along one line.   We need not stop to
discuss how far the fact justifies the exercise of
criticism by the modern Church.   For our present
purpose it is enough to keep in mind that our
Book of Jeremiah is the result of a long development through some centuries and on more than
one line, though the two divergent movements
started with, and carried down, a large body of
material in common.

Moreover, this common material bears evidence of having already undergone similar treatment, *before* it passed out on those two lines
of further development which resulted in the
canonical Hebrew text and the Greek Version
respectively.   The signs of gradual compilation
are everywhere upon the material which they
share in common.   Now and then a chronological
order appears, and indeed there are traces of a
purpose to pursue that order throughout.   But
this has been disturbed by cross-arrangements
according to subject,[1] and by the intrusion of

[1] Oracles on the King, xxii. 1-xxiii. 8 and on the Prophets,
xxiii. 9-40.

later oracles and episodes among earlier ones[1] or *vice versa*[2] as if their materials had come into the hands of the compilers or editors of the Book only gradually.   Another proof of the gradual growth of those contents, which are common to the Hebrew and the Greek, is the fashion in which they tend to run away from the titles prefixed to them. Take the title to the whole Book,[3] Ch. I. 2, *Which was the Word of the Lord to Jeremiah in the days of Josiah, son of Amon, King of Judah, in the thirteenth year of his reign.*   This covers only the narrative of the Prophet's call in Ch. I, or at most a few of the Oracles in the following chapters.   The supplementary title in verse 3—*It came also in the days of Jehoiakim, the son of Josiah, King of Judah, up to [the end of]*[4] *the eleventh year of Ṣedekiah, the son of Josiah, King of Judah, up to the exile of Jerusalem, in the fifth month*—is probably a later addition, added when the later Oracles of Jeremiah were attached to some collection of those which he had delivered under Josiah; but even then the title fails to cover those words in the Book which

---

[1] The Oracles under Jehoiakim, chs. vii-x, before those on the enforcement of Deuteronomy under Josiah xi. 6-8.

[2] The Oracle for Baruch, dated in the fourth year of Jehoiakim, 604 B.C., is not given till ch. xlv, a long way off from ch. xxxvi to which it belongs by date and subject, and only after chs. xl-xliv, the story of Jeremiah's life after the fall of Jerusalem.

[3] So far as it is common to the Hebrew and the Greek.

[4] *The end of* is wanting in the Greek.

2

Jeremiah spake after Jerusalem had gone into exile, and even after he had been hurried down into Egypt by a base remnant of his people.[1] Moreover, the historical appendix to the Book carries the history it contains on to 561 B.C. at least.[2] Again there are passages, the subjects of which are irrelevant to their context, and which break the clear connection of the parts of the context between which they have intruded.[3] The shorter sentences, that also disturb the connection as they stand, appear to have been written originally as marginal notes which a later editor or copyist has incorporated in the text.[4] To this class, too, may belong those brief passages which appear twice, once in their natural connection in some later chapter and once out of their natural connection in some earlier chapter.[5] And again in VII. 1-28 and XXVI. 1-9 we have two accounts, apparently from different hands, of what may or may not be the same episode in Jeremiah's ministry.

[1] Chs. xl-xliv. And between them the title and its supplement ignore the Oracles which Jeremiah uttered under Josiah after the thirteenth year of the King, perhaps iii. 6-18, and certainly xi. 1-5, 6-8.

[2] Ch. lii.

[3] E.g. iii. 6-18 ; ix. 23-26 with x. 1-16 ; xxi. 11-12 with (probably) 13-14.

[4] E.g. ii. 26 ; v. 13 ; x. 11, the last written in Aramaic.

[5] Cp. xxiii. 7, 8 with xvi. 14, 15, and xxx. 23, 24 with xxiii. 19, 20.

These data clearly prove that not only from the time when the Hebrew and Greek editions of the Book started upon their separate lines of development, but from the very beginnings of the Book's history, the work of accumulation, arrangement and re-arrangement, with other editorial processes, had been busy upon it.

The next question is, have we any criteria by which to discriminate between the elements in the Book that belong either to Jeremiah himself or to his contemporaries and others that are due to editors or compilers between his death soon after 586 and the close of the Prophetic Canon in 200 B.C. ? The answer is that we have such criteria. All Oracles or Narratives in the Book, which (apart from obvious intrusions) imply that the Exile is well advanced or that the Return from Exile has already happened, or which reflect the circumstances of the later Exile and subsequent periods or the spirit of Israel and the teaching of her prophets and scribes in those periods, we may rule out of the material on which we can rely for our knowledge of Jeremiah's life and his teaching. Of such Exilic and post-Exilic contents there is a considerable, but not a preponderant, amount. These various items break into their context, their style and substance are not conformable to the style and substance of the Oracles, which (as we shall see) are reasonably attributed to Jeremiah, but they

so closely resemble those of other writings from
the eve of the Return from Exile or from after
the Return that they seem to be based on the
latter.   In any case they reflect the situation and
feelings of Israel in Babylonia about 540 B.C.
Some find place in our Book among the earlier
Oracles of Jeremiah,[1] others in his later,[2] but the
most in the group of Oracles on Foreign Nations.[3]
And, finally, there are the long extracts from the
Second Book of Kings, bringing, as I have said,
the history down to at least 561.[4]

All these, then, we lay aside, so far as our search
for Jeremiah himself and his doctrine is concerned,

---

[1] x. 1-16; xvii. 19-27 (on the Sabbath—unlike Jeremiah,
who did not lay stress on single laws but very like post-exilic
teaching, e.g. Neh. xiii and Is. lviii), possibly xxiii. 1-8 ; xxv.
12-14 (the obviously late *as at this day* in verse 18 and verse 26*b*
are omitt d by the Greek).

[2] Parts of xxx and xxxi, especially xxxi. 7-14, the spirit of
which is so much that of the Eve of the Return from Exile and
the style so akin to that of the Great Prophet of that Eve that
some take it as dependent on his prophecies.

[3] xlvi-li, especially on Moab, xlviii. 40-47, which is based
on the earlier prophecy, Is. xv-xvi ; on Edom, xlix. 7-22,
based on Obadiah ; Elam, xlix. 34-39 ; and the long prophecy
on Babylon, l. 1-58, which reflects like Is. xl. ff. the historical situation just before the Medes overthrew Babylon, and
expresses an attitude towards the latter very different from Jeremiah's own fifty years earlier.   The compiler, or an editor of
the Book, has (li. 60) erred in attributing this long prophecy to
Jeremiah.   In all these there may be genuine nuclei.

[4] Ch. lii.

and we do so the more easily that they are largely devoid of the style and the spiritual value of his undoubted Oracles and Discourses. They are more or less diffuse and vagrant, while his are concise and to the point. They do not reveal, as his do, a man fresh from agonising debates with God upon the poverty of his qualifications for the mission to which God calls him, or upon the contents of that mission, or upon his own sufferings and rights; nor do they recount his adventures with his contemporaries. They are not the outpourings of a single soul but rather the expression of the feelings of a generation or of the doctrines of a school. We have in our Bible other and better utterances of the truths, questions, threats and hopes which they contain.

But once more—in what remains of the Book, what belongs to Jeremiah himself or to his time, we have again proofs of compilation from more sources than one. Some of this is in verse— among the finest in the Old Testament—some in prose orations; some in simple narrative. Some Oracles are introduced by the Prophet himself, and he utters them in the first person, some are reported of him by others. And any chronological or topical order lasts only through groups of prophecies or narratives. Fortunately, however, included among these are more than one account of how the writing of them and the collection of them came about.

In 604-603 B.C., twenty-one, or it may have been twenty-three, years after Jeremiah had begun to prophesy, the history of Western Asia rose to a crisis. Pharoah Necoh who had marched north to the Euphrates was defeated in a battle for empire by Nebuchadrezzar, son of the King of Babylon. From the turmoil of nations which filled the period Babylon emerged as that executioner of the Divine judgments on the world, whom Jeremiah since 627 or 625 had been describing generally as *out of the North*. His predictions were justified, and he was able to put a sharper edge on them. Henceforth in place of the *enemy from the North* Jeremiah could speak definitely of the *King of Babylon* and of his people *the Chaldeans*.

In Ch. XXV we read accordingly that in that year, 604-3, he delivered to the people of Jerusalem a summary of his previous oracles. He told them that the cup of the Lord's wrath was given into his hand; Judah and other nations, especially Egypt, must drink it and so stagger to their doom.

But a spoken and a summary discourse was not enough. Like Amos and Isaiah, Jeremiah was moved to commit his previous Oracles to writing. In Ch. XXXVI is a narrative presumably by an eyewitness of the transactions it recounts, and this most probably the scribe who was associated with the Prophet in these transactions. Jeremiah was commanded to *take a roll of a book and write on it all the words which* the Lord *had spoken to him concerning Jerusalem*[1] *and Judah and all the nations from the day* the Lord first *spake to him, in the days of Josiah, even unto this day.* For this purpose he employed Baruch, the son of Neriah, afterwards designated the Scribe, and Baruch wrote on the Roll to his dictation. Being unable himself to enter the Temple he charged Baruch to go there and to read the Roll on a fast-day *in the ears of all the people of Judah who have come in from their cities.* Baruch found his opportunity in the following December, and read the Roll from the New Gate of the Temple to the multitude. This was reported to some of the princes in the Palace below, who sent for Baruch and had him read the Roll over to them. Divided between alarm at its contents and their duty to the king, they sent Jeremiah and Baruch into hiding while they made report to Jehoiakim. The king had the Roll read out once more to himself as he sat in his room in front of a lighted brasier, for it was winter. The reading incensed him, and as the reader finished each three or four columns he cut them up and threw them on the fire till the whole was consumed. But Jeremiah, in safe hiding with Baruch, took another Roll and dictated again the contents of the first; *and there were added besides unto them many like words.*

[1] So Greek, Hebrew has *Israel.*

The story has been questioned, but by very few, and on no grounds that are perceptible to common sense. One critic imagines that it ascribes miraculous power to the Prophet in 'its natural impression that the Prophet reproduces from memory and dictates all the words which the Lord has spoken to him.'[1] There is no trace of miracle in the story. It is a straight tale of credible transactions, very natural (as we have seen) at the crisis which the Prophet had reached. No improbability infects it, no reflection of a later time, no idealising as by a writer at a distance from the events he recounts. On the contrary it gives a number of details which only a contemporary could have supplied. Nor can we forget the power and accuracy of an Oriental's memory, especially at periods when writing was not a common practice.

There is, of course, more room for difference of opinion as to the contents of each of the successive Rolls, and as to how much of these contents is included in our Book of Jeremiah. But to such questions the most probable answer is as follows.

There cannot have been many of the Prophet's previous Oracles on the first Roll. This was read three times over in the same day and was probably limited to such Oracles as were sufficient for its

---

[1] N. Schmidt in the 'Encyclopædia Biblica.'

practical purpose of moving the people of Judah
to repentance at a Fast, when their hearts would
be most inclined that way.　But when the first
Roll was destroyed, the immediate occasion for
which it was written was past, and the second Roll
would naturally have a wider aim.　It repeated
the first, but in view of the additions to it seems
to have been dictated with the purpose of giving
a permanent form to *all* the fruits of Jeremiah's
previous ministry.　The battle of Carchemish had
confirmed his predictions and put edge upon
them.　The destruction of the Jewish people was
imminent and the Prophet's own life in danger.
His enforced retirement along with Baruch lent
him freedom to make a larger selection, if not the
full tale, of his previous prophecies.　Hence the
phrase *there were added many words like* those on
the first Roll.[1]

If such a Roll as the second existed in the care
of Baruch then the use of it in the compilation of
our Book of Jeremiah is extremely probable, and
the probability is confirmed by some features of the
Book.　Among the Oracles which can be assigned

[1] Professor Schmidt, in the article already quoted, takes this
to mean only that Jeremiah 'retouched under fresh provocation'
the contents of the first Roll.　This interpretation would imply
that *words* means nouns, verbs, adjectives and so forth, whereas
words can only carry the same sense as it carries in the rest of
the Book, viz. *whole* Oracles or Discourses.　Note the phrase
words like them, viz. like *the words* or Oracles on the first Roll.

to Jeremiah's activity before the fourth year of Jehoiakim there is on the whole more fidelity to chronological order than in those which were delivered later, and while the former are nearly all given without narrative attached to them, and are reported as from Jeremiah himself in the first person, the latter for the most part are embedded in narratives, in which he appears in the third person.[1]

Further let us note that if some of the Oracles in the earlier part of the Book—after the account of the Prophet's call—are undated, while the dates of others are stated vaguely ; and again, if some, including the story of the call, appear to be tinged with reflections from experiences of the Prophet later than the early years of his career, then these two features support the belief that the Oracles were first reduced to writing at a distance from their composition and first delivery—a belief in harmony with the theory of their inclusion and preservation in the Prophet's *second* Roll.

Let us now turn to the biographical portions of the Book. We have proved the trustworthiness of Ch. XXXVI as the narrative of an eyewitness, in all probability Baruch the Scribe, who for the first time is introduced to us. But if Baruch wrote Ch. XXXVI it is certain that a great deal more of the biographical matter in the Book is from

[1] Cp. A. B. Davidson, ' Jeremiah,' in Hastings, ' D. B.,' ii. 522.

his hand. This is couched in the same style; it contains likewise details which a later writer could hardly have invented, and it is equally free from those efforts to idealise events and personalities, by which later writers betray their distance from the subjects of which they treat. It is true that, as an objector remarks, 'the Book does not contain a single line that claims to be written by Baruch.'[1] But this is evidence rather for, than against, Baruch's authorship. Most of the biographical portions of the Old Testament are anonymous. It was later ages that fixed names to Books as they have fixed Baruch's own to certain apocryphal works. Moreover, the suppression of his name by this scribe is in harmony with the modest manner in which he appears throughout, as though he had taken to heart Jeremiah's words to him : *Seekest thou great things for thyself? Seek them not. Only thy life will I give thee for a prey in all places whither thou goest.*[2] But there is still more conclusive evidence. That Baruch had not been associated with Jeremiah before 603-4 is a fair inference from the fact that the Prophet had to dictate to him all his previous Oracles. Now it is striking that up to that year and the introduction of Baruch as Jeremiah's scribe, we have few narratives of the Prophet's experience and activity —being left in ignorance as to the greater part of his life under Josiah—and that these few narratives

---

[1] Schmidt, *op. cit.*   [2] xlv. 5.

—of his call, of his share in the propagation of Deuteronomy, of the plot of the men of Anathoth against him, of his symbolic action with his waist-cloth, and of his visit to the house of the Potter— are (except in the formal titles to some of them) told in the first person by Jeremiah himself,[1] while from 604-3 onwards the biographical narratives are much more numerous and, except in three of them,[2] the Prophet appears only in the third person. This coincidence of the first appearance of Baruch as the Prophet's associate with the start of a numerous series of narratives of the Prophet's life in which he appears in the third person can hardly be accidental.

Such, then, are the data which the Book of Jeremiah offers for the task of determining the origins and authenticity of its very diverse contents. After our survey of them, those of you who are ignorant of the course of recent criticism will not be surprised to learn that virtual agreement now exists on certain main lines, while great differences of opinion continue as to details— differences perhaps irreconcilable. It is agreed that the book is the result of a long and a slow growth, stretching far beyond Jeremiah's time,

[1] Chs. i., xi., 1-8, 18-xii. 6; xiii. 1-17; xviii. 1-12.
[2] Chs. xxiv, xxviii, xxxii (except for the introductory verses 1-5).

out of various sources; and that these sources are in the main three :—

A. Collections of genuine Oracles and Discourses of Jeremiah—partly made by himself.

B. Narratives of his life and times by a contemporary writer or writers, the principal, if not the only, contributor to which is (in the opinion of most) the Scribe Baruch.

C. Exilic and Post-Exilic additions in various forms: long prophecies and narratives; shorter pieces included among the Prophet's own Oracles; and scattered titles, dates, notes and glosses.

Moreover, there is also general agreement as to which of these classes a very considerable number of the sections of the Book belong to. There is not, and cannot be, any doubt about the bulk of those which are apparently exilic or post-exilic. It is equally certain that a large number of the Oracles are Jeremiah's own, and that the most of the Narratives are from his time and trustworthy. But questions have been raised and are still receiving opposite answers as to whether or not some of the Oracles and Narratives have had their original matter coloured or expanded by later hands; or have even in whole been foisted upon the Prophet or his contemporary biographer from legendary sources.

Of these questions some, however they be answered, so little affect our estimates of the Prophet and his teaching that we may leave them alone. But there are at least four of them on the answers to which does depend the accurate measure of the stature of Jeremiah as a man and a prophet, of the extent and variety of his gifts and interests, of the simplicity or complexity of his temperament, and of his growth, and of his teaching through his long ministry of over forty years.

These four questions are

(1) The authenticity of the account of his call in Ch. I.

(2) The authenticity of the account of his support of the promulgation of Deuteronomy, the Old Covenant, in Ch. XI.

(3) The authenticity of his Oracle on the New Covenant in Ch. XXXI.

(4) And an even larger question—Whether indeed any of the prose Oracles attributed to him in the Book are his, or whether we must confine ourselves to the passages in verse as alone his genuine deliverances?

The first three of these questions we may leave for discussion to their proper places in our survey of his ministry. The fourth is even more fundamental to our judgment both of the Book and of the Man; and I shall deal with it in the introduction to the next lecture on 'The Poet Jeremiah.'

LECTURE II.

THE POET.

FROM last lecture I left over to this the discussion of a literary question, the answer to which is fundamental to our understanding both of the Book and of the Man, but especially of the Man.

The Book of Jeremiah has come to us with all its contents laid down as prose, with no metrical nor musical punctuation; not divided into *stichoi* or poetical lines nor marked off into stanzas or strophes. Yet many passages read as metrically, and are as musical in sound, and in spirit as poetic as the Psalms, the Canticles, or the Lamentations. Their language bears the marks that usually distinguish verse from prose in Hebrew as in other literatures. It beats out with a more or less regular proportion of stresses or heavy accents. It diverts into an order of words different from the order normal in prose. Sometimes it is elliptic, sometimes it contains particles unnecessary to the meaning—both signs of an attempt at metre. Though almost constantly unrhymed, it carries alliteration and assonance to a degree beyond what is usual in prose, and prefers forms of words more

sonorous than the ordinary.   But these many and
distinct passages of poetry issue from and run into
contexts of prose unmistakable.   For two reasons
we are not always able to trace the exact border
between the prose and the verse—*first* because of
the frequent uncertainties of the text, and *second*
because the prose, like most of that of the prophets,
has often a rhythm approximating to metre.   And
thus it happens that, while on the one hand much
agreement has been reached as to what Oracles
in the Book are in verse, and what, however
rhythmical, are in prose, some passages remain,
on the original literary form of which a variety
of opinion is possible.   This is not all in dispute.
Even the admitted poems are variously scanned—
that is either read in different metres or, if in the
same metre, either with or without irregularities.
Such differences of literary judgment are due
partly to our still imperfect knowledge of the laws
of Hebrew metre and partly to the variety of
possible readings of the text.   Nor is even that
all.   The claim has been made not only to confine
Jeremiah's genuine Oracles to the metrical portions
of the Book, but, by drastic emendations of the
text, to reduce them to one single, exact, unvary-
ing metre.

These questions and claims—all-important as
they are for the definition of the range and character of the prophet's activity—we can decide only
after a preliminary consideration of the few clear

and admitted principles of Hebrew poetry, of their consequences, and of analogies to them in other literatures.

In Hebrew poetry there are some principles about which no doubt exists. *First*, its dominant feature is Parallelism, Parallelism of meaning, which, though found in all human song, is carried through this poetry with a constancy unmatched in any other save the Babylonian. The lines of a couplet or a triplet of Hebrew verse may be Synonymous, that is identical in meaning, or Supplementary and Progressive, or Antithetic. But at least their meanings respond or correspond to each other in a way, for which no better name has been found than that given it by Bishop Lowth more than a century and a half ago, 'Parallelismus Membrorum.'[1] *Second*, this rhythm of meaning is wedded to a rhythm of sound which is achieved by the observance of a varying proportion between stressed or heavily accented syllables and unstressed. That is clear even though we are unable to discriminate the proportion in every case or even to tell whether there were fixed rules for it; the vowel-system of our Hebrew text being possibly different from what prevailed in ancient Hebrew. But on the whole it is probable that as in other primitive poetries[2] there were no exact or rigorous

[1] 'De Sacra Pœsi Hebræorum,' 1753.

[2] Writing of the early German lyric, Dr. John Lees says in his volume on 'The German Lyric' (London, Dent & Sons, 1914)·

3

rules as to the proportion of beats or stresses in
the single lines. For the rhythm of sense is the
main thing—the ruling factor—and though the
effort to express this in equal or regularly pro-
portioned lines is always perceptible, yet in the
more primitive forms of the poetry just as in some
English folk-songs and ballads the effort did not
constantly succeed. The art of the poet was not
always equal to the strength of his passion or the
length of his vision, or the urgency of his meaning. The meaning was the main thing and had
to be beat out, even though to effect this was to
make the lines irregular. As I have said in my
Schweich Lectures : 'If the Hebrew poet be so
constantly bent on a rhythm of sense this must
inevitably modify his rhythms of sound. If his
first aim be to produce lines each more or less
complete in meaning, but so as to run parallel to
its fellow, it follows that these lines cannot be
always exactly regular in length or measure of
time. If the governing principle of the poetry
requires each line to be a clause or sentence in
itself, the lines will frequently tend, of course

'In regard to the length of the lines, their number, and the
arrangement of the rhymes, the poet has absolute freedom in all
three classes ;' and again of the Volkslied 'theie is no mechanical counting of syllables ; the variation in the number of accented and unaccented syllables is the secret of the verse.'
And he quotes from Herder on the Volkslieder : 'songs of the
people . . . songs which often do not scan and are badly
rhymed.'

within limits, to have more or fewer stresses than
are normal throughout the poem.'

But there are other explanations of the metrical
irregularities in the traditional text of Hebrew
poems, which make it probable that these irregularities are often original and not always (as they
sometimes are) the blunders of copyists. In all
forms of Eastern art we trace the influence of what
we may call Symmetriphobia, an aversion to
absolute symmetry which expresses itself in more
or less arbitrary disturbances of the style or
pattern of the work. The visitor to the East
knows how this influence operates in weaving and
architecture. But its opportunities are more frequent, and may be used more gracefully, in the
art of poetry. For instance, in many an Old
Testament poem in which a single form of metre
prevails there is introduced at intervals, and especially at the end of a strophe, a longer and
heavier line, similar to what the Germans call the
' Schwellvers' in their primitive ballads. And
this metrical irregularity is generally to the profit
both of the music and of the meaning.

Further, the fact that poems, such as we now
deal with, were not composed in writing, but
were sung or chanted is another proof of the
possibility that the irregularities in their metre
are original. In the songs of the peasants of
Palestine at the present day the lines vary as
much as from two to five accents, and within the

same metrical form from three to four; lines with
three accents as written will, when sung to music,
be stressed with four, or with four as written will
be stressed with five in order to suit the melody.[1]

Nor are such irregularities confined to Eastern
or primitive poetry. In the later blank verse of
Shakespeare, broken lines and redundant syllables
are numerous, but under his hand they become
things of beauty, and 'the irregularity is the
foundation of the larger and nobler rule.' To
quote the historian of English prosody—'These
are quite deliberate indulgences in excess or defect,
over or under a regular norm, which is so pervad-
ing and so thoroughly marked that it carries
them off on its wings.'[2] Heine in his unrhymed
'Nordseebilder,' has many irregular lines—irregularities suitable to the variety of the subjects
of his verse.

Again, in relevance to the mixture of poetry
with prose in the prophetic parts of the Book of
Jeremiah, it is just to note that the early pre-
Islamic rhapsodists of Arabia used prose narratives to illustrate the subjects of their chants;
that many later works in Arabic literature are
medleys of prose and verse; that in particular the
prose of the 'Arabian Nights' frequently breaks
into metre; while the singing women of Mecca

[1] Dalman, 'Palästinischer Diwan.'
[2] Saintsbury, 'History of English Prosody,' vol. ii. 53, 54.

'often put metre aside and employ the easier form of rhymed prose'[1] the 'Saj'' as it is called.

If I may offer a somewhat rough illustration, the works of some Eastern poets are like canoe voyages in Canada, in which the canoe now glides down a stream and is again carried overland by what are called portages to other streams or other branches of the same stream. Similarly these works have their clear streams of poetry, but every now and again their portages of prose. I may say at once that we shall find this true also of the Book of Jeremiah.

All these phenomena, both of Eastern and of Western poetry, justify us in regarding with scepticism recent attempts whether to eliminate— by purely arbitrary omissions and additions, not founded on the evidence of the Manuscripts and Versions—the irregularities in the metrical portions of the Book of Jeremiah, or to confine the Prophet's genuine Oracles to these metrical portions, and to deny that he ever passed from metre into rhythmical prose. And our scepticism becomes stronger when we observe to what different results these attempts have led, especially in the particular form or forms of metre employed.

Professor Duhm, for instance, confines our prophet to one invariable form, that of the Qînah or Hebrew Elegy, each stanza of which consists

[1] Snouck Hurgronje, 'Mekka,' vol. ii. 62.

of four lines of alternately *three* and *two* accents or beats; and by drastic and often quite arbitrary emendation of the text he removes from this every irregularity whether of defect or redundance in the separate lines.[1] On the other hand Cornill concludes that 'the metrical pieces in the book are written throughout in *Oktastichs*,' or eight lines a piece, but admits (and rightly) that 'in the metrical structure of the individual lines there prevails a certain freedom, due to the fact that for the prophet verse-making (*Dichten*) was not an end in itself.' While he allows, as all must, that Jeremiah frequently used the Qînah metre, he emphasises the presence of the irregular line, almost as though it were the real basis of the prophetic metre.[2] Other modern scholars, by starting from other presuppositions or by employing various degrees of the textual evidence of the Versions, have reached results different from those of Duhm and Cornill.[3] But at the same time it is remarkable how much agreement prevails as to

[1] 'Kurzer Hand-Commentar,' 1901; and 'Das Buch Jeremia,' a translation, 1903.

[2] 'Das Buch Jeremia,' 1905, p. xlvi.

[3] E.g. Sievers, 'Metrische Studien,' in the 'Transactions of Saxon Society of the Sciences,' vol. xxi (which relies too much on the Massoretic or Canonical text); Erbt, 'Jeremia u. seine Zeit,' p. 298; Giesebrecht, 'Jeremia's Metrik,' iii. ff.; Karl Budde's relevant pages in his 'Geschichte der althebräischen Litteratur,' 1906, reached me after I had expressed the views I have given above. They agree in the main with these views.

the frequent presence of the Qînah measure or its near equivalent.

To sum up : in view of the argument adduced from the obvious principles of Hebrew verse and of the primitive poetic practice of other nations —not to speak of Shakespeare and some modern poets—I am persuaded after close study of the text that, though Jeremiah takes most readily to the specific Qînah metre, it is a gross and pedantic error to suppose that he confined himself to this, or that when it appears in our Book it is always to be read in the same exact form without irregularities. The conclusion is reasonable that this rural prophet, brought up in a country village and addressing a people of peasants, used the same license with his metres that we have observed in other poetries of his own race. Nor is it credible that whatever the purpose of his message was—reminiscence, or dirge, or threat of doom or call to repent, or a didactic purpose— Jeremiah, throughout the very various conditions of his long ministry of forty years, employed but one metre and that only in its strictest form allowing of no irregularities. This, I say, is not credible.[1]

[1] Certainly the evidence of both the Hebrew text and the Versions are against it, and the sense supports the text. More than once when sharp questions or challenges are thrown out, we have very appropriately two parallel lines of *two* accents each instead of the usual Qînah couplet of *three* and *two :* e.g.

The other question, whether in addition Jeremiah ever used prose in addressing his people, may be still more confidently answered. Duhm maintains that with the exception of the letter to the Jewish exiles in Babylonia,[1] the Prophet never spoke or wrote to his people in prose, and that the Book contains no Oracles from him, beyond some sixty short poems in a uniform measure. These Duhm alleges—and this is all that he finds in them—reveal Jeremiah as a man of modest, tender, shrinking temper, 'no ruler of spirits, a delicate observer, a sincere exhorter and counsellor, a hero only in suffering and not in attack.'[2] Every passage of the Book, which presents him in any character beyond this—as an advocate for the Law or as a didactic prophet—is the dream of a later age, definitely separable from his own Oracles not more by its inconsistence with the temper displayed in these than by its prose form; for in prose, according to Duhm, Jeremiah never prophesied. On the evidence we have reviewed this also is not credible. That Jeremiah never passed from verse to prose when addressing his people is a theory at variance with the practice of other poets of his

---

ii. 14 and iii. 5. See below, pp. 46 ff. Compare the variety of metres, which Schiller employs to such good effect in his 'Song of the Bell'—a variety in beautiful harmony with that of the different aspects of life on which he touches; and see above, p. 36, on the irregularity of metre in Heine's *Nordseebilder*.

[1] Ch. xxix. [2] *Op. cit.*, p. xii.

race ; and the more unlikely in his case, who was
not only a poet but a prophet, charged with truths
heavier than could always be carried to the heart
of his nation upon a single form of folk-song. Not
one of the older prophets, upon whom at first he
leant, but used both prose and verse ; and besides
there had burst upon his young ear a new style of
prophetic prose, rhythmical and catching beyond
any hitherto publicly heard in Israel. At least
some portions of our Book of Deuteronomy were
discovered in the Temple a few years after his call,
and by order of King Josiah were being recited
throughout Judah. Is it probable that he, whose
teaching proves him to have been in sympathy
with the temper and the practical purpose of that
Book, should never have yielded to the use of its
distinctive and haunting style ?

It is true that, while the lyrics which are
undoubtedly the prophet's own are terse, concrete, poignant and graceful, the style of many—
not of all—of the prose discourses attributed
to him is copious, diffuse, and sometimes
cold. But then it is verse which is most
accurately gripped by the memory and firmly
preserved in tradition ; it is verse, too, which
best guards the original fire. Prose discourses,
whether in their first reporting or in their subsequent tradition more readily tend to dilate and
to relax their style. Nor is any style of prose
so open as the Deuteronomic to additions,

parentheses, qualifications, needless recurrence of formulas and favourite phrases, and the like.

Therefore in the selection of materials available for estimating the range and character of Jeremiah's activities as a prophet, we must not reject any prose Oracles offered by the Book as his, simply because they are in prose. This reasonable caution will be of use when we come to consider the question of the authenticity of such important passages as those which recount his call, or represent him as assisting in the promulgation of Deuteronomy, and uttering the Oracle on the New Covenant.[1]

But, while it has been necessary to reject as groundless the theory that Jeremiah was exclusively a poet of a limited temper and a single form of verse and was not the author of any of the prose attributed to him, we must keep in mind that he did pour himself forth in verse; that it was natural for a rural priest such as he, aiming at the heart of what was mainly a nation of peasants, to use the form or forms of folk-song most familiar to them[2]—in fact

[1] Chs. i, xi and xxxi.

[2] 'It is an understatement of the case to say that the folk-song has been a source of inspiration. In the very greatest lyricists we simply find the folksong in a new shape : it has become more polished and artistic, and it has been made the instrument of personal lyrical utterance.'—John Lees, M.A., D.Litt., 'The German Lyric' (London, etc., Dent & Sons, 1914)

the only literary forms with which they were familiar; and that in all probability more of the man himself comes out in the poetry than in the prose which he has left to us. By his native gifts and his earliest associations he was a poet to begin with; and therefore the form and character of his poetry, especially as revealing himself, demand our attention.

From what has been said it is clear that we must not seek too high for Jeremiah's rank as a poet. The temptation to this—which has overcome some recent writers—is due partly to a recoil from older, unjust depreciations of his prophetic style and partly to the sublimity of the truths which that mixed style frequently conveys. But those truths apart, his verse was just that of the folksongs of the peasants among whom he was reared—sometimes of an exquisite exactness of tone and delicacy of feeling, but sometimes full both of what are metrical irregularities according to modern standards, and of coarse images and similes. To reduce the metrical irregularities, by such arbitrary methods as Duhm's, may occasionally enhance the music and sharpen the edge of an Oracle yet oftener dulls the melody and weakens the emphasis.[1] The figures again

[1] And in particular sins against the fundamental principle of parallelism, e.g. in iv. 3, where even with the help of part of an obvious title to the Oracle he gets only three lines and supposes

are always simple and homely, but sometimes even ugly, as is not infrequent in the rural poetries of all peoples. Even the dung on the pastures and the tempers of breeding animals are as readily used as are the cleaner details of domestic life and of farming—the house-candle, the house-mill, the wine skins, the ornaments of women, the yoke, the plough, and so forth. And there are abrupt changes of metaphor as in our early ballads, due to the rush of a quick imagination and the crowd of concrete figures it catches.

Some of Jeremiah's verse indeed shows no irregularity. The following, for instance, which recalls as Hosea loved to do the innocence and loyalty of Israel's desert days, is in the normal Qînah rhythm of lines with alternately *three* and *two* accents each. The two first lines are rhymed, the rest not.

II. 2f. :—

> The troth of thy youth I remember,
>   Thy love as a bride,
> Thy follow of Me through the desert,
>   The land unsown.

the fourth to be lost; and though the sense-parallelism is generally within a couplet he divides it between the last line of his first couplet and the first of his second. Again, if we keep in mind what is said above (p. 35) of the recurrence in Hebrew poems of longer, heavier lines at intervals—especially at the end of a strophe or a poem, we must feel a number of Duhm's emendations to be not only unnecessary but harmful to the effectiveness of the verse.

Holy to the Lord was Israel,
  Of His income the firstling,
All that would eat it stood guilty,
  Evil came on them.

Or II. 32 :—

Can a maiden forget her adorning,
  Or her girdle the bride ?
Yet Me have My people forgotten,
  Days without number.
How fine hast thou fashioned thy ways,
  To seek after love !
Thus 't was thyself[1] to [those] evils
  Didst train[2] thy ways.
Yea on thy skirts is found blood
  Of innocent[3] souls.
Not only on felons (?) I find it,[4]
  But over all these.

Here again is a passage which, with slight
emendations and these not arbitrary, yields a fair
constancy of metre (IV. 29-31) :—

From the noise of the horse and the bowmen
  All the land is in flight,
They are into the caves, huddle in thickets,
  And are up on the crags.[5]
Every town of its folk is forsaken,
  With none to inhabit.

[1] Pointing אַתְּ for אֵת.   [2] Pointing לִמַּדְתִּי.
[3] Hebrew adds *poor*.
[4] So Duhm after the Greek ; see p 97, n. 3   [5] After the Greek

All is up! Thou destined to ruin, (?)[1]
　What doest thou now
That thou deck'st thee in deckings of gold
　And clothest in scarlet,[2]
And with stibium widenest thine eyes?
　In vain dost thou prink!
Though satyrs, they utterly loathe thee,
　Thy life are they after.
For voice as of travail I hear,
　Anguish as hers that beareth,
The voice of the Daughter of Ṣion agasp,
　She spreadeth her hands:
'Woe unto me, but it faints,
　My life to the butchers!'

On the other hand here is a metre,[3] for the irregularities of which no remedy is offered by alternative readings in the Versions, but Duhm and others reduce these only by padding the text with particles and other terms. Yet these very irregularities have reason; they suit the meaning to be expressed. Thus while some of the couplets are in the Qînah metre, it is instructive that the first three lines are *all* short, because they are mere ejaculations—that is they belong to the

---

[1] By differently arranging the Hebrew consonants, see p. 117. Other arrangements are possible. Greek omits *destined to ruin*.

[2] Hebrew and Greek have this couplet in the reverse order.

[3] ii. 14-17.

same class of happy irregularities as we recalled
in Shakespeare's blank verse.

> Israel a slave!
> Or house-born serf!
> Why he for a prey?
> Against him the young lions roar,
> Give forth their voice,
> And his land they lay waste
> Burning and tenantless.
> Is not this being done thee
> For thy leaving of Me?

Or take the broken line added to the regular
verse on Rachel's mourning, the sob upon which
the wail dies out :—

> A voice in Ramah is heard, lamentation
> And bitterest weeping,
> Rachel beweeping her children
> And will not be comforted—
> For they are not![1]

Sometimes, too, a stanza of regular metre is
preceded or followed by a passionate line of
appeal, either from Jeremiah himself or from
another—I love to think from himself, added when
his Oracles were about to be repeated to the
people in 604-3. Thus in Ch. II. 31 we find the
cry,

O generation look at the Word of the Lord!

[1] xxxi. 15.

breaking in before the following regular verse,

> Have I been a desert to Israel,
>> Or land of thick darkness?
> Why say my folk, 'We are off,
>> No more to meet Thee.'

There is another poem in which the Qînah measure prevails but with occasional lines longer than is normal—Ch. V. 1-6*a* (alternatively to end of 5 [1]).

> Run through Jerusalem's streets,
>> Look now and know,
> And search her broad places
>> If a man ye can find,
> If there be that doth justice
>> Aiming at honesty.
>> [That I may forgive her.]
> Though they say, 'As God liveth,'
>> Falsely they swear.
> Lord, are thine eyes upon lies [2]
>> And not on the truth?
> Thou hast smitten, they ail not,
>> Consumed them, they take not correction;
> Their faces set harder than rock,
>> They refuse to return.

---

[1] While Duhm and Giesebrecht reduce the text to the exact Qînah form, Erbt correctly reads it as varied by lines of four accents.

[2] After Duhm who reads לָאֵין = לְבֵן (cp. viii. 6) and transfers it to the following line.

Or take Ch. II. 5-8. A stanza of four lines in
irregular Qînah measure (verse 5) is followed by
a couplet of four-two stresses and several lines of
three each (verses 6 and 7), and then (verse 8) by
a couplet of three-two, another of four-three, and
another of three-three.[1]   In Chs. IX and X also
we shall find irregular metres.

Let us now take a passage, IX. 22, 23, which,
except for its last couplet, is of another measure
than the Qînah.   The lines have three accents
each, like those of the Book of Job :—

Boast not the wise in his wisdom,
Boast not the strong in his strength,
Boast not the rich in his riches,
But in this let him boast who would boast—
Instinct and knowledge of Me,
Me, the Lord, Who work troth
And[2] justice and right upon earth,
    For in these I delight.

Or this couplet, X. 23, in lines of four stresses
each :—

Lord, I know—not to man is his way,
Not a man's to walk or settle his steps!

Not being in the Qînah measure, both these
passages are denied to Jeremiah by Duhm.   Is
not this arbitrary ?

The sections of the Book which pass from verse
to prose and from prose to verse are frequent.

---

[1] See below, p. 92.   [2] So Greek.

One of the most striking is the narrative of the Prophet's call, Ch. I. 4-19, which I leave to be rendered in the next lecture. In Chap. VII. 28 ff. we have, to begin with, two verses :—

This is the folk that obeyed not
 The voice of the Lord,[1]
That would not accept correction ;
 Lost[2] is truth from their mouth.
Shear and scatter thy locks,
Raise a dirge on the heights,
The Lord hath refused and forsaken
The sons of His wrath.

Then these verses are followed by a prose tale of the people's sins. Is this necessarily from a later hand, as Duhm maintains, and not naturally from Jeremiah himself ?

Again Chs. VIII and IX are a medley of lyrics and prose passages. While some of the prose is certainly not Jeremiah's, being irrelevant to the lyrics and showing the colour of a later age, the rest may well be from himself.

Ch. XIV is also a medley of verse and prose. After the Dirge on the Drought (which we take later), comes a passage in rhythmical prose (verses 11-16), broken only by the metrical utterance of the false prophets in verse 13 :—

[1] So Greek ; Hebrew adds *their God.*
[2] Hebrew adds *and is cut off.*

Sword or famine ye shall not see,
They shall not be yours;
But peace and staith shall I give you
Within this Place.[1]

And verse comes in again in verses 17-18, an
Oracle of Jeremiah's own :—

Let mine eyes with tears run down,
By night and by day,
Let them not cease from weeping[2]
For great is the breach—
Broken the Virgin, Daughter of my people,
Most sore the wound!
Fare I forth to the field,
Lo, the slain of the sword;
If I enter the city,
Lo, anguish of famine.
Priest and prophet alike are gone begging
In a land they know not.
Hast Thou utterly cast away Judah,
Loathes Şion Thy soul?
Why then hast Thou smitten us,
Past our healing?
Hoped we for peace—no good,
For time to heal—and lo panic!
Lord we acknowledge our evil,
The guilt of our fathers—
To Thee have we sinned.

[1] The Hebrew *makôm* must here as elsewhere be given as
equivalent to the Arabic *makâm* (literally like the Hebrew
standing-place but) generally *sacred site*.

[2] After Duhm.

And now the measure changes to one of longer irregular lines, hardly distinguishable from rhythmical prose, which Duhm therefore takes, precariously, as from a later hand (vv. 21, 22).

For Thy Name's sake do not despise,
Demean not the Throne of Thy Glory,
Remember and break not Thy Covenant with us!
Can any of the gentile Bubbles bring rain,
Or the Heavens give the showers?
Art not Thou He [1] on whom we must wait?
 For all these Thou hast made.

Again in Ch. XV. 1-2, prose is followed by a couplet, this by more prose (verses 3, 4) and this by verse again (verses 5-9). But these parts are relevant to each other, and some of Duhm's objections to the prose seem inadequate and even trifling. For while the heavy judgment is suitably detailed by the prose, the following dirge is as naturally in verse:—

Jerusalem, who shall pity,
 Who shall bemoan thee?
Who shall but turn him to ask
 After thy welfare?

And once more, in the Oracle Ch. III. 1-6 the first verse, a quotation from the law on a divorced wife, is in prose, and no one doubts that Jeremiah himself is the quoter, while the rest, recounting

[1] Hebrew adds *the Lord our God;* not in the Greek.

Israel's unfaithfulness to her Husband is in
verse.   See below, pages 98, 99.

So much for the varied and often irregular
streams of the Prophet's verse and their interruptions and connections by "portages" of prose.
Let us turn now from the measures to the sub-
tance and tempers of the poetry.

As in all folk-song the language is simple, but
its general inevitableness—just the fit and ringing
word—stamps the verse as a true poet's.   Hence
the difficulty of translating.   So much depends
on the music of the Hebrew word chosen, so much
on the angle at which it is aimed at the ear, the
exact note which it sings through the air.   It is
seldom possible to echo these in another language ;
and therefore all versions, metrical or in prose, must
seem tame and dull beside the ring of the original.
Before taking some of the Prophet's renderings of
the more concrete aspects of life I give, as even
more difficult to render, one of his moral reflections
in verse—Ch. XVII. 5 f.   Mark the scarceness of
abstract terms, the concreteness of the figures :—

> Curséd the wight that trusteth in man
> Making flesh his stay !
> [And his heart from the Lord is turned]
> Like some desert-scrub shall he be,
> Nor see any coming of good,
> But dwell in the aridest desert,
> A salt, uninhabited land.

Blesséd the wight that trusts in the Lord,
And the Lord is his trust!
He like a tree shall be planted by waters,
That stretches its roots to the stream,
Unafraid [1] at the coming of heat,
His leaf shall be green.
Sans care in a year of drought,
He fails not in yielding his fruit.

As here, so generally, the simplicity of the poet's diction is matched by that of his metaphors, similes, and parables. A girl and her ornaments, a man and his waist-cloth—thus he figures what ought to be the clinging relations between Israel and their God. The stunted desert-shrub in contrast to the river-side oaks, the incomparable olive, the dropped sheaf and even the dung upon the fields; the vulture, stork, crane and swift; the lion, wolf and spotted leopard coming up from the desert or the jungles of Jordan; the hinnying stallions and the heifer in her heat; the black Ethiopian, already familiar in the streets of Jerusalem, the potter and his wheel, the shepherd, plowman and vinedresser, the driver with his ox's yoke upon his shoulders; the harlot by the wayside; the light in the home and sound of the hand-mill—all everyday objects of his people's sight and hearing as they herded, ploughed, sowed, reaped or went to market in the city—he brings them in simply and with natural

---

[1] So Greek and Vulg. ; Hebrew has *he shall not see.*

ease as figures of the truths he is enforcing. They are never bald or uncouth, though in translation they may sometimes sound so.

In the very bareness of his use of them there lurks an occasional irony as in the following—a passage of prose broken by a single line of verse.[1] The Deity is addressing the prophet :—

> And thou shalt say unto this people,
> ' Every jar shall be filled with wine,'

and it shall be if they say unto thee, ' Don't we know of course [2] that

> ' Every jar shall be filled with wine,'

then thou shalt say unto them : Thus saith the Lord, Lo, I am about to fill the inhabitants of this land, the kings and princes, the priests and prophets, even Judah and all the inhabitants of Jerusalem, with drunkenness [the drunkenness, that is, of horror at impending judgments] and I will dash them one against another, fathers and sons together. I will not pity, saith the Lord, not spare nor have compassion that I should not destroy them.

How one catches the irritation of the crowd on being told what seems to them such a commonplace—till it is interpreted!

---

[1] xiii. 12-14. The above rendering follows the Greek version
[2] A Hebrew idiom, literally *don't, knowing, we know ?*

Like his fellow-prophets, whose moral atmosphere was as burning as their physical summer, who living on the edge of the desert under a downright sun *drew breath* (as Isaiah puts it) *in the fear of the Lord* and saw the world in the blaze of His justice, Jeremiah brings home to the hearts of his people the truths and judgments, with which he was charged, in the hard, hot realism of their austere world. Through his verse we see the barer landscapes of Benjamin and Judah without shadow or other relief, every ugly detail exposed by the ruthless noon, and beyond them the desert hills shimmering through the heat. Drought, famine, pestilence and especially war sweep over the land and the ghastly prostrate things, human as well as animal, which their skirts leave behind are rendered with vividness, poignancy and horror of detail.

Take, to begin with, the following, XIV. 1 ff. :—

The Word of the Lord to Jeremiah Concerning the Drought.

Jerusalem's cry is gone up,
Judah is mourning,
The gates thereof faint in
Black grief to the ground.

Her nobles sent their menials for water,
They came to the pits;
Water found none and returned,

Empty their vessels.
[Abashed and confounded
They cover their heads.] [1]

The tillers [2] of the ground are dismayed,
For no rain hath been [3];
And abashed are the ploughmen,
They cover their heads.

The hind on the moor calves and abandons,
For the grass has not come.
On the bare heights stand the wild asses,
Gasping for air
With glazen eyes—
Herb there is none!

Though our sins do witness against us,
Lord act for the sake of Thy Name!
[For many have been our backslidings,
   'Fore Thee have we sinned.]

Hope of Israel, His Saviour
   In time of trouble,
Why be like a traveller [4] thorough the land,
   Or wayfaring guest of a night?
Why art Thou as one that is stunned,—
   Strong yet unable to save?

[1] This couplet is wanting in the Greek.
[2] So rightly Duhm after the Greek.
[3] Hebrew uselessly adds *in the land*.
[4] So Duhm, reading *gār* for *gēr*.

Yet Lord, Thou art in our midst,
[O'er us Thy Name hath been called]
  Do not forsake us!

Thus saith the Lord of this people :—

So fond to wander are they,
  Their feet they restrain not,
The Lord hath no pleasure in them,
  He remembers their guilt.[1]

The following dirge is on either a war or a pestilence, or on both, for they often came together. The text of the first lines is uncertain, the Hebrew and Greek differing considerably :—

Call ye the keening women to come,
  And send for the wise ones,
That they hasten and sing us a dirge,
Till with tears our eyes run down,
  Our eyelids with water.

  .   .   .   .   .   .

For death has come up by our windows,
  And into our palaces,
Cutting off from the streets the children,
  The youths from the places.
And fallen are the corpses of men
  Like dung on the field,
Or sheaves left after the reaper,
  And nobody gathers.[2]

[1] Hebrew adds, *and will make visitation on their sins*, which the Greek omits.
[2] ix. 17 f., 21 f. ; see also pp. 205, 206.

The minatory discourses are sombre and lurid. Sometimes the terror foretold is nameless and mystic, yet even then the Prophet's simplicity does not fail but rather contributes to the vague, undefined horror.   In the following it is premature night which creeps over the hills—night without shelter for the weary or refuge for the hunted.

Hear and give ear, be not proud,
   For the Lord hath spoken!
Give glory to the Lord your God
   Before it grows dark,
And before your feet stumble—
   On the mountains of dusk.

While ye look for light, He turns it to gloom
   And sets it thick darkness.[1]

There this poem leaves the Doom, but in others Jeremiah leaps in a moment from the vague and far-looming to the near and exact.   He follows a line which songs of vengeance or deliverance often take among unsophisticated peoples in touch with nature.   They will paint you a coming judgment first in the figure of a lowering cloud or bursting storm and then in the twinkling of an eye they turn the clouds or the lightnings into the ranks and flashing arms of invaders arrived.   I remember an instance of this within one verse of a negro song from the time of the American Civil War :—

[1] xiii. 15-16.

Don't you see de lightning flashing in de cane-
    brakes ?
  Don't you think we'se gwine to have a storm ?
No you is mistaken—dem's de darkies' bayonets,
  And de buttons on de uniform !

Examples of this sudden turn from the vague to
the real are found throughout Jeremiah's Oracles
of Doom. Here are some of them :—

Wind off the glow of the bare desert heights,
  Right on the Daughter of My people,
It is neither to winnow nor to cleanse,
  In full blast it meets me . . . :
Lo, like the clouds he is mounting,
  Like the whirlwind his chariots !
Swifter than vultures his horses ;
  Woe ! We are undone !

    .   .   .   .

For hark a signal from Dan,
  Mount Ephraim echoes disaster,
Warn the folk ! 'They are come !'[1]
  Make heard o'er Jerusalem.
Lo, the beleaguerers (?) come
  From a land far-off,
They let forth their voice on the townships of
  Judah.
  [Close] as the guards on her suburbs

[1] So the Greek.

They are on and around her,
    For Me she defied.[1]

There is a similar leap from the vagueness of
IV. 23-26, which here follows, to the vivid detail
of verses 29-31 already rendered on page 45.

I looked to the earth, and lo, chaos,
    To the heavens, their light was gone,
I looked to the mountains, they quivered,
    The hills were all shuddering.
I looked and behold not a man,
    All the birds of the heavens had fled.
I looked for the gardens, lo desert,
    All the townships were burning.

Or take a similar effect from the Oracle on the
Philistines, Ch. XLVII. 2, 3.

Lo, the waters are up in the North,
    The torrents are plunging,
O'erwhelming the land and her fulness,
    The city and her dwellers.
Mankind is crying and howling,
    Every man in the land,
At the noise of the stamp of the hoofs of his steeds
    At the rush of his cars,
    The rumble of his wheels.

[1] iv. 11-13, 15-17. The text and so the metre of 16, 17 are
uncertain. For *besiegers* Duhm proposes by the change of one
letter to read *panthers*, to which in v. 6 Jeremiah likens the same
foes. Skinner, *leopards*. See below, p. 114.

Fathers look not back for their children,
So helpless their hands![1]

Or take the Prophet's second vision on his call,
Ch. I. 13 ff., the boiling cauldron with its face from
the North, which is to boil out over the land;
then the concrete explanation, *I am calling to all
the kingdoms of the North, and they shall come and every
one set his throne in the gates of Jerusalem.* There
you have it—that vague trouble brewing in the
far North and then in a moment the northern
invaders settled in the gates of the City.

But the poetry of Jeremiah had other strains.
I conclude this lecture with selections which deal
with the same impending judgment, yet are wistful
and tender, the poet taking as his own the sin
and sufferings of the people with whose doom he
was charged.

The first of these passages is as devoid of hope
as any we have already seen, but like Christ's
mourning over the City breathes the regret of a
great love—a profound and tender Alas!

Jerusalem, who shall pity,
Who shall bemoan thee?
Or who will but turn him to ask
After thy welfare?

Then follow lines of doom without reprieve
and the close comes:—

[1] Lit. *Because of the feebleness of their hands.*

She that bore seven hath fainted,
> She breathes out her life.
Set is her sun in the daytime,
> Baffled and shaméd ;
And their remnant I give to the sword
> In face of their foes.[1]

In the following also the poet's heart is with
his people even while he despairs of them. The
lines, viii. 14—IX. 1, of which 17 and 19*b* are
possibly later insertions, are addressed to the
country-folk of Judah and Benjamin :—

For what sit we still ?
> Sweep together,
And into the fortified cities,
> That there we may perish !
For our God[2] hath doomed us to perish,
And given us poison to drink,
> For to Him[2] have we sinned.
Hope for peace there was once—
> But no good—
For a season of healing—
> Lo, panic.[3]
From Dan the sound has been heard,[4]
> The hinnying of his horses ;

[1] xv. 5-9.

[2] Greek ; in both cases Hebrew adds *the Lord*.

[3] This verse is uncertain ; for Hebrew בעתה read with the
Greek בהלה. For another arrangement see above, p 51.

[4] So Greek ; Hebrew omits *sound*.

With the noise of the neighing of his stallions
    All the land is aquake.
For that this grief hath no comfort,[1]
    Sickens my heart upon me.
Hark to the cry of my people
    Wide o'er the land—
' Is the Lord not in Şion,
    Is there no King there ? '[2]

Harvest is over, summer is ended
    And we are not saved !
For the breach of the Daughter of my people
    I break, I darken,
Horror hath seized upon me,
    Pangs as of her that beareth.[3]
Is there no balm in Gilead,
    Is there no healer ?
Why will the wounds never stanch
    Of the daughter of my people ?
O that my head were waters,
    Mine eyes a fountain of tears,
That day and night I might weep
    For the slain of my people !

Such in the simple melodies of his music and
in the variety of his moods—now sombre, stern
and relentless, now tender and pleading, now in
despair of his people yet identifying himself with

---

[1] This line is uncertain.   [2] Greek.
[3] So Greek ; Hebrew omits this line.

them—was this rural poet, who was called to
carry the burdens of prophecy through forty of
the most critical and disastrous years of Israel's
history.   In next lecture we shall follow the
earlier stages which his great heart pursued
beneath those burdens.

LECTURE III.

THE PROPHET—HIS YOUTH AND HIS CALL.

JEREMIAH was born soon after 650 B.C. of a priestly house at Anathoth, a village in the country of Benjamin near Jerusalem. Just before his birth Egypt and the small states of Palestine broke from allegiance to Assyria. War was imminent, and it may have been because of some hope in Israel of Divine intervention that several children born about the time received the name Yirmyahu—*Yahweh hurls* or *shoots*.[1] The boy's name and his father's, Hilkiah, *Yahweh my portion*,[2] are tokens of the family's loyalty to the God of Israel, at a time when the outburst in Jewry of a very different class of personal names betrays on the part of many a lapse from the true faith, and when the loyal remnant of the people were being persecuted by King Manasseh. Probably the family were descended from Eli. For

---

[1] (1) Jeremiah of Libnah, father of Hamutal, II. Kings xxiii. 31 ; xxiv. 18 ; (2) Jeremiah, father of Jaazaniah, the Rechabite, Jer. xxxv. 3 ; (3) Jeremiah the prophet, son of Hilkiah.

[2] Not to be confounded with the temple-priest, Hilkiah, who was concerned with the finding of the Law.

Abiathar, the last of that descent to hold office as Priest of the Ark, had an ancestral estate at Anathoth, to which he retired upon his dismissal by Solomon.[1] The child of such a home would be brought up under godly influence and in high family traditions, with which much of the national history was interwoven. It may have been from his father that Jeremiah gained that knowledge of Israel's past, of her ideal days in the desert, of her subsequent declensions, and of the rallying prophecies of the eighth century, which is manifest in his earlier Oracles. Some have claimed a literary habit for the stock of Abiathar.[2] Yet the first words of God to Jeremiah—*before I formed thee in the body I knew thee, and before thou camest forth from the womb I hallowed thee*[3]—as well as the singular originality he developed, rather turn us away from his family traditions and influence.

What is more significant, for its effects appear over all his earlier prophecies, is the country-side on which the boy was born and reared.

'Anathoth, which still keeps its ancient name 'Anata, is a little village not four miles north-north-east of Jerusalem, upon the first of the rocky shelves by which the central range of Palestine declines through desert to the valley of the Jordan. The village is hidden from the main road between Jerusalem and the North, and lies

---

[1] I. Kings ii. 26 f.   [2] Duhm, p. 3.   [3] Jer. i. 5.

on no cross-road to the East.　One of its influences
on the spirit of its greatest son was its exposure
to the East and the Desert.　The fields of
Anathoth face the sunrise and quickly merge into
the falling wilderness of Benjamin.　It is the
same open, arid landscape as that on which
several prophets were bred : Amos a few miles
farther south at Tekoa, John Baptist, and during
His Temptation our Lord Himself.　The tops of
the broken desert hills to the east are lower than
the village.　The floor of the Jordan valley is not
visible, but across its felt gulf the mountains of
Gilead form a lofty horizon.

The descending foreground with no shelter
against the hot desert winds, the village herds
straying into the wilderness, the waste and
crumbling hills shimmering in the heat, the open
heavens and far line of the Gilead highlands, the
hungry wolves from the waste and lions from the
jungles of Jordan are all reflected in Jeremiah's
poems :—

Light o' heel young camel,
　　Zig-zagging her tracks,
Heifer gone to school to the desert—
　　In the heat of her passion,
Snapping the breeze in her lust,
　　Who is to turn her ?

Wind off the glow of the bare desert heights,
　　Direct on my people,

Neither to winnow nor to sift,
In full blast it meets me.

A lion from the jungle shall smite,
A wolf from the wastes undo them,
The leopard shall prowl round their towns,
All faring forth shall be torn.

Even the stork in the heavens
Knoweth her seasons,
And dove, swift and swallow
Keep time of their coming.

Is there no balm in Gilead,
No healer there? [1]

We need not search the botany of that province
for the suggestion of this last verse. Gilead was
the highland margin of the young prophet's view,
his threshold of hope. The sun rose across it.
The tribal territory in which Anathoth lay
was Benjamin's. Even where not actually desert
the bleak and stony soil accords with the character
given to the tribe and its few historical personages.
Benjamin shall ravin as a wolf. [2] Of Benjamin were
the mad King Saul, the cursing Shimei, Jeremiah's
persecutors in Anathoth, and the other Saul who
breathed threatenings and slaughter against the
Church—while Jeremiah himself, in his moods of
despair, seems to have caught the temper of the

[1] ii. 23, 24; iv. 11; v. 6; viii. 7, 22   [2] Gen. xlix. 27.

tribe among whom his family dwelt. Whether in the land or in its sons it was hard, thorny soil that needed deep ploughing.[1] It was, too, as Isaiah had predicted, the main path of invasion from the North,[2] by Ai, Migron, Michmash, the Pass, Geba, Ramah, Gibeah of Saul, Laish, and *poor* Anathoth herself. It had been the scene of many massacres, and above all of the death of the Mother of the people, who returns to bewail their new disasters :—

> A voice in Ramah is heard, lamentation
> And bitterest weeping,
> Rachel beweeping her children,
> And will not be comforted,
> For they are not.[3]

The cold northern rains and the tears of a nation's history alike swept these bare uplands. The boy grew up with many ghosts about him— not Rachel's only but the Levite and his murdered wife, the slaughtered troops at Gibeah and Rimmon, Saul's sullen figure, Asahel stricken like a roe in the wilderness of Gibeon, and the other nameless fugitives, whom through more than one page of the earlier books we see cut down among the rocks of Benjamin.

The empty, shimmering desert and the stony land thronged with such tragedies—Jeremiah

---

[1] iv. 3.   [2] Is. x. 28-32.   [3] xxxi. 15.

was born and brought up on the edge between them.

It was a nursery not unfit for one, who might have been (as many think), the greatest poet of his people, had not something deeper and wider been opened to him, with which Anathoth was also in touch. The village is not more than an hour's walk from Jerusalem. Social conditions change little in the East; then, as now, the traffic between village and city was daily and close—country produce taken to the capital; pottery, salted fish, spices, and the better cloths brought back in exchange. We see how the history of Jerusalem may have influenced the boy. Solomon's Temple was nearly four hundred years' old. There were the city walls, some of them still older, the Palace and the Tombs of the Kings—perhaps also access to the written rolls of chroniclers and prophets. Above all, Anathoth lay within the swirl of rumour of which the capital was the centre. Jerusalem has always been a tryst of the winds. It gathers echoes from the desert far into Arabia, and news blown up and down the great roads between Egypt and Damascus and beyond to the Euphrates; or when these roads are deserted and men fear to leave their villages, news vibrating as it vibrates only in the tremulous East, from hamlet to hamlet and camp to camp across incredible spaces. As one has finely said of a rumour of invasion:—

I saw the tents of Cushán in affliction,
The curtains of Midian's land were trembling.[1]

To the north lay the more fruitful Ephraim—
more fruitful and more famous in the past than
her sister of Benjamin, but now in foreign hands,
her own people long gone into exile. It was
natural that her fate should lie heavy on the still
free but threatened homes of Benjamin, whose
northern windows looked towards her ; and that
a heart like Jeremiah's should exercise itself upon
God's meaning by such a fate and the warning it
carried for the two surviving tribes.[2] Moreover,
Shiloh lay there, Shiloh where Eli and other
priestly ancestors had served the Ark in a sanctuary now ruined.[3]

It was, too, across Ephraim with its mixed
population in touch with the court and markets
of Nineveh, that rumours of war usually reached
Benjamin and Judah :—

Hark ! They signal from Dan,
Mount Ephraim echoes disaster.[4]

After a period of peace, and as Jeremiah was
growing to manhood, such rumours began to
blow south again from the Euphrates. Some
thirteen years or so earlier, Asshurbanipal, the
Sardanapalus of the Greeks, had accomplished
the last Assyrian conquest in Palestine, 641 B.C.,

[1] Hab. iii. 7.   [2] See below on ch. iii.
[3] vii. 12-15 ; xxvi. 6.   [4] iv. 15.

and for an interval the land was quiet. But
towards 625 word came that the Medes were
threatening Nineveh, and, though they were repelled, in that year Asshurbanipal died and
Nabopolassar of Babylon threw off the Assyrian
yoke. Palestine felt the grasp of Nineveh relax.
There was a stir in the air and men began to
dream. But quick upon hope fell fear. Hordes
of a new race whom—after the Greeks—we call
Scythians, the Ashguzai of the Assyrian monuments, had half a century before swarmed over
or round the Caucasus, and since then had been
in touch, and even in some kind of alliance, with
the Assyrians. Soon after 624 they forced the
Medes to relinquish the siege of Nineveh. They
were horsemen and archers, living in the saddle,
and carrying their supplies behind them in wagons.
After (as it seems) their effective appearance at
Nineveh, they swept over the lands to the south,
as Herodotus tells us;[1] and riding by the Syrian
coast were only brought up by bribes on the
border of Egypt.[2] This must have been soon
after the young prophet's call in 627-6. In
short, the world, and especially the North, was
(to use Jeremiah's word) *boiling* with events
and possibilities of which God alone knew the
end. Prophets had been produced in Israel from

[1] i. 103-107 (after Hecatæus).
[2] See Appendix I—Medes and Scythians.

like conditions in the previous century, and now after a silence of nigh seventy years, prophets were again to appear: Zephaniah, Nahum, Habakkuk, and Jeremiah.

For these northern omens conspired with others, ethical and therefore more articulate, within Judah herself. It was two generations since Isaiah and Hezekiah had died, and with them the human possibilities of reform. For nearly fifty years Manasseh had opposed the pure religion of the prophets of the eighth century, by persecution, by the introduction of foreign and sensual cults, and especially by reviving in the name of Israel's God[1] the ancient sacrifice of children, in order to propitiate His anger. Thus it appears that the happier interests of religion—family feasts, pieties of seed-time and harvest, gratitude for light, fountains and rain, and for good fortune—were scattered among a host both of local and of foreign deities; while for the God of Israel, the God of Abraham, Moses and Isaiah, the most horrible of superstitious rites were reserved, as if all that His people could expect of Him was the abatement of a jealous and hungry wrath.

A few voices crying through the night had indeed reminded Judah of what He was and what He required. *He hath showed thee, O man,*

---

[1] 'Jerusalem,' ii. 263, 264.

what is good; and what doth the Lord require but to do justly, and love mercy, and walk humbly with thy God.[1] At last with the overthrow of Manasseh's successor, Amon, signs of a dawn appeared. The child of eight years who was heir to the throne was secured, perhaps through his mother's influence, by a party in Court and Temple that had kept loyal to the higher faith; and the people, probably weary of the fanatic extravagance of Manasseh, were content to have it so.

The young King Josiah, who to the end was to prove himself worthy of his training, and the boy in the priest's home at Anathoth were of an age: a fact not to be omitted from any estimate of the influences which moulded Jeremiah in his youth. But no trace of this appears in what he has left us; as a boy he may never have seen the King, and to the close of Josiah's reign he seems to have remained too obscure to be noticed by his monarch; yet at the last he has only good to say of Josiah:—

Did he not eat and drink,
And do judgment and justice?
The cause of the poor and the needy he judged—
Then was it well.[2]

Attempts at reform were made soon after Josiah's accession,[3] but little was achieved, and that little only in the capital and its Temple.

---

[1] Micah vi. 8. [2] xxii. 15, 16. [3] 'Jerusalem,' ii.

In the latter for four hundred years no deity of
the land had been worshipped save Yahweh, and
He in no material form. It would be easy to remove from the streets of Jerusalem any recently
introduced Baals and possibly, as Assyria's sovereignty relaxed, the worship of the Host of Heaven.
But beyond Jerusalem the task was more difficult.
Every village had the shrine of a deity before the
God of Israel came to the land. The names of
these local Baalim, or Lords, had mostly vanished,[1]
and Israel claimed the rural sanctuaries for
Yahweh. But the old rites, with the old conceptions of deity attached to them, seem to have
been transferred to Him by the ignorant wor-
shippers, till instead of one Yahweh—one Lord—
unique in character and in power, there were as
many as there had been Baalim, and they bore the
same inferior and sometimes repulsive characters.
We cannot exaggerate this division of the God-
head into countless local forms :—

> As many as thy cities in number
> So many O Judah thy gods![2]

Their high places lay all round the Prophet and
each had its bad influence, not religious only but
ethical, not only idolatrous but immoral, with
impure rites and orgies.

[1] Though not in every case, for Anathoth itself is but the
plural of the Syrian goddess Anath, as Ashtaroth is the plural of
Astart or Astarte.

[2] ii. 28 ; xi. 13.

Lift to the bare heights thine eyes,
Where not wast thou tumbled?
The land thou hast fouled with thy whoredoms,[1]

—spiritual and physical both; the one led to the other.

This dissipation of the national mind upon many deities was reflected in the nation's politics. With no faith in One Supreme God the statesmen of Judah, just as in Isaiah's earlier days, fluttered between the great powers which were bidding for the empire of the world. Egypt under Psamtik's vigorous direction pressed north, flying high promises for the restless vassals of Assyria. But Assyria, though weakened, had not become negligible. Between the two the anchorless policy of Judah helplessly drifted. To use Jeremiah's figure, suitable alike to her politics and her religion, she was a faithless wife, off from her husband to one paramour after another.

All this was chaos worse than the desert that crumbled before Anathoth, a tragedy more bitter than the past which moaned through the land behind. What had God to say? It was a singular mark of Israel, that the hope of a great prophet never died from her heart. Where earnest souls were left they prayed for his coming and looked for the Word of the Lord by him more than they who wait for the morning. The same

[1] iii. 2.

conditions prevailed out of which a century before had come an Amos, a Hosea, a Micah and an Isaiah. Israel needed judgment and the North again stirred with its possibilities. Who would rise and spell into a clear Word of God the thunder which to all ears was rumbling there?

The call came to Jeremiah and, as he tells the story, came sudden and abrupt yet charged with the full range and weight of its ultimate meaning, so far as he himself was concerned :—

Before in the body I built thee, I knew thee,
Before thou wast forth of the womb, I had
    hallowed thee,
And a prophet to the nations had set thee.[1]

A thought of God, ere time had anything to do with him, or the things of time, even father or mother, could make or could mar him; God's alone, and sent to the world; out of the eternities with the Divine will for these days of confusion and panic and for the peoples, small and great, that were struggling through them. It was a stupendous consciousness—this that then broke in the village of Anathoth and in the breast of the young son of one of its priests; the spring of it deeper and the range of it wider than even that similar assurance which centuries later filled another priest's home in the same hill country :—

[1] i. 5.

And thou, child, shalt be called the prophet of the
    Highest,
For thou shalt go before the face of the Lord,
    To prepare His ways.[1]

The questions of foreknowledge and predestination, with which Jeremiah engaged himself
not a little, I leave for a future lecture.[2] Here
we may consider the range of his mission.

This was very wide—not for Judah only, but
a prophet to the nations had I set thee. The objection
has been taken, that it is too wide to be original,
and the alternative inferences drawn : either that
it is the impression of his earliest consciousness as
a prophet but formed by Jeremiah only after years
of experience revealed all that had been involved
in his call; or that it is not Jeremiah's own but
the notion formed of him by a later exaggerating
generation. It is true that Jeremiah did not
dictate the first words of the Lord to him till some
twenty-three years after he heard them, when it
was possible and natural for him to expand them
in terms of his intervening experience. And we
must remember the summary bent of the Hebrew
mind—how natural it was to that mind to describe
processes as if they were acts of a day, done by a
fiat as in the story of the Creation; or to state a
system of law and custom, which took centuries
to develop, as though it were the edict of a single

---

[1] Luke i. 76.   [2] See Lecture vii.

lawgiver and all spoken at once, when the development entered on a new and higher stage, as we see in the case of Deuteronomy and its attribution to Moses.

Yet the forebodings at least of a task so vast as that of *prophet to the nations* were anything but impossible to the moment of Jeremiah's call; for the time surged, as we have seen, with the movements of the nations and their omens for his own people. Indeed it would have been strange if the soul of any prophet, conscious of a charge from the Almighty, had not the instinct, that as the meaning of this charge was gradually unfolded to him, it would reveal, and require from him the utterance of, Divine purposes throughout a world so full even to the uninspired eye of the possibilities both of the ruin of old states and of the rise of new ones—a world so close about his own people, and so fraught with fate for them, that in speaking of *them* he could not fail to speak of the *whole of it* also. If at that time a Jew had at all the conviction that he was called to be a prophet, it must have been with a sense of the same responsibilities, to which the older prophets had felt themselves bound : men who knew themselves to be ministers of the Lord of Hosts, Lord of the Powers of the Universe, who had dealt not with Israel only but with Moab and Ammon and Aram, with Tyre and the Philistines and Egypt, and who had spoken of Assyria herself as

His staff and the rod of His judgment. Jeremiah's three contemporaries, Ṣephaniah, Nahum and Habakkuk, all deal with the foreign powers of their day—why should he in such an age not have been conscious from the first that his call from the Lord of Hosts involved a mission as wide as theirs? I am sure that if we had lived with this prophet through his pregnant times, as we have lived through these last ten years and have been compelled to think constantly not of our own nation alone—concentrated as we had to be on our duties to her—but of *all* the nations of the world as equally involved in the vast spiritual interests at stake, we should have no difficulty in understanding how possible and natural it was for Jeremiah to hear his mission *to the nations* clearly indicated in the very moment of his call.

And in fact Jeremiah's acknowledged Oracles—some of them among his earliest—travel far beyond Judah and show not merely a knowledge of, and vivid interest in, the qualities and fortunes of other peoples, but a wise judgment of their policies and therefore of what should be Judah's prudent attitude and duty towards them. For long before his call she had been intriguing with Egypt and Assyria.[1] Just then or immediately later the Scythians, after threatening the Medes, were sweeping over Western Asia as far as the frontier

[1] ii. 18.

of Egypt, and in his Scythian songs Jeremiah[1]
shows an intimate knowledge of their habits.   In
his Parable of the Potter (for which unfortunately
there is no date) he declares God's power to
mould or re-mould *any* nation.[2]   And Baruch,
writing of Jeremiah's earlier ministry, says that
he spoke *concerning all nations.*[3]

No wonder that Jeremiah shrank from such a
task: *Ah, Lord God, I know not to speak, I am too
young.*[4]   His excuse is interesting.   Had he not
developed his gift for verse?   Or, conscious
of its rustic simplicity, did he fear to take the
prophet's thunder on lips, that had hitherto moved
only to the music of his country-side?   In the
light of his later experience the second alternative
is not impossible.   When much practice must have
made him confident of his art as a singer, he tells
us how burning he felt the Word of the Lord to
be.   But whatever was the motive of his reluctance it was overcome.   As he afterwards said :—

> Ah, Lord, Thou didst beguile me,
> And beguiled I let myself be;
> Thou wast too strong for me
> And hast prevailed.[5]

[1] See his seven Scythian songs below, pp. 110 ff.

[2] xviii.

[3] xxxvi. 2, a clause which Duhm merely on the grounds of his
theory is obliged to regard as a later intrusion, though it bears
no marks of being such.

[4] So Cornill after the Greek.   [5] xx. 7.

The following shows how this came about :—

> And the Lord said unto me, Say not I am
> too young, for to all to which I send thee
> thou shalt go, and all I command thee thou
> shalt speak,
>
> > Be not afraid before them
> > For with thee am I to deliver,
>
> Rede of the Lord. And the Lord put forth
> His hand and caused it to touch my mouth,
> and the Lord said to me, Lo, I have set My
> Word in thy mouth,
>
> > See I appoint thee this day
> > Over the nations and kingdoms,
> > To pull up and tear down and destroy,[1]
> > To build and to plant.

To this also objection has been taken as still more
incredible in the spiritual experience of so youthful a rustic. It has been deemed the exaggeration of a later age, and described as the 'gigantic
figure' of a 'plenipotentiary to the nations,'
utterly inconsistent with the modest singer of
the genuine oracles of Jeremiah, 'a hero only in
suffering, not in assault.'[2] Such an objection rather
strains the meaning of the passage. According
to this Jeremiah is to be the carrier of the Word
of the Lord. That Word, rather than the mar.

[1] Hebrew adds the redundant *to pull down;* Greek omits
[2] Duhm ; see above, p. 40.

himself, is the power *to pull up and tear down and destroy, to build and to plant*[1]—that Word which no Hebrew prophet received without an instinct of its world-wide range and its powers of both destruction and creation.

Two visions follow. To appreciate the first we must remember the natural anxiety of the prophets when charged with pronouncements so weighty and definite. The Word, the ethical purpose of God for Israel was clear, but how was it to be fulfilled? No strength appeared in the nation itself. The party, or parties, loyal to the Lord had been in power a dozen years and effected little in Jerusalem and nothing beyond. The people were not stirred and seemed hopeless. Living in a village where little changed through the years, but men followed the habits of their fathers, Jeremiah felt everything dead. Winter was on and the world asleep.

> Then the Word of the Lord came to me saying, What art thou seeing, Jeremiah? and I said, I am seeing the branch of an almond tree. And the Lord said to me, Well hast thou seen, for I am awake over My Word to perform it.

The Hebrew for almond tree is *shākēdh*, which also means *awakeness* or *watchfulness*,[2] and the

---

[1] This is clear from other passages, v. 14 ; xviii. 7-10, etc.

[2] Ball happily translates *wake-tree*.

Lord was *awake* or was *watchful—shōkēdh—*the
difference only of a vowel. In that first token of
spring which a Palestine winter affords, the Prophet received the sacrament of his call and of the
assurance that God was awake! That the sacrament took this form was natural. That of Isaiah
of Jerusalem was the vision of a Throne and an
Altar. That of Ezekiel, the exile, shone in the
stormy skies of his captivity. This to the prophet
of Anathoth burst with the first blossom on his
wintry fields. The sense of unity in which he
and his people conceived the natural and spiritual
worlds came to his help; neither in the one world
nor in the other did God slumber. God was
watching.

The Second Vision needs no comment after
our survey of the political conditions of the time.
The North held the forces for the fulfilling of the
Word. The Vision is followed by a charge to
the Prophet himself.

> And the word of the Lord came to me
> the second time, What art thou seeing?
> And I said, A caldron boiling and its face is
> from (?) the North.[1] And the Lord said unto
> me :—

---

[1] The text reads, *its face is from the face of northwards,*
which some would emend to *its face is turned northwards,* i.e.
the side on which it is blown upon and made to boil. *Boiling* or
bubbling, lit. *blown upon, fanned.*

Out of the North shall evil boil **forth**[1]
On all that dwell in the land;
For behold, I am calling
All the realms[2] of the North.

They shall come and each set his throne
In the openings of the gates of Jerusalem,
On all of her walls round about,
And every township of Judah.

And My judgments by them[3] shall I **utter**
On the evil of those who have left **Me,**
Who have burned to other gods
And bowed to the works of their **hands.**

But thou shalt gird up thy loins,
Stand up and speak[4] all I charge **thee.**
Be not dismayed before them,
Lest to their face I dismay thee.
See I have set thee this day
A fenced city and walls of bronze
To the kings and princes of Judah,
Her priests and the folk of the land;
They shall fight but master thee **never,**
For with thee am I to deliver—
Rede of the Lord.[5]

---

[1] After the Greek; Hebrew has *be opened.*
[2] Hebrew has *races and kingdoms* and adds *Rede of the Lord.*
[3] Read אֹתָם.
[4] Hebrew adds *to them;* Greek omits.
[5] The last three couplets are uncertain. In v. 18 Hebrew adds *a basalt pillar* and, after *bronze, against all the land.*

Jeremiah was silenced and went forth to his ministry—the Word upon his lips and the Lord by his side.

Two further observations are natural.

First, note the contrast between the two Visions—the blossoming twig and the boiling caldron brewing tempests from the North. Unrelated as these seem, they symbolise together Jeremiah's prophesying throughout. For in fact this was all blossom and storm, beauty and terror, tender yearning and thunders of doom—up to the very end. Or to state the same more deeply: while the caldron of the North never ceased boiling out over his world—consuming the peoples, his own among them, and finally sweeping him into exile and night—he never, for himself or for Israel, lost the clear note of his first Vision, that all was watched and controlled. There is his value to ourselves. Jeremiah was no prophet of hope, but he was the prophet of that without which hope is impossible—faith in Control—that be the times dark and confused as they may, and the world's movements ruthless, ruinous and inevitable, God yet watches and rules all to the fulfilment of His Will—though how we see not, nor can any prophet tell us.

Second, note how the story leaves the issue, not with one will only, but with two—God's and the Man's, whom God has called His family has been discounted, his people and their authorities, political and religious, are to be against him. *He* is to stand up and speak, *He* is not to let himself be dismayed before them, lest God make him dismayed. Under God, then, the Individual becomes everything. Here, at the start of his ministry, Jeremiah has pressed upon him, the separateness, the awful responsibility, the power, of the Single Soul. We shall see how the significance of this developed not for himself only, but for the whole religion of Israel.

LECTURE IV.

THE PROPHET IN THE REIGN OF JOSIAH.

627-26—608 B.C.

THIS period of the Prophet's career may be taken in three divisions :—

First, His Earliest Oracles, which reflect the lavish distribution of the high-places in Judah and Benjamin, and may therefore be dated before the suppression of these by King Josiah, in obedience to the Law-Book discovered in the Temple in 621-20 B.C.

Second, His Oracles on the Scythians, whose invasions also preceded that year ; with additions.

Third, Oracles which imply that the enforcement of the Law-Book had already begun, and reveal Jeremiah's attitude to it and to the course of the reforms which it inspired.

We must keep in mind that the Prophet did not dictate his early Oracles till the year 604-03, and that he added to them on the Second Roll *many like words*.[1] We shall thus be prepared for the appearance among them of references to the

---

[1] xxxvi. 32 ; see pp. 22 ff.

changed conditions of this later date, when the
Scythians had long come and gone, the Assyrian
Empire had collapsed, its rival Egypt had been
defeated at the Battle of Carchemish, and
Nebuchadrezzar and his Chaldeans were masters
of Western Asia.

1. His Earliest Oracles.

(II. 2—IV. 4.)

These bear few marks of the later date at which
they were dictated by Jeremiah—in fact only a
probable reference to Egypt's invasion of Palestine
in 608, Ch. II. 16, and part, if not all, of Ch. III.
6-18. The general theme is a historical retrospect
—Israel's early loyalty to her God, and her subsequent declension to the worship of other gods,
figured as adultery; along with a profession of
penitence by the people, to which God responds
by a stern call to a deeper repentance and
thorough reform; failing this, her doom, though
vaguely described as yet, is inevitable. The
nation is addressed as a whole at first in the
second person singular feminine, but soon also
in the plural, and the plural prevails towards the
end. The nation answers as a whole, sometimes
as *I* but sometimes also as *We*.

Before expounding the truths conveyed by
these early Oracles it is well to translate them in
full, for though not originally uttered at the same
time. they run now in a continuous stream of

verse—save for one of those 'portages' of prose
which I have described.[1]   There is no reason for
denying the whole of this passage to Jeremiah,
whether because it is in prose or because it treats
of Northern Israel as well as Judah.[2] But on
parts of it the colours are distinctly of a period
later than that of the Prophet.   All the rest of
the Oracles may be taken to be from himself.
Duhm after much hesitation has come to doubt
the genuineness of Ch. II. 5-13, but his suspicions
of deuteronomic influence seem groundless, and
even if they were sound they would be insufficient
for denying the verses to Jeremiah.[3]
II. 1, 2, And he said, Thus sayeth the Lord :[4]

> I remember the troth of thy youth,
>   Thy love as a bride,
> Thy following Me through the desert,
>   The land unsown.
> 3 Holy to the Lord was Israel,
>   First-fruit of His income ;
> All that would eat it stood guilty,
>   Evil came on them.
> Rede of the Lord—

---

[1] P. 37.   [2] See pp. 40 f., 72.   [3] See p. 41.

[4] So simply the Greek; the Hebrew, *And the word of the Lord
came unto me saying, Go and proclaim in the ears of Jerusalem
saying,* not only betrays an editorial redundancy, but what follows
is addressed not to Jerusalem but to all Israel.   Here if anywhere
the Greek has the original.   Jeremiah begins thus to dictate to
Baruch.

4 Hear the Lord's Word, House of Jacob.
  All clans of Israel's race!
5 [Thus sayeth the Lord]
  What wrong found your fathers in Me,
    That so far they broke from Me,
  And following after the Bubble[1]
  Bubbles became.
6 Nor said they:
  Where is the Lord who carried us up
    From the land of Miṣraim?[2]
  Who led us thorough the desert,
  Land of waste and chasms,
  Land of drought and barren,[3]
  A land which nobody crosses,
  Nor mankind settles upon it.
7 And I brought you into a garden,
    To feed on its fruit and its wealth.
  But coming ye fouled My land,
    My heritage turned to loathing.
8 The priests never said,
    Where is the Lord?
  They who handle the Law knew Me not,
    The rulers[4] rebelled against Me;
  By Baal the prophets did prophesy,
    And followed the worthless.
9 So still with you must I strive,[5]
    And strive with your sons.[6]

---

[1] Hebrew *hebel* = *breath*.   [2] Egypt .   [3] So Greek.
[4] Lit. *shepherds*.   [5] Hebrew adds *Rede of the Lord.*
[6] Some Hebrew MSS. and Vulgate.

10 For cross to the isles of Kittîm and look
   Send to Kedár, and think for yourselves,[1]
   And see, was ever like this?
11 Have any nations[2] changed their gods,
   And these no gods at all?
   Yet My people exchanged their[3] Glory
   For that which is worthless.
12 Be heavy,[4] O heavens, for this,
   Shudder and shudder again!
13 Twain the wrongs My people have wrought—
   Me have they left,
   The Fount of live water,
   To hew themselves cisterns,
   Cisterns broken,
   That cannot hold water!

14   Israel a slave!
         Or house-born serf!
         Why he for a prey?
15 Against him the young lions roar,
   Give forth their voice,
   And his land they lay waste,
   Burned are his towns and tenantless.

---

[1] Cyprus = Kittim and Kedár, an Arab tribe, are the extremes of the world then known to the Jews.

[2] So Greek.   [3] Hebrew marg. *my*.

[4] Or *heave* (Ball), lit. *be aghast* but the Hebrew is alliterative, *shommû shamaim*.

16 The sons, too, of Noph and Taḥpanḥes **have**
     forced,
   Have abused thee.[1]
17 Is not all this being done thee
     For thy leaving of Me?[2]
   And now what to thee is the road to Miṣraim,[3]
     Nile's waters to drink?
   Or what is to thee the road to Asshúr,
     To drink of the River?
19 Be thy scourge thine own sin,
     Thy doublings convict thee!
   Know and see how sore for thyself,
     How bitter to leave Me!
   But never was awe of Me thine—
     Rede of the Lord thy God.[4]

20 From of old thou hast broken **thy yoke,**
     Hast burst thy bonds,
   Saying, 'I will not serve!'
   While upon every high hill,
   And under each rustling tree,
     Harlot thou sprawlest!

[1] This couplet is after the Greek, Hebrew has *browsed on thy skull* for *forced*.   Noph = Memphis, Egypt's capital; Taḥpanḥes = Daphne on the Egyptian road to Palestine. Either 14-19 or more probably 16 alone is one of Jeremiah's additions to his earlier Oracles after Egypt's invasion of Palestine in 608.

[2] So Greek; Hebrew adds, *when he led thee by the way.*

[3] Miṣraim = Egypt.

[4] These last four lines follow the Greek

21 Yet a noble vine did I plant thee,
 Wholly true seed;
How could'st thou change to a corrupt,[1]
 A wildling grape?

22 Yea, though thou scour thee with nitre,
 And heap to thee lye,
Ingrained is thy guilt before Me,
 Rede of the Lord, thy God.[2]

23 How sayest thou, 'I'm not defiled,
 Nor gone after the Baals.'
Look at thy ways in the Valley,
 And own thy deeds!
A young camel, light o' heel,[3]
 Zig-zagging her tracks,

24 A heifer, schooled to the desert—
 In the heat of her lust,
Snapping the wind in her passion,
 Who is to turn her?
None that would seek her need strain them,
 In her month they shall find her.

25 Save thou thy feet from the peeling,
 Thy throat from thirst!
But thou sayest, 'No use![4]
For with strangers I'm fallen in love,
 Them must I after!'

[1] So Duhm by a better division of words.
[2] So the Greek.
[3] The Hebrew *kal* seems to combine here its two meanings of *swift* and *trifling*.
[4] Hebrew *no' ash;* with Greek delete the second *no.*

26 Like the shame of the thief when he's caught,
   Shall Israel's sons[1] be shamed.
   [They and their kings and their princes,
   Their priests and their prophets][2]
27 Who say to a stock 'Thou my Father!'
   To a stone 'Thou hast borne me!'
   Their[3] backs they have turned to Me
   Never their[3] faces.
   Yet in time of their trouble they say
   'Rise up and save us!'
28 Where be thy gods thou hast made thee?
   Let them rise, if so they may save thee
   In time of thy trouble;
   For as thy townships in number,[4]
   So be, O Judah, thy gods!
29 What quarrel have you against Me?
   All you are the sinners;[5]
   Against Me you all have rebelled—
   Rede of the Lord.
30 In vain have I smitten your sons
   Ye[6] took not correction
   Your[7] sword has devoured your prophets,
   Like a ravaging lion.

[1] So Greek.

[2] The insertion (by a copyist?) of this formula rather weakens the connection.

[3] So some Versions.

[4] Greek adds *and as the number of streets in Jerusalem they burn to Baal;* cp. xi. 13.

[5] So Greek.   [6] Greek.   [7] Greek *the.*

31 O generation—you!—look at the Word of the
    Lord![1]
  Have I been a desert to Israel,
    Or land of thick darkness?
  Why say My folk 'We are off,
    No more to meet Thee!'

32 Can a maiden forget her adorning,
    Or her girdle a bride?
  Yet Me have My people forgotten,
    Days without number!

33 Why trimmest thou still thy ways
    To seek after love?
  Therefore thou also to evil
    Thy ways hast trained:[2]

34 Yea, on thy skirts is found blood
    Of innocent souls,
  Not only on felons(?) I find it
    But over all these.[3]

35 Yet thou said'st, 'I am assoiled,
    Sure His wrath turns from me!'
  Behold I am going to judge thee
    For saying, 'I'm sinless!'

[1] Prose, probably a later insertion when the prophet dictated
his Oracles.   See pp. 47 f.

[2] The text of this quatrain is corrupt, the rendering above
makes use of the versions.

[3] The text of this verse too is uncertain.   For *skirts* Greek has
hands; to *innocent* Hebrew adds *needy*.   Some read the second
couplet [*though*] *thou did'st not catch them breaking in, but
because of all these*, i.e. thy sins against Me, thou did'st
murder them.

7

36 How very light dost thou take it,
   To change thy ways!
  E'en of Miṣraim shalt thou be ashamed[1]
   As ashamed of Ashshúr.
37 Out of this too shalt thou come
   With thy hands on thy head,
  For spurned hath the Lord the things of thy
      trust,
   Not by them shalt thou prosper!

III. 1 [Saying]:—
  If a man dismiss his wife and she go from him
  and become another man's, shall she return to
  him?[2] Is that woman[3] not too polluted?
  But thou hast played the harlot with many
  lovers and—wouldest return unto Me? Rede
  of the Lord.

2 Lift to the clearings thine eyes,
   Where not wast thou tumbled?
  For them by the roads thou hast sate,
   Like an Arab in desert,
  Thou hast fouled the land with thy whore-
      doms
   And with thy vices;
3 With thy lovers so many
   It has meant but thy snare.[4]
  The brow of a harlot was thine,
   Shame thou hadst done with.

---

[1] Or *balked*.   [2] Greek.   [3] Greek ; Hebrew *land*.
[4] So Duhm after the Greek.   Hebrew is impossible.

4 But now—thou callest me 'Father,
   Friend of my youth!'
5 'Bears *He* a grudge for ever,
   Stands on His guard for aye?'[1]
Lo, so thou hast spoken, yet done
Ills to thine utmost.

6 And the Lord said unto me in the days of
Josiah, the king,[2] Hast thou seen what recreant Israel did to Me[3] going up every high
hill and under each rustling tree, and there
7 playing the harlot; and I said, After she has
done all these things can she return to Me?—
and she did not return.   And her treacherous
8 sister Judah saw, yes she saw,[4] that, all because recreant Israel committed adultery, I
had dismissed her and given her the bill of
her divorce; yet her sister treacherous Judah

---

[1] The two Hebrew verbs in this couplet, *natar* and *shamar*
mean *to keep* (or *maintain*) and *to watch;* they are usually
transitive and (in the sense here intended) are followed by a
noun, *anger* or *wrath*, which English versions supply here.
But its absence from *both* the Hebrew and Greek texts leads us
to take the verbs as intransitive, as is the case with *natar* in New-
Hebrew.

[2] Verses 6-18, in prose break the connection both of style and
meaning between 5 and 19 and cannot in whole be Jeremiah's or
from his period.   This is especially true of 16-18 which assume
the destruction of the Ark and the Exile of Judah as well as
of Israel as already actual.   But the passage probably contains
genuine fragments from Jeremiah.

[3] So Greek.   [4] So one Hebrew MS. and Syriac.

was not afraid, but also went and played the
9 harlot.   And it came to pass that, through the
wantonness of her harlotry, she polluted the
land, committing adultery with stones and with
10 stocks.   And yet, for all this, treacherous
Judah[1] has not returned to Me with all her
heart, but only in feigning.[2]
11　　And the Lord said to me, Recreant Israel
hath justified herself more than treacherous
12 Judah.   Go and call out these words toward
the North and say,

Turn thee to Me,[3] recreant Israel,
　　I frown[4] not upon thee;
For gracious am I (Rede of the Lord),
　　Nor for ever bear grudge.
13 Only acknowledge thy guilt,
　　That defying the Lord thy God,
Thou hast scattered to strangers thy ways
　　Under each rustling tree,
And hast[5] not obeyed My voice—
　　Rede of the Lord.

14 [Return ye backsliding children, Rede of the
Lord, for I am your Baal,[6] and I will take
you, one from a city and two from a clan, and

[1] Hebrew adds *her sister.*
[2] Hebrew adds *Rede of the Lord.*
[3] So Greek.　　　[4] Lit. *make not My face to fall.*
[5] Greek; Hebrew *ye have.*
[6] That is *Lord* and *Husband.*

15 will bring you to Ṣion. And I will give you
Shepherds after My heart, and they shall
shepherd you with knowledge and with skill.

16 And it shall be, when ye multiply and increase
in the land in those days (Rede of the Lord),
they shall not again say, 'The Ark of the
Covenant of the Lord!' It shall not come to
mind, it shall be neither remembered nor
missed,[1] nor shall it be made again.

17   At that time they shall call Jerusalem the
Throne of the Lord and all nations shall
gather to her,[2] nor walk any more after the

18 stubbornness of their evil hearts. In those
days the House of Judah shall walk with the
House of Israel, that together they may come
from the land of the North to the land which
I gave their [3] fathers for a heritage.]

19   But I [4] had declared the How (?)
        I should set thee [5] among the sons,
    And should give thee a land of delight,
        Fairest domain of the nations.

---

[1] So Greek.

[2] Hebrew adds *to the Name of the Lord to Jerusalem.*

[3] So Greek ; Hebrew *your*; after *North* Greek has *and from
all lands.*

[4] In antithesis to verse 5 of which it is the immediate sequel
both in sense and metre.

[5] Feminine, i.e. Judah was a daughter, and a son's portion was
designed for her.

And said, Thou would'st call Me Father,
Nor from after Me turn.
20 As a woman plays false to her fere,[1]
So to Me ye played false!
[O House of Israel, Rede of the Lord.]

21 Hark!
From the clearings weeping is heard,
Wailing of Israel's sons,
That they have perverted their way,
Forgotten the Lord their God.
22 Return ye oft-turning children,
Let me heal your back-turnings!
'Here are we! to Thee we are come,
Thou Lord art our God.
23 'Surely the heights are a fraud
The hills and their hubbub![2]
'Alone in the Lord our God
Is Israel's safety.
24 'The Baal hath devoured our toil
And our sires' from their youth,
'Their flocks and their herds,
Their sons and daughters—
25 'Lie we low in our shame,
Our dishonour enshroud us!
'For to our God[3] have we sinned,
'[We and our sires from our youth]

[1] So finely Ball.
[2] The riotous festivals on the high-places.
[3] Hebrew adds *the Lord*.

Up to this day!
'Nor have heeded the voice
    Of the Lord our God.'

IV. 1 [Israel, if thou wilt return,
        Return to Me,
    And thy loathly things put from thy mouth
        Nor stray from My face.[1]
  2 If in truth thou swear by the life of the Lord,
        Honest and straight,
    Then the nations shall bless them by Him
        And in Him shall they glory.][2]

3 Thus saith the Lord to the men of Judah and
to the inhabitants of[3] Jerusalem:

Fallow up your fallow-ground,[4]
    And sow not on thorns!
4 To your God[5] circumcise ye,
    Off from your heart with the foreskin!
[O men of Judah and inhabitants of Jerusalem]
    Lest My fury break out like fire,
        And burn with none to quench!
    [Because of the ill of your doings.]

[1] This couplet after the Greek.

[2] I agree with Cornill and Skinner that these two verses
are a later addition. The answer to the people's confession
comes in verses 3 and 4.

[3] So some Hebrew MSS. and versions.

[4] Hebrew *nirû lakeh nîr;* also in English the noun and verb
are the same—*to fallow* or *fallow up* = *to break* or *plough up.*

[5] So Greek and other versions.

From his call the Prophet went forth, as we
saw, with a heavy sense of the responsibility and
the power of the single soul, so far as he himself
was concerned ; and while we study his ministry
we shall find him coming to feel the same for
each of his fellow-men. But in these his earliest
utterances he follows his predecessors, and
especially Hosea, in addressing his people as a
whole, and treating Israel as a moral unit from
the beginning of her history to the moment of
his charge to her. He continues the figures
which Hosea had used. Long ago in Egypt God
chose Israel for His child, for His bride, and led
her through the desert to a fair and fruitful land
of her own. Then her love was true. The term
used for it, *hesedh*, is more than an affection ; it is
loyalty to a relation. To translate it but *kindness*
or *mercy*, as is usually done, is wrong—*troth* is
our nearest word.

> I remember the troth of thy youth,
>   Thy love as a bride,
> Thy following Me through the desert,
>   The land unsown.

Upon the unsown land there were no rival
gods. But in fertile Canaan the nation encountered innumerable local deities, the Baalîm,
husbands of the land, begetters of its fruits and
lords of its waters. We conceive how tempting
these Baalîm were both to the superstitious

prudence of tribes strange to agriculture and anxious to conciliate the traditional powers thereof; and to the people's passions through the sensuous rites and feasts of the rural shrines. Among such distractions Israel lost her innocence, forgot what her own God was or had done for her, and ceased to enquire of Him. Hence her present vices and misery in contrast with her early troth and safety. Hence the twin evils of the time—on the one hand the nation's trust in heathen powers and silly oscillation between Egypt and Assyria; on the other the gross immoralities to which the Baals had seduced its sons. There was a double prostitution, to gods and to men, so foul that the young prophet uses the rankest facts in the rural life which he is addressing in order to describe it.

The cardinal sin of the people, the source of all their woes is religious,

> Is not this being done thee
> For thy leaving of Me ?

This was so, not only because He was their ancestral God—though such an apostasy was unheard of among the nations—but because He was such a God and had done so much for them ; because from the first He had wrought both with grace and with might, while the gods they went after had neither character nor efficiency—mere breaths, mere bubbles!

The nerve of the faith of the prophets was this memory—that their God was love and in love had wrought for His people. The frequent expression of this by the prophets and by Deuteronomy, the prophetic edition of the Law, is the answer to those abstractions to which some academic moderns have sought to reduce the Object of Israel's religion—such as, ' a tendency not ourselves that makes for righteousness.' The God of Israel was Righteous and demanded righteousness from men ; but to begin with He was Love which sought their love in return. First the Exodus then Sinai ; first Redemption then Law ; first Love then Discipline. Through His Deeds and His Word by the prophets He had made all this clear and very plain.

> What wrong found your fathers in Me,
>   That so far they broke from Me ?
> Have I been a desert to Israel,
>   Or land of thick darkness ?
> Why say My folk, ' We are off,
>   To meet Thee no more.'

Jeremiah has prefaced this Divine challenge with a passionate exclamation in prose—*O Generation —you !—look at the Word of the Lord !*—which (as I have said) I like to think was added to his earlier verses when he dictated these to Baruch. Cannot you see, cannot you see ? He is amazed by the stupidity, the callousness, the abandonment with

which his people from their leaders down l... ...
treated a guidance so clear, a love so constant
and yearning. And again his soul sways upon
the contrast between the early innocence and the
present corruption of Israel.

> A noble vine did I plant thee,
>   Wholly true seed,
> How could'st thou change to a corrupt,
>   A wildling grape ?

The sense of their terrible guilt governs him, and
of their indifference to it, saying we are clean,
to which he answers :—

> Yea though thou scour thee with nitre
>   And heap to thee lye,
> Ingrained is thy guilt before Me—
>   Rede of the Lord.

Yet the fervency with which he pleads the
Divine Love reveals a heart of hunger, if hardly
of hope, for his nation's repentance. Indeed apart
from his own love for them he could not have
followed Hosea so closely as he does at this stage
of his career, without feeling some possibility of
their recovery from even this, their awful worst ;
and his ear strains for a sign of it. Like Hosea
he hears what sounds like the surge of a national
repentance [1]—was it when Judah listened to the

----

[1] iii. 22*b*, 25 ; Hos. v. 15-vi. 3.

pleadings and warnings of the discovered Book of the Law and *all the people stood to the Covenant?* But he does not say whether he found this sincere or whether it was merely a shallow stir of the feelings. Probably he suspected the latter, for in answer to it he gives not God's gracious acceptance, but a stern call to a deeper repentance and to a thorough trenching of their hearts.

> Fallow up the fallow-ground,
>   Sow not on thorns!
> To your God [1] circumcise ye,
>   Off from your heart with the foreskin!
> Lest My wrath break out like the fire,
>   And burn with none to quench.[2]

Jeremiah has been called the blackest of pessimists, and among his best-known sayings some seem to justify the charge :—

> Can the Ethiop change his skin,
>   Or the leopard his spots ?
> Then also may ye do good,
>   Who are wont to do evil.[3]

And again,

> False above all is the heart,
>   And sick to despair,
> Who is to know it ?

[1] So Greek.   [2] iv. 3, 4.   [3] xiii. 23.

But to his question came the answer :—

> I, the Lord, searching the heart,
>   And trying the reins,
> To give to each man as his ways,
>   As the fruit of his doings.[1]

In this answer there is awfulness but not final doom. The affirmation of a man's dread responsibility for his fate implies, too, the liberty to change his ways. In the dim mystery of the heart freedom is clear. Similarly, and even more plainly, is this expressed in the earlier call to *break up the fallow-ground*. This implies that beneath those surfaces of the national life, whether of callous indifference on the one hand or of shallow feeling on the other, there is soil which, if thoroughly ploughed, will be hospitable to the good seed and fit to bring forth fruits meet for repentance. Human nature even at its worst has tracts other than those on which there has been careless sowing among thorns, moral possibilities below those of its abused or neglected surfaces. Let us mark this depth, which the Prophet's insight has already reached. Much will come out of it; this is the matrix of all developments by himself and others of the doctrine of man and his possibilities under God. And for all time the truth is valid that many spoiled or wasted lives are spoiled or wasted

------

[1] xvii. 9, 10.

only on the surface; and that it is worth while
ploughing deeper for their possibilities.[1]

In what form the deep ploughing required was
at first imagined by the Prophet we see from the
immediately following Oracles.

2. ORACLES ON THE SCYTHIANS.

(With some others : IV. 5-VI. 29.)

The invasion of Western Asia by the Scythians
happened some time between 627 and 620 B.C.[2]
The following series of brief poems unfold the
panic actually caused, or to the Prophet's imagination likely to be caused, in Judah by the advance
of these marauding hordes, and clearly reflect
their appearance and manner of raiding. It is
indeed doubtful that Judah was visited by the
Scythians, who appear to have swept only the
maritime plain of Palestine. And once more we
must remember that when the Prophet dictated
his early Oracles to Baruch for the second time
in 604, and *added to them many more like words*,[3]
the impending enemy from the North was no
longer the Scythians but Nebuchadrezzar and his
Chaldeans; for this will explain features of the
poems that are not suited to the Scythians and
their peculiar warfare, which avoided the siege
of fortified towns but kept to the open country

---

[1] See further, Lecture viii.   [2] See above, p. 73.
[3] xxxvi. 32.

and the ruin of its villages and fields. Jeremiah
does not give the feared invaders a name. The
Scythians were utterly new to his world; yet
their name may have occurred in the poems as
originally delivered and have been removed in
604, when the Scythians were no longer a force
to be reckoned with.[1]

1. As it has reached us, the First Scythian
Song, Ch. IV. 5-8, opens with the general
formula—

> Proclaim in Judah and Jerusalem,
> Make heard and say!

which may be the addition of a later hand, but
is as probably Jeremiah's own; for the capital,
though not likely to be besieged by the Scythians,
was just as concerned with their threatened invasion as the country folk, to whom, in the first

---

[1] On the subject of this paragraph see the appendix on 'The
Medes and Scythians.' The following may be consulted:
N. Schmidt in 'Enc. Bibl.' on 'Jeremiah' and 'Scythians;'
Driver, 'The Book of the Prophet Jeremiah,' p. 21; J. R.
Gillies, 'Jeremiah, the Man and His Message,' pp. 63 ff., who
thinks that the Scythians did invade Judah, and W. R.
Thomson, 'The Burden of the Lord,' pp. 46 ff., who thinks
they did not. A thorough study of the question will be found
in Skinner's 'Prophecy and Religion, Studies in the Life of
Jeremiah,' ch. iii. The case against the Scythians being the
enemy from the North that Jeremiah describes is best presented
by J. F. McCurdy in 'History, Prophecy, and the Monuments,'
vol. ii. pp. 395 ff., and Wilke, see below, p. 383.

place, the lines are addressed. The *trump* or *horn* of the first line was the signal of alarm, kept ready by the watchman of every village, as Amos and Joel indicate.[1]

IV. 5*b* Strike up the trump through the land,
    Call with full voice,
    And say, Sweep together and into
    The fortified towns.

6   Hoist the signal towards Ṣion,
    Pack off and stay not!
    For evil I bring from the North
    And ruin immense.

7   The Lion is up from his thicket,
    Mauler of nations;
    He is off and forth from his place,
    Thy land[2] to lay waste;
    That thy townships be burned
    With none to inhabit!

8   Gird ye with sackcloth for this,
    Howl and lament,
    For the glow of the wrath of the Lord
    Turns not from us.

These lines are followed by a verse with an introduction to itself, and therefore too separate from the context, and indeed too general to have belonged to so vivid a song:—

---

[1] Amos iii. 6; Joel ii. 1.   [2] Greek *the earth.*

9 And it shall be in that day—Rede of the
Lord—

> The heart of the king shall perish,
> And the heart of the princes,
> And the priests they shall be aghast
> And the prophets dismayed!

And this is followed by one of the sudden protests to God, which are characteristic of Jeremiah :—

10 And I said, Ah Lord God, surely Thou hast
wholly deceived this people and Jerusalem
saying, ' Peace shall be yours,' while the
sword strikes through to the life!

2. The Second Scythian Song is like the first,
prefaced by a double address, which there is no
reason to deny to Jeremiah.   Jerusalem is named
twice in the song, and naturally, since the whole
land is threatened with waste and the raiders
come up to the suburbs of the capital.   The
Prophet speaks, but as so often the Voice of the
Lord breaks through his own and calls directly
to the city and people (though the last line of
verse 12 may be a later addition).   On the other
hand, the Prophet melts into his people ; their
panic and pangs become his.   This is one of the
earliest instances of Jeremiah's bearing of the
sins of his people and of their punishment.

8

IV. 11 At that time it was said to this people and
to Jerusalem,

A wind off the blaze of the bare desert
heights,
Straight on the Daughter of my people,
Neither to winnow nor to sift,
12　　In full blast it meets me.
[Now will I speak My judgments upon them]
13 Lo, like the clouds he is mounting,
Like the whirlwind his cars!
Swifter than vultures his horses,
Woe, we are undone!
14 Jerusalem, cleanse thou thy heart,[1]
That thou be saved!
How long shalt thou harbour within thee
Thy guilty devices.
15 For hark! They signal from Dan,
Mount Ephraim echoes disaster.
16 Warn the folk, 'They are come!'[2]
Make heard o'er Jerusalem.
Behold,[3] beleaguerers (?) coming
From a land far away;
They give out their voice on the townships of
Judah;
17　　Like the guards on her fields

---

[1] The text adds *from evil*, one wonders if *Jerusalem* was added
in 604; without it the line is regular.
[2] After the Greek.
[3] So Syr., transferred from previous couplet.

They are round and upon her,
For Me she defied![1]

18 Thy ways and thy deeds have done
These things to thee.
This evil of thine how bitter!
It strikes to the heart.

19 O my bowels! My bowels, I writhe!
O walls of my heart!
My heart is in storm upon me,
I cannot keep silence.[2]
For the sound of the trump thou hast heard,
O my soul,
The uproar of battle.

20 Ruin upon ruin is summoned,
The land is undone!
Suddenly undone my tents,
In a moment my curtains!

21 How long must I look for the signal
And hark for the sound of the trump!

22 [Yea, fools are My people
Nor Me do they fear.[3]
Children besotted are they,
Void of discretion.
Clever they are to do evil,
To do good they know not.]

---

[1] Metre and meaning of 16 and 17 uncertain. For beleaguerers (?) Duhm reads *panthers* or *leopards;* cp. v. 6.

[2] Duhm after Greek renders, My soul is in storm, my heart throbs.

[3] Greek; Hebrew *know.*

3. The Third of the Scythian Songs is without introduction. Whether the waste, darkness, earth-quake and emptiness described are imminent or have happened is still left uncertain, as in the previous songs. The Prophet speaks, but as before the Voice of God peals out at the end.

23 I looked to the earth, and lo chaos,
    To the heavens, their light was gone.
24 I looked to the hills and[1] they quivered,
    All the heights were a-shuddering.
25 I looked—and behold not a man!
    All the birds of heaven were fled.
26 I looked to the gardens, lo desert,
    All the townships destroyed,
  Before the face of the Lord,
    The glow of His wrath.
27 [For thus hath the Lord said,
    All the land shall be waste
    Yet full end I make not][2]
28 For this let the Earth lament,
    And black be Heaven above!
  I have spoken and will not relent,
    Purposed and turn not from it.[3]

4. The Fourth Scythian Song follows immediately, also without introduction. The first four couplets vividly describe the flight of the peasantry,

[1] Greek ; Hebrew adds *lo !*
[2] Probably a later addition.
[3] The order of verbs in this couplet is that of the Greek.

actual or imagined, before the invaders.   The rest
seems addressed to the City as though being
threatened she sought to reduce her foes with a
woman's wiles, only to find that it was not her
love but her life they were after, and so expired
at their hands in despair.   All this is more suitable to the Chaldean than to the Scythian invasion,
and may be one of the Prophet's additions in 604
to his earlier Oracles.   However we take it, the
figure is of Jeremiah's boldest and most vivid.
The irony is keen.

IV. 29 From the noise of the horse and the bow-
          men,
       All the land [1] is in flight,
     They are into the caves, huddle in thickets, [2]
       Are up on the crags.
     Every town of its folk is forsaken
       No habitant in it.
30 All is up ! Thou destined to ruin (?) [3]
       What doest thou now ?
     That thou dressest in scarlet,
       And deck'st thee in deckings of gold,
     With stibium widenest thine eyes.
       In vain dost thou prink !

[1] So Greek ; Hebrew *city*, a change possibly made after the
fall of Jerusalem.

[2] So Greek.

[3] Text uncertain ; this reading is derived by differently dividing
the consonants—*bah no' ash for bahen 'ish.*

> Though satyrs they utterly loathe thee,
> Thy life are they after!
> 31 For voice as of travail I hear,
> Anguish as hers that beareth,
> The voice of the daughter of Ṣion agasp,
> She spreadeth her hands:
> 'Woe unto me, but it faints,
> My life to the butchers!'

The next poem, Ch. V. 1-13, says little of the Scythians, possibly only in verse 6, but details the moral reasons for the doom with which they threatened the people. It describes the Prophet's search through Jerusalem for an honest, God-fearing man and his failure to find one. Hence the fresh utterance of judgment. Perjury and whoredom are rife, with a callousness to chastisement already inflicted. Some have relegated Jeremiah's visit to the capital to a year after 621-20 when the deuteronomic reforms had begun and Josiah had removed the rural priests to the Temple.[1] But, as we have seen, Anathoth lay so near to Jerusalem, and intercourse between them was naturally so constant, that Jeremiah may well have gained the following experience before he left his village for residence in the city. The position of the poem among the Scythian Songs, along with the possible allusion to the Scythians

[1] P. 134.

in verse 6, suggests a date before 620.   There is
no introduction.

V. 1 Range ye the streets of Jerusalem,
    Look now and know,
  And search her broad places,
    If a man ye can find—
  If there be that does justice,
    Aiming at honesty.
  [That I may forgive them [1]]
2 Though they say, 'As God liveth,'
    Falsely [2] they swear
3 LORD, are Thine eyes upon lies (?)
    And not on the truth [3]?
  Thou hast smitten, they ail not,
    Consumed them, they take not correction.
  Their faces set harder than rock,
    They refuse to return.
4 But I said, 'Ah, they are the poor,
    And therefore [4] the foolish!
  'They know not the Way of the Lord,
    The Rule of their God.
5 'To the great I will get me,
    With them let me speak.
  'For they know the Way of the Lord,
    And the Rule of their God.'
  Ah, together they have broken the yoke,
    They have burst the bonds!

[1] Greek ; Hebrew *her*.   The clause seems an addition.
[2] Hebrew adds *therefore*.
[3] So Duhm after the Greek ; p. 48, n. 2.   [4] So Greek.

6 So a lion from the jungle shall smite them,
  A wolf of the waste destroy,
The leopard shall prowl round their towns,
  All faring forth shall be torn.
For many have been their rebellions,
  Profuse their backslidings.
7 How shall I pardon thee this—
  Thy children have left Me,
  And swear by no-gods.
I gave them their fill and they whored,
  And trooped to the house of the harlot.
8 Rampant[1] stallions they be,
  Neighing each for the wife of his friend.
9 Shall I not visit on such,
  Rede of the Lord,
Nor on a people like this
  Myself take vengeance?

10 Up to her vine-rows, destroy,
  And make[2] a full end,
Away with her branches,
  They are not the Lord's.
11 For betraying they have betrayed Me
  Judah and Israel both [Rede of the Lord]
12 The Lord they have belied,
  Saying 'Not He!

---

[1] The text is uncertain, the Hebrew margin and versions pointing to an untranslatable original.

[2] The text has *make not*, but this is inconsistent with the context, and *not* seems a later addition.

Evil shall never come on us,
Nor famine nor sword shall we see.

13 'The prophets! they are nothing but wind
The Word is not with them!'[1]

14 Therefore thus hath the Lord of Hosts said,
because of their speaking this word—[2]

Behold I am setting My Word
In thy mouth for fire,
And this people for wood,
And it shall devour them.

5. The Fifth Song upon the Scythians, Ch. V.
15-17, besides still leaving them nameless,
emphasises their strangeness to Israel's world.
There was a common language in Western Asia,
Aramean, the *lingua franca* of traders from Nineveh
to Memphis; and Jew, Assyrian and Egyptian con-
versed in it. But the tongue of these raiders from
over the Caucasus was unintelligible. Yet how
they would set their teeth into the land! Mixed
with the verses which thus describe them are
others which suit not them but the Chaldeans and
must have been added by the Prophet in 604.
A people so new to the Jews might hardly have
been called by Jeremiah *an ancient nation, from of old
a nation*, and in fact these phrases are wanting in
the Greek version.

---

[1] Hebrew adds, *thus be it done them;* Greek omits.
[2] Hebrew has *God* after *Lord* and *your* for *their.*

V. 15 Behold, I am bringing upon you
          A nation from far,
      [O house of Israel, Rede of the Lord
          An ancient nation it is,
          From of old a nation,]¹
   16 A nation thou knowest not its tongue,
          Nor canst hear what it says,
          Its quiver an open grave,²
          All of it stalwarts.³
   17 It shall eat up thy harvest and bread,
          Eat thy sons and thy daughters,
      It shall eat up thy flocks and thy cattle,
          Eat thy vines and thy figs.
      It shall beat down thy fortified towns,
          Wherein thou dost trust, with the sword.

The last couplet is unsuitable to the Scythians,
incapable as they were of sieges and avoiding
fortified towns—though once they rushed
Askalon. It is probably, therefore, another of
the additions of 604 referring to the Chaldeans.
The prose which follows is certainly from the
Chaldean period, for it was not Scythians but
Chaldeans who threatened with exile the peoples
whom they overran.

V. 18 Yet even in those days—Rede of the
          Lord—I will not make a full end of you.

¹ This couplet the Greek lacks.
² Eloquent of death : Ps. v. 9.
³ For these four lines the Greek has only *A nation thou
hearest not its tongue, all of them mighty.*

19 And it shall be when they say, For what
hath the Lord our God done to us all these
things ?—that thou shalt say to them, Just as
ye have left Me and have served foreign gods
in your own land, so shall ye serve strangers
in a land not yours.

There follows a poem, verses 20-31, that has
nothing to do with the Scythian series ; and that
with the preceding prose, with which also it has no
connection, shows us what a conglomeration of
Oracles the Book of Jeremiah is.   It seems as
though the compiler, searching for a place for it,
had seen the catch-word *harvest* in the previous
Scythian song and, this one having the same word,
he had copied it in here.   The Book shows signs
elsewhere of the same mechanical method.   But
like all the Oracles this has for its theme the
foolish dulness of Israel to their God and His
Word, and the truth that it is their crimes which
are the cause of all their afflictions yet now not in
history but in Nature.   There is no reason to doubt
that the verses are Jeremiah's, and nothing against
our dating them in the early years of his ministry

V. 20 Declare ye this in the House of Jacob,
        Through Judah let it be heard :[1]
21 Hear ye now this, people most foolish,
        And void of sense.[2]

[1] Hebrew adds *saying*.

[2] Lit. *with no heart*, the seat not only of feeling, but of the
practical intelligence.

[They have eyes but they do not see,
Ears but they hear not.]

22 Fear ye not Me, Rede of the Lord,
Nor tremble before Me ?—
Who have set the sand a bound for the sea,
An eternal decree it cannot transgress ;
Though (its waters)[1] toss, they shall not pre-
vail,
And its rollers boom, they cannot break over.

23 Yet this people heart-hard and rebellious,
Have swerved and gone off ;

24 For not with their hearts do they say,
' Now fear we the Lord our God,
' Who giveth the rain in its season,
The early and latter ;
' And the weeks appointed for harvest
Secureth for us.'

25 These have your crimes deranged,
Your sins withholden your luck.

26 For scoundrels are found in My folk,
Who prowl with the crouch of a fowler (?)[2]
And set their traps to destroy,
'Tis men they would catch !

27 Like a cage that is full of birds,
Their houses are filled with deceit,[3]

28 And so they wax wealthy and great—
They are fat, they are sleek !—

---

[1] Something like this has obviously slipped from the text.
[2] Text uncertain.
[3] Either with the spoils or with the victims thereof.

Overflowing with things of evil (?),
 They defend not the right,
The right of the orphan to prosper,
 Nor justice judge for the needy.[1]
29 Shall I not visit on these,
 Rede of the Lord,
Nor on a people like this
 Myself be avenged?[2]
30 Appalling and ghastly it is
 That has come to pass in the land:
31 The prophets prophesy lies,
 The priests bear rule at their hand,
And My people—they love so to have it;
 But what will ye do in the end?

6. In the Sixth Song on the Scythians, VI. 1-8, which also is given without introduction, Jerusalem is threatened—even Jerusalem to which in the previous songs the country-folk had been bidden to fly for shelter—and the foes are described in the attempt to rush her, as they rushed Askalon according to Herodotus. That they are represented as faltering and no success is predicted for them, and also that they are called *shepherds*, are signs that it is the Scythians, though still nameless, who are meant in verses 3-5. The next three verses, separately introduced, point rather to

---

[1] The text of the whole verse is uncertain. Greek omits *things of evil* and *to prosper*.
[2] Or *take vengeance Myself*.

a Chaldean invasion by their picture of besiegers
throwing up a mound against the walls, and may
therefore be one of the additions to his earlier
Oracles made by the Prophet, when in 604 the
enemy from the North was clearly seen to be
Nebuchadrezzar, with the siege-trains familiar
to us from the Assyrian and Babylonian monuments; upon which are represented just such a
hewing of timber and heaping of mounds against
a city's walls.

VI. 1 Pack off, O Benjamin's sons,
    Out of Jerusalem !
  Strike up the trump in Tekoa,[1]
    O'er Beth-hakkérem lift up the signal!
  For evil glowers out of the North,
    And ruin immense.
2 O the charming (?) the pampered height [2]
    Of the daughter of Ṣion !
3 Unto her shepherds are coming,
    With their flocks around,[3]
  They pitch against her their tents,
    Each crops at his hand.
  ' Hallow [4] the battle against her,
    Up, let us on by noon.'

---

[1] Hebrew biṭĕkô'a tiḳĕ'û ; a play upon words.

[2] After the Greek ; the Hebrew text is corrupt.

[3] Transferred from the next line to suit the metre.

[4] The Hebrew idiom for starting a campaign or a siege, which
was formally sanctioned by a religious rite.

4 'Woe unto us!   The day is turning,
   The shadows of evening stretch.'
5 'Up then and on by night,
   That we ruin her palaces!'
6 For thus said the Lord of Hosts:
   Hew down her [1] trees and heap
   Against Jerusalem a mound;
   Woe to the City of Falsehood,[2]
   Nought but oppression within her!
7 As a well keeps its waters fresh
   She keeps fresh her evil;
   Violence and spoil are heard throughout her,
   Ever before Me sickness and wounds.
8 Jerusalem, be thou corrected,
   Lest from thee My soul doth break,
   Lest I lay thee a desolate waste,
   Uninhabited land.

Here follows another and separately introduced
Oracle :—

9 Thus hath the Lord [3] said:
   Glean, let them glean as a vine
   Israel's remnant ;
   Like the grape-gleaner turn thy hand
   Again to its [4] tendrils.
10 'To whom shall I utter myself,
   And witness that they may hear ?

---

[1] So some MSS.
[2] So Greek : Hebrew, *She is a city to be visited.*
[3] Hebrew adds *of Hosts.*   [4] So Greek.

'Lo, uncircumcised is their ear,
   They cannot give heed.
'The Word of the Lord is their scorn,
   No pleasure have they therein.
11 'I am full of the rage of the Lord,
   Weary with holding it back!'
Pour [1] it out on the child in the street,
   On the youths where they gather;
Both husband and wife shall be taken,
   The old with the full of days.
12 Their homes shall be turned to others,
   Their fields and wives together,
When I stretch forth My Hand
   On those that dwell in this [2] land.
      [Rede of the Lord.]
13 Because from the least to the greatest
   All are greedy of gain,
Right on from prophet to priest
   Every one worketh lies.
14 They would heal the breach of My people,
   As though it were trifling,
Saying, 'It is well, it is well'—
   When—where [3] is it well?
15 Were they shamed of their loathsome deeds?
   Nay, not at all ashamed!

---

[1] It is difficult to discriminate in these lines between the Lord and the Prophet as speakers.   If the Greek *I will pour* is correct, the Prophet still speaks, otherwise the Lord who began in verse 9 and was followed by the Prophet in 10 and 11*a*, resumes in 11*b*.
   [2] So Greek.   [3] *Ibid.*

They know not even to blush!
So they with the fallen shall fall,
And shall reel in the time that I visit,
Rede of the Lord.

Still another Oracle which gives no glimpse of
the Scythians, but threatens a vague disaster and
once more states the moral reasons for Judah's
doom. Its allusion to incense and sacrifices is
no reason for dating it after the discovery of
Deuteronomy.[1]

16 Thus hath the Lord said—
Halt on the ways and look,
And ask for the ancient paths:
Where is[2] the way that is good?
Go ye in that,
And rest shall ye find to your soul,
But they—'We go not!'
17 I raised up sentinels for you—
Heed the sound of the trump![3]
But they—'We heed not!'
18 Therefore, O nations, hearken,
And own My record against them (?)[4]

[1] Hans Schmidt, quoted by Dr. Skinner, does so, and takes it
as the earliest evidence of Jeremiah's opposition to Deuteronomy,
and Dr. Skinner in his Chapter ' In the Wake of the Reform,'
says it is almost certainly post-deuteronomic. I am not convinced. See below, p. 133.

[2] Greek *mark ye*.   [3] See above, p. 112.

[4] Text both of Greek and Hebrew uncertain; the above is
adapted from the Greek.

19 Hear thou, O Earth,
 Lo, evil I bring to this people,
  The fruit of their own devices,[1]
 Since they have not heeded My Word,
  And My Law have despised.
20 To Me what is incense that cometh from Sheba,
  Sweet-cane from a far-off land?
 Your holocausts are not acceptable,
  Nor your sacrifice pleasing.
21 Therefore thus hath the Lord said:
 Behold I set for this people
  Blocks upon which to stumble;
 Fathers and children together,
  Neighbour and friend shall perish.

None of the foregoing brief and separate Oracles diverts from the moral theme of all these earlier utterances of the Prophet, that Judah's afflictions, whether from Nature or from invaders, are due to her own wickedness. And this record even the foreign peoples are called to witness—another proof that from the first Jeremiah had a sense of a mission to *the nations* as well as to his own countrymen.

7. There follows the Seventh, the last of the Songs which may be referred to the Scythian invasion, Ch. VI. 22-26. It repeats the distance from which, in the fateful North, those hordes have been *stirred* to their work of judgment, their

---

[1] Greek has *backslidings*.

ruthlessness and terrific tumult, the panic they
produce, and bitter mourning.   The usual formula
introduces the verses.

22 Thus hath the Lord said:

> Lo, a people comes out of the North,
>   A nation[1] astir from the ends of the earth,

23 The bow and the javelin they grasp,
>   Cruel and ruthless,
> The noise of them booms like the sea,
>   On horses they ride—
> Arrayed as one man for the battle
>   On thee, O Daughter of Ṣion!

24   We have heard their fame,
>   Limp are our hands;
>   Anguish hath gripped us,
>   Pangs as of travail.

25   Fare not forth to the field,
>   Nor walk on the way,
>   For the sword of a foe,
>   Terror all round!

26 Daughter of My people, gird on thee sackcloth
>   And wallow in ashes!
> Mourn as for an only-begotten,
>   Wail of the bitterest!
> For of a sudden there cometh
>   The spoiler upon us.[2]

---

[1] Hebrew adds *great*, which Greek omits.
[2] Greek *you*.

This is the last of Jeremiah's Oracles on the Scythians. There is little or no doubt of their date—before 621-20. What knowledge of this new people and their warfare the Prophet displays! What conscience of the ethical purpose of the Lord of Hosts in threatening Judah with them! Yet some still refuse to credit the story of his Call, that from the first he heard himself appointed as a prophet *to the nations.*[1]

This section of Jeremiah's earlier Oracles concludes with one addressed to himself, Ch. VI. 27-30. It describes the task assigned him during the most of his time under Josiah, whether before the discovery and promulgation of the Book of the Law in 621-20, or subsequently to this while he watched the nation's new endeavour to repent and reform. During the years from 621-20 till 608 when Josiah was defeated and slain at Megiddo, there can have been but little for him to do except to follow, as his searching eyes and detached mind alone in Israel could follow, the great venture of Judah in obedience to the Book of the Law. For this interval the outside world had ceased to threaten Israel. The Assyrian control of her was relaxed: the people of God were free, and had their first opportunity for over a century to work out their own salvation.

[1] See above, pp. 79 ff.

27 Assayer among My people I set thee,[1]
  To know and assay their ways,
28 All of them utterly recreant,
  Gadding about to slander.
  Brass and iron are all of them (?),
  Wasters they be!
29 Fiercely blow the bellows,
  The lead is consumed of the fire (?)
In vain docs the smelter smelt,
  Their dross [2] is not drawn.
' Refuse silver' men call them,
  For the Lord hath refused them.[3]

To take these lines as subsequent to the
institution of Deuteronomy and expressive of
the judgment of the Prophet upon the failure of
the reformation under Josiah to reach the depth
of a real repentance,[4] is unnecessary.   The young

[1] Hebrew adds, *a fortress*, obviously borrowed by some scribe
from other appointments by God of Jeremiah, e.g. i. 18.   For
ways in next line Duhm by change of a letter reads *value*.

[2] Greek and Turg. read *their evil* for *the evil ones* of the
Hebrew.

[3] The general meaning is clear, the details obscure for the text
is uncertain.   Driver's note is the most instructive.   In refining,
the silver was mixed with lead and the mass, fused in the furnace,
had a current of air turned upon it ; the lead oxidising acted as
a flux, carrying off the alloy or dross.   But in Israel's case the
dross is too closely mixed with the silver, so that though the
bellows blow and the lead is oxidised, the dross is not drawn and
the silver remains impure.

[4] As Erbt ('Jeremia u. seine Zeit') and Skinner (p. 160) do.

Jeremiah had already tested his people and in his earliest Oracles reached conclusions as hopeless as that here. At least he had already been called to test the people; and in next section we shall see how he continued to fulfil his duty after the discovery of Deuteronomy, and onwards through the attempts at reformation which it inspired.

3. Jeremiah and Deuteronomy.
(Chs. VII, VIII. 8, XI.)

We are not told when or why Jeremiah left Anathoth for Jerusalem. His early poem denouncing the citizens[1] reveals a close observation of their morals but no trace of the reforms begun by Josiah soon after 621 B.C. Some therefore hold that he had settled in the City before that year.[2] Anathoth, however, lay so near Jerusalem that even from his boyhood Jeremiah must have been familiar with the life and trade of the capital; and as his name is not mentioned in connection with the discovery of the Law-Book on which the reforms were based, and neither he nor his biographer speaks of that discovery, it is probable that as yet he had not entered upon residence in the Temple-precincts. A natural occasion for the migration of his family and himself would be upon Josiah's disestablishment of the rural sanctuaries and provision for their priests beside the priests

[1] v. 1-8, see p. 119.　　　　[2] So Duhm.

of the Temple.[1] In any case we find Jeremiah
henceforth in Jerusalem, delivering his Words in
the gateways or courts of the Temple to all classes
of the citizens as well as to the country-folk, who
under the new laws of worship thronged more
than ever the City and her great Shrine

There is general agreement that *the Book of the
Law* discovered by the Temple-priests in 621-20
was our Book of Deuteronomy in whole or in
part—more probably in part, for Deuteronomy
has been compiled from at least two editions of
the same original, and the compilation may not
have been made till some time later. Many of its
laws, including some peculiar to itself, have been
woven out of more than one form, and there are
two Introductions to the Book, each hortatory
and historical and each covering to some extent
the same ground as the other. We cannot tell
how much of this compilation was contained in
the discovered Book of the Law. But this Book
included certainly *first* the laws of worship peculiar
to Deuteronomy, because the reforms which it
inspired carried out these laws, and probably
second some of the denunciations which precede or
follow the laws, for such would explain the consternation of the King when the Book was read
to him.[2]

---

[1] Deut. xviii. 6, II Kings xxiii. 8, 9.

[2] On this and the following paragraphs see the writer's
"Deuteronomy" in the Cambridge Bible for Schools.

Deuteronomy is fairly described as a fresh codification of the ancient laws of Israel in the spirit of the Prophets of the Eighth Century The Book is not only Law but Prophecy, in the proper sense of this word, and a prophetic interpretation of Israel's history. It not only restates old and adds new laws but enforces the basal truths of the prophets, and in this enforcement breathes the ethical fervour of Amos and Isaiah as well as Hosea's tenderness and his zeal for education.

Deuteronomy has three cardinal doctrines : The One God, The One Altar, and The One People.

First, The One God. Though slightly tinged with popular conceptions of the existence of other gods,[1] the monotheism of the Book is strenuously moral and warmly spiritual. The God of Israel is to be served and loved because He is Love—the One and Only God not more by His Righteousness and His Power than by His Grace, manifest as all three have been throughout His dealings with Israel. The worship of other gods is forbidden and so is every attempt to represent Himself in a material form. His ritual is purged of foolish, unclean and cruel elements. Witchcraft and necromancy are utterly condemned.

Second—and this is original to Deuteronomy—The One Altar, at that time an inevitable corollary

---

[1] Deut. iv. 19.

both to the need for purity in the worship of God and to the truth of His Unity. The long license of sacrifices at a multitude of shrines had resulted not only in the debasement of His worship, but in the popular confusion of Himself with a number of local deities.[1] The removal of the high-places, the concentration of sacrifice upon One Altar had, by the bitter experience of centuries, become a religious and an ethical necessity.

Third, The One People. Save for possible proselytes from the neighbouring heathen, Israel is alone legislated for—a free nation owning no foreign king as it bows to no foreign deity, but governing itself in obedience to the revealed Will of its own God. This Will is applied to every detail of its life in as comprehensive a system of national religion as the world has known. And thus next to devotion to the Deity comes pride in the nation. Because of their possession of the Divine Law Israel are *the* righteous people and wise above all others. The patriotism of the Book must have been one cause of its immediate acceptance by the people, when Josiah brought it before them and upon it they made Covenant with their God. Throughout the Book treats the nation as a moral unit. It enforces indeed justice as between man and man. It gives woman a

---

[1] See above, pp. 76, 104 ff.

higher position than is assumed for her by other
Hebrew codes. It cares for the individual poor,
stranger, debtor and dependent priest with a
humanity all its own, and it exhorts to the
education of children. Above all it forbids base
thoughts as well as base deeds. Yet, while thus
enforcing the elements of a searching personal
morality, Deuteronomy deals with the individual
only through his relations to the nation and the
national worship. The Book has no promise for
the individual beyond the grave. Nor is there
pity nor charity for other peoples nor any sense
of a place for them in the Divine Providence.
There is no missionary spirit nor hope for mankind outside of Israel.

Further it is due to the almost exclusively
national outlook and interest of the Book that it
has no guidance or comfort to offer for another
element of personal experience—question and
doubt. While it illustrates from the nation's
history the purifying discipline of suffering because of sin it says nothing of the sufferings of
righteous individuals, but by the absoluteness of
its doctrines of morality and Providence suggests,
if indeed it does not inculcate, the dogma that
right-doing will always meet with prosperity and
wrong-doing with pain and disaster—a dogma
which provoked the thoughtful to scepticism, as
we shall see with Jeremiah himself.

Again, the fact that the Book, while superbly

insistent upon justice, holiness and humanity, lays equal emphasis on a definite ritual, with One Altar and an exclusive system of sacrifices, tempted the popular mind to a superstitious confidence in these institutions. And while it was of practical advantage to have the principles of the prophets reduced to a written system, which could be enforced as public law and taught to the young— two ends on which the authors of Deuteronomy are earnestly bent—there was danger of the people coming thereby to trust rather in the letter than in the spirit of the new revelation. Both these dangers were soon realised. As Dr. A. B. Davidson has said, 'Pharisæism and Deuteronomy came into the world on the same day.'

Such was the Book discovered in the Temple in 621-20 and accepted as Divine by King and Nation. Modern efforts to connect Jeremiah with its discovery and introduction to the Monarch, and even with its composition, may be ignored. Had there been a particle of evidence for this, it would have been seized and magnified by the legalists in Israel, not to speak of those apocryphal writers who foist so much else on Jeremiah and Baruch.[1] That they have not even attempted this is proof—if proof were needed—that Jeremiah, the youthful son of a rural family, and probably

[1] See p. 8.

still unknown to the authorities in the Capital, had nothing whatever to do either with the origins, or with the discovery, of the Book of the Law or with its presentation to the King by the priests of the Temple.

Yet so great a discovery, so full a volume of truth poured forth in a style so original and compelling, cannot have left unmoved a young prophet of the conscience and heart of Jeremiah.[1] That he was in sympathy with the temper and the general truths of Deuteronomy we need not doubt. As for its ethics, its authors were of the same school as himself and among their teachers they had the same favourite, Hosea. In his earliest Oracles Jeremiah had expressed the same view as theirs of God's constant and clear guidance of Israel and of the nation's obstinacy in relapsing from this. His heart, too, must have hailed the Book's august enforcement of that abolition of the high places and their pagan ritual, which he had ventured to urge from his obscure position in Anathoth. Nor did he ever throughout his ministry protest against the substitute which the Book prescribed for those—the concentration of the national worship upon a single sanctuary. On the contrary in a later Oracle he looks for the day when that shall be observed by all Israel and the watchmen on Mount Ephraim shall cry,

[1] Cp. Thomson, *op. cit.*, p. 61.

Rise, let us up to Sion,
  To the Lord our God![1]

On the other hand, the emphasis which Deuteronomy equally lays upon ethics and upon ritual,
and its absolute doctrines of morality and
Providence were bound to provoke questions in
a mind so restlessly questioning as his.   Then
there was the movement of reform which followed
upon the appeal of the Book to the whole nation.
Jeremiah himself had called for a national repentance and here, in the people's acceptance of the
Covenant and consent to the reforms it demanded,
were the signs of such a repentance.   No opposition appears to have been offered to those
reforms.   The King who led them was sincere;
a better monarch Judah never knew, and his
reign was signalised by Jeremiah at its close as a
reign of justice when *all was well.*   Yet can we
doubt that the Prophet, who had already preached
so rigorous a repentance and had heard himself
appointed by God as the tester of His people,
would use that detached position jealously to
watch the progress of the reforms which the
nation had so hurriedly acclaimed and to test
their moral value ?

In modern opinion of Jeremiah's attitude to the
discovered Law-Book there are two extremes.
One is of those who regard him as a legalist and

[1] xxxi. 6.

throughout his career the strenuous advocate of the Book and the system it enforced.   The other is of those who maintain that he had no sympathy with legal systems or official reforms, and that the passages in the Book of Jeremiah which allege his assent to, and his proclamation of, the Deuteronomic Covenant, or represent him as using the language of Deuteronomy, are not worthy of credit.[1]   Of these extremes we may say at once that if with both we neglect the twofold character of Deuteronomy—its emphasis now on ethics and now on ritual—and again, if with both we assume that Jeremiah's attitude to the Law-Book and to the reforms it inspired never changed, then the evidences for that attitude offered by the Book of Jeremiah are inconsistent and we may despair of a conclusion.   But a more reasonable course is open to us.   If we keep in mind the two faces of Deuteronomy as well as the doubtful progress for many years of the reforms started by it, and if we also remember that a prophet like all the works of God was subject to growth; if we allow to Jeremiah the same freedom to change his purpose in face of fresh developments of his people's character as in the Parable of the Potter he imputes to his God; if we recall how in 604 the new events in the history of Western

---

[1] These two extremes are represented by Winckler and Duhm respectively.

Asia led him to adapt his earlier Oracles on the
Scythians to the Chaldeans who had succeeded
the Scythians as the expected Doom from the
North—then our way through the evidence becomes tolerably clear, except for the difficulty of
dating a number of his undated Oracles. What
we must not forget is the double, divergent
intention and influence of Deuteronomy, and the
fact that Josiah's reformation, though divinely
inspired, was in its progress an experiment upon
the people, whose mind and conduct beneath it
Jeremiah was appointed by God to watch and to
test.

These considerations prepare us *first* for the
story in Ch. XI. 1-8 of Jeremiah's fervent assent
to the ethical principles of Deuteronomy and of
the charge to him to proclaim these throughout
Judah; and *then* for his later attitude to the
written Law, to the Temple and to sacrifices.

XI. 1 The Word which came to Jeremiah from
the Lord, saying:

2 Hear thou[1] the words of this Covenant, and
speak[1] them to the men of Judah, and to the
3 inhabitants of Jerusalem. And thou shalt
say to them, Thus saith the Lord, the God
of Israel: Cursed be the man who hears not
4 the words of this Covenant, which I commanded your fathers in the day that I brought

[1] Sing. as partly in Greek and wholly in Syriac.

them out of the land of Egypt, out of the iron-
furnace, saying, Hearken to My Voice and
do[1] according to all that I command you,
and ye shall be to Me a people, and I will be
5 God to you; in order to establish the oath
which I sware unto your fathers, to give them
a land flowing with milk and honey, as at
this day.
And I answered and said, Amen, O Lord!
6 And the Lord said unto me, Proclaim[2] these
words in the cities of •Judah and in the
streets of Jerusalem, saying, Hear ye the
8 words of this Covenant and do them, but
they did them not.[3]

The story has its difficulties. It is undated;
it is followed by verses 9-17, apparently from the
reign of Jehoiakim; what the Prophet is called
to hear and gives his solemn assent to is generally
described as *this Covenant;* and in verses 7 and 8
there is what may be a mere editorial addition
since the Greek Version omits it, which has led
some to assert the editorial character of the
whole. But for the reasons given above, there is
no cause to doubt the substantial truthfulness of
the story, unless with Duhm we were capable of
believing that Jeremiah never spoke in prose, nor

[1] With Greek omit *them* of the Hebrew text.

[2] Hebrew adds *all.*

[3] As above, Greek omits all of the Hebrew verses **7, 8** except
the last clause which follows naturally on verse 6.

can be conceived as, at any time in his life the advocate of what was a legal as well as a prophetic book. Of the first of these assertions we have already disposed;[1] the second is met by the fact that what Jeremiah was called to assent to was not a legal programme but a spiritual covenant, of which ethical obedience alone was stated as the condition. In Josiah's reign what else could *this Covenant* mean than the Covenant set forth in the recently discovered Book of the Law and solemnly avouched by the whole people?[2] That its essence was spiritual and ethical is expressed in the Deuteronomic phrases which follow, and the quotation of these is most relevant to the occasion. Nor do the recollections, the command and the promise which they convey go beyond what Jeremiah had already enforced in his earlier Oracles.[3]

[1] See above, pp. 40 ff.

[2] This consideration seems to dispose of König's claim that Jeremiah here maintains the Sinai-Covenant (with the Decalogue) in opposition to the Moab-Covenant set forth in Deuteronomy. How could the former be defined in the time of Josiah as *this Covenant* or described in Deuteronomic phrases? See also G. Douglas, 'Book of Jeremiah,' p. 156.

[3] Dr. Skinner (*op. cit.*, p. 100) thinks that ' the accumulation of distinctively Deuteronomic phrases and ideas in verses 4, 5 implies a dependence on that book which savours strongly of editorial workmanship.' But if *this Covenant* be the Deuteronomic, as he admits, what more natural than to state it in Deuteronomic terms, expressive as these are only of its spiritual

Therefore we may believe that, as recorded, Jeremiah heard in the heart of Deuteronomy the call of God, that he uttered his Amen to it; and that, from his experience of the evils of the high-places, he felt obliged, as he also records, to proclaim *this Covenant* throughout Judah.[1]

In the same chapter as the charge to the Prophet concerning *this Covenant* there is mention of a con-spiracy against his life by the men of Anathoth, XI. 21. Some suppose that these were enraged by his support of reforms which abolished rural sanctuaries like their own. But his earlier de-nunciations of such shrines, delivered inde-

essence? I would also refer to what I have said on p. 41 as to the effect on the Prophet of the new and haunting style of Deuteronomy.

[1] Dr. Skinner's authoritative support to the substance of the thesis maintained above is very welcome, strengthened as it is by the point which he makes in the first of the following sentences : 'The deliberate invention of an incident, which had no point of contact in the authentic record of his life, is a procedure of which no assured parallel is found in the book. We must at least believe that a trustworthy tradition lies behind the passage in ch. xi ; and the conclusion to which it naturally points is that Jeremiah was at first strongly in favour of the law of Deuteronomy, and lent his moral support to the reformation of Josiah' (pp. 102-3). Wellhausen, 'Isr. u. Jüdische Gesch.' (1894, p. 97): 'An der Einführung des Deuteronomiums hatte er mitgewirkt, zeitlebens eiferte er gegen die illegitimen Altäre in den Städten Judas . . . Aber mit den Wirkungen der Reforma-tion war er keineswegs zufrieden.' So too J. R. Gillies, 'Jeremiah,' p. 113, and W. R. Thomson, 'The Burden of the Lord,' p. 66; and virtually so, Peake, i. 11-14.

pendently of Deuteronomy, had been enough to rouse his fellow-villagers against him as a traitor to their local interests and pieties.

Another address, VII. 1-15, said to have been delivered to all Judah, rebukes the people for their false confidence in the Temple and their abuse of it, and threatens its destruction. Editorial additions may exist in both the Hebrew and Greek texts of this address, but it contains phrases non-deuteronomic and peculiar to Jeremiah, while its echoes of Deuteronomy were natural to the occasion. Except for a formula or two, I take the address to be his own. Nor am I persuaded by the majority of modern critics that it is a mere variant of the Temple address reported in Ch. XXVI as given *in the beginning of the reign of Jehoiakim.* Why may Jeremiah not have spoken more than once on the same theme to the same, or a similar effect? Moreover, the phrase *We are delivered!* VII. 10, which does not recur in XXVI, suits the conditions before, rather than those after, the Battle of Megiddo. For parallel with the increased faith in the Temple, due mainly to the people's consciousness of their obedience to the Law-Book, was their experience of deliverance from the Assyrian yoke. I am inclined, therefore, to refer VII. 1-15 to the reign of Josiah, rather than with XXVI to that of Jehoiakim.[1] But,

[1] So, too, H. P. Smith, 'O.T. History,' p. 278, n. 2; while Duhm, Giesebrecht, Davidson, Driver, Gillies, Peake and Skinner

whatever be its date, VII. 1-15 is relevant to our present discussion.

VII. 2, 3 Hear ye the Word of the Lord, all Judah![1] Thus saith the Lord, the God of Israel—

Better your ways and your doings that I 4 may leave you to dwell in this Place. Put not your trust on lying words,[2] saying to your-selves,[3] 'The Temple of the Lord, The Temple 5 of the Lord, The Temple of the Lord—are those!'[4] But if ye throughly better your ways and your doings, if ye indeed do justice 6 between a man and his fellow, and oppress not the sojourner, the orphan, and the widow, and shed not innocent blood [in this Place], 7 nor go after other gods to your hurt, then I shall leave you to abide in this Place [in

all take vii. 1-15 and xxvi. to refer to the same occasion early in Jehoiakim's reign. Duhm and Skinner remark on an apparently incoherent association of Place (= Holy Place) and Land in vii. 3-7. The clause about the Land may be a later addition. Yet in verses 13-15 (the substance of which Skinner admits to be genuine) the destruction of the Holy Place and ejection of the people from the Land are *both* threatened.

[1] So simply the Greek ; the longer Hebrew title, verses 1, 2 may be an expansion by an editor, who took vii. 1-15 as reporting the same speech as xxvi. 1 ff. In verse 3 Hebrew reads *Lord of Hosts.*

[2] Greek adds *for they will be absolutely of no avail to you.*

[3] So Syriac.

[4] Or *there they are!*—plural because of the complex of buildings.

the land which I gave to your fathers from
8 of old for ever].   Behold, you put your trust
9 on lying words that cannot profit.   What?
Steal, murder, fornicate, swear falsely, and
burn[1] to Baal, and go after other gods whom
10 ye knew not, yet come and stand before
Me in this House upon which My Name has
been called and say 'We are delivered'—in
11 order to work all these abominations!   Is it
a robbers' den that My[2] House [upon which
My Name has been called] has become in
your eyes?   I also, behold I have seen it
—Rede of the Lord.
12 For go now to My Place which was in Shiloh,
where at first I caused My Name to dwell,
and see what I did to it because of the
13 wickedness of My people Israel.   And now
because of your doing of all these deeds [Rede
of the Lord, though I spake unto you rising
early and speaking, but ye hearkened not, and
14 I called you, but ye did not answer],[3] I shall
do to the House [on which My Name has
been called] in which you are trusting, and to
the Place which I gave to you and to your

[1] It is doubtful whether this verb, meaning in earlier Hebrew
to make any burnt offering was already confined to its later
meaning, *to burn incense.*

[2] So Greek.

[3] Much within these brackets is lacking in the Greek.

15 fathers, as I did to Shiloh. And I shall cast
you out from before My Face as I cast out[1]
your brethren, all the seed of Ephraim.

In this address there is nothing that contradicts
Deuteronomy. The sacredness with which the
Book had invested the One Sanctuary is acknowledged. But the people have no moral sense
of that sacredness. Their confidence in the
Temple is material and superstitious, fostered, we
may believe, by the peace they were enjoying and
their relief from a foreign sovereignty, as well as
by their formal observance of the institutions
which the Book prescribed. What had been
founded to rally and to guide a spiritual faith they
turned into a fetish and even to an 'indulgence'
for their wickedness. The House, in which Isaiah
had bent beneath the seraphs' adoration of the
Divine Holiness, and, confessing his own and his
people's sin, had received from its altar the
sacrament of pardon and of cleansing, was by this
generation not only debased to a mere pledge of
their political security but debauched into a shelter
for sins as gross as ever polluted their worship
upon the high places. So ready, as in all other
ages, were formality and vice to conspire with
each other! Jeremiah scorns the people's *trust* in
the Temple as utterly as he had scorned their
trust (it is the same word) in the Baals or in Egypt

---

[1] Hebrew *all*.

and Assyria. The change in the pivot of their false confidence is to be marked. So much at least had Deuteronomy effected—shifting their trust from foreign gods and states to something founded by their own God, yet leaving it material, and unable to restrain them from bringing along with it their old obdurate vices.

Whether, then, this address was delivered in Josiah's reign or early in Jehoiakim's it affords no reason for our denying it to Jeremiah. As God's tester of the people he has been watching their response to the Revelation they had accepted, and has proved that their obedience was to the letter of this and not to its spirit, that while they superstitiously revered its institutions they shamelessly ignored its ethics. For just such vices as they still practised God Himself must take vengeance. As those had deranged the very seasons and were leading to the overthrow of the state,[1] no one could hope that the Temple would escape their consequences. And there was that precedent of the destruction of Israel's first sanctuary in Shiloh, the ruins of which, as we have seen, lay not far from Jeremiah's home at Anathoth.[2]

Another Oracle, XI. 15, 16, also undated, seems, like the last passage, best explained as delivered by Jeremiah while he watched during the close of Josiah's reign the hardening of the people's trust in their religious institutions and felt its

[1] Verses 9, 25, 29, etc.   [2] See above, p. 72.

futility; or alternatively when that futility was exposed by the defeat at Megiddo. It has, however, been woven by some hand or other into a passage reflecting the revival of the Baal-worship under Jehoiakim (verse 17; its connection with the prose sentence preceding is also doubtful). Copyists have wrought havoc with the Hebrew text, but as the marginal note of our Revisers indicates, the sense may be restored from the Greek. *My Beloved* is, of course, Israel.

XI. 15 What has My Beloved to do in My house,
    Working out mischief?
    Vows, holy flesh! Can such things turn
    Calamity from thee;
    Or by these thou escape?[1]
16 Flourishing olive, fair with fruit,
    God called thy name.
    To the noise of a mighty roaring
    He sets her on fire—
    Blasted her branches!

The first of these verses repeats the charge of VII. 2-11: the people use the Temple for their sins. The word rendered *mischief* is literally *devices.* and the meaning may be intrigues hatched from their false ideas of the Temple's security. But the word is mostly used of *evil devices* and here the Greek has *abomination.* As with their

---

[1] *Vows*, so Greek, but Lucian *fat pieces* (Lev. vi. 5); *by these thou escape*, so Greek, Hebrew *then mightest thou rejoice*.

Temple so with their vows and sacrifices. All are useless because of their wickedness. The nation must be punished. The second verse may well have been uttered after the defeat at Megiddo, or may be a prediction on the eve of that disaster to *the branches* of the nation, which the nation as a whole survived.

This leads to another and more difficult question. Jeremiah has spoken doom on the Temple and the Nation ; has he come to doubt the Law-Book itself or any part of it ? As to that there are two passages one of which speaks of a falsification of the Law by its guardians, while the other denies the Divine origin not only of the deuteronomic but of all sacrifices and burnt offerings.

Even before the discovery of the Law-Book the young prophet had said of *those who handle the Law* that *they did not know the Lord.*[1] And now in an Oracle, apparently of date after the discovery, he charges the scribes with manipulating *the Law*, the *Torah*, so as to turn it to falsehood. The Oracle is addressed to the people of whom he has just said that they do not know *the Rule, the Mishpaṭ, of the Lord.*

> VIII. 8 How say you, 'We are the Wise,
> The Law of the Lord is with us.'
> But lo, the falsing pen of the scribes
> Hath wrought it to falsehood.

[1] ii. 8, see above, p. 92.

Torah, literally *direction* or *instruction*, is either a single law or a body of law, revealed by God through priests or prophets, for the religious and moral practice of men. Here it is some traditional or official form of such law, for which the people have rejected the Word of the Lord—His living Word by the prophets of the time (verse 9).

> 9 Put to shame are the wise,
>   Dismayed and taken.
>   Lo, they have spurned the Word of the Lord—
>   What wisdom is theirs?

Was this *Torah* oral or written? And if written was it the discovered Book of the *Torah*, which in part at least was our Deuteronomy?

So far as the text goes the original *Torah* may have been either oral or written, and the scribes have *falsified* it, by amplification or distortion,[1] either when reducing it for the first time to writing or when copying and editing it from an already written form. This leaves open these further questions. If written was the *Torah* the very *Book of the Torah* discovered in the Temple in 621-20? And if so did the falsification affect the whole or only part of the Book? To these questions some answer No, on the ground of Jeremiah's assent to *this Covenant*, and the command to him

---

[1] Cp. the similar charge of Christ against the scribes.

to proclaim it.[1] Others answer Yes; in their
view Jeremiah was opposed to the deuteronomic
system as a whole, or at least to the detailed laws
of ritual added to the prophetic and spiritual
principles of the Book.[2] Another possibility is
that Jeremiah had in view those first essays in
writing of a purely priestly law-book, which resulted during the Exile in the so-called Priests'
Code now incorporated in the Pentateuch. In
our ignorance both of the original form of Deuteronomy and of the extent and character of the
activity of the scribes during the reign of Josiah
we might hesitate to decide among these possibilities were it not for the following address
which there is no good reason for denying to
Jeremiah.

VII. 21 Thus saith the Lord,[3] Your burnt
offerings add to your sacrifices and eat
22 flesh[4]! For I spake not with your fathers nor
charged them, in the day that I brought them
forth from the land of Egypt, concerning
23 burnt-offering and sacrifice. But with this
Word I charged them, saying, Hearken to
My Voice, and I shall be to you God, and

---

[1] xi. 1 ff. ; so Giesebrecht on viii. 8.

[2] Marti, *Gesch. der Isr. Religion*, 154, 166 ; Duhm, and especially Cornill, *in loco*.

[3] Hebrew adds *of Hosts, the God of Israel*.

[4] The former were not, the latter were in part, eaten by the
worshipper ; but it does not matter if now he eats them all alike !

ye shall be to Me a people, and ye shall walk
in every way that I charge you, that it may
be well with you.

Whether from Jeremiah or not, this is one of the
most critical texts of the Old Testament because
while repeating what the Prophet has already
fervently accepted,[1] that the terms of the deuteronomic Covenant were simply obedience to the
ethical demands of God, it contradicts Deuteronomy and even more strongly Leviticus, in their repeated statements that in the wilderness God
also commanded sacrifices. The issue is so grave
that there have been attempts to evade it. None,
however, can be regarded as successful. That
which would weaken the Hebrew phrase, rightly
rendered *concerning* by our versions, into *for the
sake of* or *in the interest of* (as if all the speaker
intended was that animal sacrifice was not the
chief end or main interest of the Divine legislation)
is doubtful philologically, nor meets the fact that
all the Hebrew codes assign an indispensable
value to sacrifice. Inadmissible also is the suggestion that the phrase means *concerning the details
of*, for Deuteronomy and especially Leviticus emphasise the details of burnt-offering and sacrifice.
Nor is the plausible argument convincing that
the Prophet spoke relatively, and meant only
what Samuel meant by *Obedience is better than sacri-*

----

[1] **xi.** 1 ff. : above, pp. 143 ff.

fice, or Hosea by *The Knowledge of God is more than burnt-offerings.*[1] Nor are there grounds for thinking that the Prophet had in view only the Ten Commandments; while finally to claim that he spoke in hyperbole is a forlorn hope of an argument. In answer to all these evasions it is enough to point out that the question is not merely that of the value of sacrifice, but whether during the Exodus the God of Israel gave any charge concerning sacrifice; as well as the fact that others than Jeremiah had either explicitly questioned this or implicitly denied it. When Amos, in God's Name repelled the burnt-offerings of his generation he asked, *Did ye bring unto Me sacrifices and offerings in the wilderness forty years, O House of Israel?* and obviously expected a negative answer And the following passages only render more general the truth that Israel's God has no pleasure at any time in the sacrifices offered to Him, with the institution of which—the natural inference is—He can have had nothing to do. *Will the Lord be pleased with thousands of rams or with ten thousands of rivers of oil. Shall I give my first-born for my transgression, the fruit of my body for the sin of my soul? He hath declared to thee, O man, what is good : and what doth the Lord require of thee but to do justly, and to love mercy, and to walk humbly with thy God.*

[1] Sam. xv. 22, Hos. vi. 6. Those who take the passage relatively also quote Paul's words that Christ sent him not to baptize but to preach the gospel, 1 Cor. i. 17.

And these two utterances in the Psalms: *Shall I eat the flesh of bulls or drink the blood of goats? Offer unto God thanksgiving and pay thy vows to the Most High;* and *Thou desirest not sacrifice else would I give it, Thou delightest not in burnt-offering, The sacrifices of God are a broken spirit.*[1]

For the accuracy of these assertions or implications by a succession of prophets and psalmists there is a remarkable body of historical evidence The sacrificial system of Israel is in its origins of far earlier date than the days of Moses and the Exodus from Egypt. It has so much, both of form and meaning, in common with the systems of kindred nations as to prove it to be part of the heritage naturally derived by all of them from their Semitic forefathers. And the new element brought into the traditional religion of Israel at Sinai was just that on which Jeremiah lays stress—the ethical, which in time purified the ritual of sacrifice and burnt-offering but had nothing to do with the origins of this.

Therefore it is certain *first* that Amos and Jeremiah meant literally what they stated or implicitly led their hearers to infer—God gave no commands at the Exodus concerning burnt-offerings and sacrifices—and *second* that historically they were correct. But, of course, their interest in so saying was not historical but spiritual.

---

[1] Amos v. 25 ; Micah vi. 6-8 ; Ps. l. 13, 14 ; li. 16, 17.

Their aim was practical—to destroy their generation's materialist belief that animal sacrifice was the indispensable part of religion and worship. Still his way of putting it involves on the part of Jeremiah a repudiation of the statements of Deuteronomy on the subject. So far, then, Jeremiah opposed the new Book of the Law.[1]

But with all this do not let us forget something more. While thus anticipating by more than six centuries the abolition of animal sacrifices, Jeremiah, by his example of service and suffering, was illustrating the substitute for them—the *human* sacrifice, the surrender by man himself of will and temper, and if need be of life, for the cause of righteousness and the salvation of his fellow-men. The recognition of this in Jeremiah by a later generation in Israel led to the conception of the suffering Servant of the Lord, and of the power of His innocent sufferings to atone for sinners and to redeem them.

This starts a kindred point—and the last—upon which Jeremiah offers, if not a contradiction, at least a contrast and a supplement to the teaching of Deuteronomy. We have noted the absoluteness—or idealism—of that Book's doctrines of

[1] See Robertson Smith, "The O.T. in the Jewish Church," 2nd ed., 203, 295 (1892), and Edghill, "The Evidential Value of Prophecy" (1904), 274, one of the best works on the O.T. in our time.

Morality and Providence; they leave no room for certain problems, raised by the facts of life. But Jeremiah had bitter experience of those facts, and it moved him to state the problems to God Himself. He owns the perfect justice of God; but this only makes his questioning more urgent

XII. 1 Too righteous art Thou O Lord,
  That with Thee I should argue,
  Yet cases there are I must speak to Thee of:
  The way of the wicked—why doth it prosper,
  And the treacherous all be at ease?
  2 Thou hast planted them, yea they take root,
  They get on, yea they make fruit;
  Near in their mouths art Thou,
  But far from their hearts.

We shall have to deal with these questions and God's answer to them, when in a later lecture we analyse Jeremiah's religious experience and struggles. Here we only note the contrast which they present to Deuteronomy—a contrast between the Man and the System, between Experience and Dogma, between the Actual and the Ideal. And, as we now see, it was the System and the Dogma that were defective and the Man and his Experience of life that started, if not for himself yet for a later generation, pondering his experience, the solution of those problems, which against the deuteronomic teaching he raised in brave agony to God's own face.

Such serious differences between Jeremiah and Deuteronomy—upon the Law, the Temple, the Sacrifices, and Doctrines of Providence and Morality—suggest an important question with regard to the methods of Divine Revelation under the Old Covenant. Do they not prove that among those methods there were others than vision or intuition springing from the direct action of the Spirit of God upon the spirits of individual men? Are they not instances of the processes by which to this day in the Providence of God truth is sifted and ultimately beaten out—namely debate and controversy between different minds or different schools of thought, between earnest supporters of various and often hostile opinions in neither of which lies the whole of the truth? The evidence for Revelation by Argument which the Book of Jeremiah affords is not the least of its contributions to the history and philosophy of religion.

LECTURE V.

UNDER JEHOIAKIM.

608—597-8 B.C.

1. FROM MEGIDDO TO CARCHEMISH, 608-605.

JOSIAH's faithful reign, and with it all thorough efforts to fulfil the National Covenant,[1] came to a tragic close on the field of Megiddo—the Flodden of Judah.

The year was 608 B.C. Medes and Chaldeans together had either taken, or were still besieging, Nineveh; and Pharaoh Něcoh,[2] eager to win for Egypt a share of the crumbling Assyrian Empire, had started north with a great army. Marching by the coast he first took Gaza, and crossing by one of the usual passes from Sharon to Esdraelon,[3] found himself opposed near Megiddo by a Jewish force led by its king in person. The Chronicler tells us that Necoh

[1] II. Chron. xxxv. 20, *when he had set the Temple again in order.*

[2] Or Nechoh or Neco as in our own versions: Heb. נְכוֹה or נְכוֹ

[3] 'H.G.H.L.,' p. 151; but see KAT³, p. 105.

(162)

sought to turn Josiah from his desperate venture
*What have I to do with thee? I am come not against
thee but against the House with which I am at war.
God hath spoken to speed me ; forbear from God who is
with me, lest He destroy thee.*[1]   But Josiah persisted.
The issue of so unequal a contest could not be
doubtful. The Jewish army was routed and
Josiah himself immediately slain.[2]

At first sight, the courage of Josiah and his
small people in facing the full force of Egypt
seems to deserve our admiration, as much as did
the courage of King Albert and his nation in opposing the faithless invasion of Belgium by the
Germans aiming at France. There was, however, a difference. Necoh was not invading
Judah, but crossing Philistine territory and a
Galilee which had long ceased to be Israel's.
Some suppose that since the Assyrian hold upon
Palestine relaxed, Josiah had gradually occupied
all Samaria. If this be so, was he now stirred by
a gallant sense of duty to assert Israel's ancient
claim to Galilee as well ? We cannot tell.[3]   But

[1] II. Chron. xxxv. 21.   This may be only the reflection of later
Jewish piety on so perplexing a disaster ; but it rings like fact.

[2] II. King xxiii. 29, *as soon as he saw him.*   For other records
of Necoh's northward march see Appendix II.

[3] The idea that Josiah fought Necoh, as an Assyrian vassal
(Benzinger on II. Kings xxiii. 28-30) is, of course, quite improbable, even if Nineveh did not fall till 606. But if the
latest datum is correct that Nineveh fell in 612 (See Appendix I) it is utterly groundless.

what we may confidently assume is that, having fulfilled by thirteen years of honest reforms his own part of the terms of the Covenant, Josiah believed that he could surely count on the Divine fulfilment of the rest, and that some miracle would bring to a righteous king and people victory over the heathen, however more powerful the heathen might be. He was only thirty-nine years of age.

His servants carried his body from the field in a chariot to Jerusalem, bringing him back, as we may realise, to a people stricken with consternation. Their trust in the Temple was shaken— they were not *delivered!*[1] In the circumstances they did their feeble best by raising to the vacant throne Josiah's son, Shallum, as Jehoahaz, *the Lord hath taken hold.* But the new name proved no omen of good. In three months Necoh had the youth in bonds at Riblah, in the land of Hamath, *that he might not reign in Jerusalem,* and afterwards took him to Egypt. Of this fresh sorrow Jeremiah sang as if it had drowned out the sorrow of Megiddo—

XXII. 10 Weep not for the dead,
Nor bemoan him,
But for him that goeth away weep sore,
For he cometh no more,
Nor seeth the land of his birth.

Jehoahaz died in Eygpt.

[1] See above, p. 149.

The next King, Jehoiakim, another of Josiah's sons, was set on the throne by Necoh, who also exacted a heavy tribute. What national disillusion! The hopes falsely kindled upon the letter of Deuteronomy lay quenched on Megiddo; and the faithful servant of the Covenant had, in spite of its promises as men would argue, been defeated and slain in the flower of his life. Judah had been released from the Assyrian yoke, only to fall into the hands of another tyrant, her new king his creature, and her people sorely burdened to pay him. The result was religious confusion. In at least a formal obedience to the deuteronomic laws of worship, the people of the land continued to resort to the Temple fasts and festivals.[1] But resenting the failure of their God to grant victory numbers relapsed into an idolatry as rank as that under Ahaz or Manasseh;[2] while others, more thoughtful but not less bewildered, conceived doubts of the worth of righteousness. And these tempers were embittered by the cruel selfishness of the new monarch and his reckless injustice. To the taxes required for the tribute to Egypt he added other exactions in order to meet his extravagance in enlarging and adorning his palace. The crime, with which Jeremiah charges him in

---

[1] xxvi. 2, xxxvi. 9.

[2] Whether the sacrifices of children in Hinnom had been resumed, viii. 31 ff., is uncertain; yet this passage may well belong to Jehoiakim's reign.

the following lines, is one to which small kings
in the East have often been tempted by their
contact with civilisations richer than their own.
On Judah Jehoiakim imposed the cruel corvée,
which in our day Ismail Pasha imposed upon
Egypt.

XXII. 13 Woe to who builds his house by in-
justice,
His storeys by wrong,
Who forces his fellows to serve for nothing,
And pays not their wage.

14 Who saith,[1]
I will build me an ampler house
And airier storeys,
Widen my windows, panel with cedar,
And paint with vermilion,

15 Wilt thou thus play the king,
Fussing with cedar?
Thy sire, did not he eat and drink,
And do justice and right,

16 And judge for the poor and the needy?
Then was it well![2]

[1] Greek omits and renders the following *I* and *my* by *thou*
and *his*.

[2] Using the Greek, Duhm, Cornill and Skinner render
this quatrain thus :—

Did not thy father eat and drink,
And do himself well?
Yet he practised justice and right,
Judged the cause of the needy and poor.

Was not this how to know Me ?—
Rede of the Lord.
17 But thine eyes and thy heart are on nought
Save thine own spoil,
And on shedding of innocent blood,
Doing outrage and murder.

Josiah had enjoyed what was enough for him
in sober, seemly parallel to his faithful discharge
of duty; his son was luxurious, unscrupulous,
bloody, and withal petty—*fussing with cedar*, and
cutting up the Prophet's roll piece by piece with
a pen-knife! Jeremiah and Baruch's sarcastic
notes on Jehoiakim find parallels in Victor Hugo's
'Châtiments' of Napoleon III. : 'l'infiniment petit,
monstreux et feroce;' 'Voici de l'or, viens pille
et vole . . . voici du sang, accours, viens boire,
petit, petit !'
XXII. 18. Therefore, thus saith the Lord of
Jehoiakim, son of Josiah, King of Judah.

Mourn him they shall not, 'Woe brother!'
'Woe sister!'
Nor beweep him, 'Woe Lord!'
Or 'Woe Highness!'
19 With the burial of an ass shall they bury him,
Dragged and flung out—
Out from the gates of Jerusalem.

Such a prophet to such a king must have been
intolerable, and through the following years
Jeremiah was pursued by the royal hatred.

There were other and more poisonous enemies.
We have found him, from the first, steadily seeing
through, and stoutly denouncing the great religious orders—the priests, natural believers in the
Temple, with a belief, since Deuteronomy came
into their hands, more dogmatic and arrogant
than ever; and the professional prophets with
their shallow optimism that all was well for
Judah, and that her God could never bring upon
her the doom which Jeremiah threatened in His
Name. *Not He!* was their answer to him.
These two classes were in conspiracy, deluding
themselves and the people; in their trust upon
the letter of the Law, they had no sense, as he
told them, of *The Living God.*[1] Roused by his
scorn they watched for an occasion to convict and
destroy him.[2]

This he bravely gave by making, in obedience
to God's call, public prediction of the ruin of the
Temple. It is uncertain whether Jeremiah did
so only once, as many think who read in Chs.
VII and XXVI reports of the same address, or
whether, as I am inclined to believe, the former
chapter reports an address delivered under Josiah,
and the latter the repetition of its substance in
the beginning of the reign of Jehoiakim.[3] However this be, Ch. XXVI alone relates the consequences of his outspoken courage. It represents

[1] ii. 8, 31, v. 30, 31, vi. 13, 14, 19, etc. ; see pp. 106, 154, etc.
[2] xx. 10.   [3] See above, pp. 147 ff.

the priests and the prophets as quoting his
sentence upon the Temple in absolute terms;
though both reports, in the form in which they
have reached us, render his own delivery of it as
conditional upon the nation's refusal to repent and
to better their ways.[1]   This, of course, was ever
their way; they were ready distorters.

XXVI. 1 In the beginning of the reign of Jehoiakim, son of Josiah, came this word from the
2 Lord: Thus saith the Lord, Stand in the
court of the Lord's House and speak unto all
Judah, all who come in to worship in the
Lord's House, all the words that I have
charged thee to speak to them; keep back
3 not a word.   Peradventure they will hearken
and turn every man from his evil way, and I
shall relent of the evil which I am purposing
to do to them because of the evil of their
4 doings.   And thou shalt say, Thus saith the
Lord: If ye will not obey Me to walk in My
5 Law, which I have set before you, to hearken
to the words of My servants, the prophets
whom I am sending to you, rising early and
6 sending—but ye have not hearkened—then

---

[1] Many take the conditional clauses in vii and xxvi to be later
insertions (e.g. Skinner, 169 f.).   But it was natural to the
malice of his foes to distort Jeremiah's conditional into an absolute, threat, and in xxvi. 13 he corrects them.   My translation
follows the Greek version, and omits the Hebrew additions
which are found in our English versions.

shall I render this House like Shiloh and this
City a thing to be cursed of all nations of the
earth.

7   And the priests and the prophets and all
the people heard Jeremiah speaking these
8 words in the House of the Lord. And it was,
when Jeremiah finished speaking all that the
Lord had charged him to speak to all the
people, that the priests and the prophets[1] laid
hold on him saying, Thou shalt surely die!
9 Because thou hast prophesied in the Name
of the Lord saying, As Shiloh this House
shall be, and this City shall be laid waste
without a dweller. And all the people were
gathered to Jeremiah in the House of the
Lord.

10   When the princes of Judah heard of these
things they came up from the king's house to
the House of the Lord and took their seats
in the opening of the New Gate of the Lord's
11 House.[2] Then said the priests and the
prophets to the princes and to all the people
—Sentence of death for this man! For he
hath prophesied against this City as ye have
heard with your ears.

[1] Both text and versions add here *and all the people ;* but this
may be the careless insertion of a copyist, for in what follows
the people are with Jeremiah.

[2] So 34 MSS., and Syr. Vulg. and Targ.

12 And Jeremiah said to the princes and to all the people, The Lord hath sent me to prophesy against this House and against this 13 City all the words which ye have heard. So now better your ways and your doings, and hearken to the Voice of the Lord, that the Lord may relent of the evil which He hath 14 spoken against you. But as for me, here am I in your hand! Do to me as is good and 15 right in your eyes. Only know for sure that if ye put me to death ye will be bringing innocent blood upon yourselves, and upon this City and upon her inhabitants; for in truth the Lord did send me unto you to speak in your ears all these words.

16 And the princes and all the people said to the priests and the prophets, Not for this man be sentence of death, because in the Name of the Lord our God hath he spoken to us.

17 Then arose some of the elders of the land and said to all the assembly of the people, 18 There was Micaiah the Morasthite in the days of Hezekiah, king of Judah, and he said to all the people of Judah, Thus saith the Lord:

Şion like a field shall be ploughed,
And Jerusalem be heaps,
And the mount of the House a mound
of the jungle.

19 Did Hezekiah and all Judah put him to death ? Did they not fear the Lord and soothe the Lord's face, and the Lord relented of the evil He had uttered against them. Yet we are about to do a great wrong upon our own lives.

Several of its features lift this story to a place among the most impressive in the Old Testament. The priests and prophets on the one side and the princes on the other both use the phrase, that Jeremiah *spoke in the Name of the Lord*. But the former quote it ironically, or in indignation at the Prophet's claim, while the princes are obviously impressed by his sincerity and apparently their impression is shared by the people. There could be no firmer measure of the pitch of personal power to which Jeremiah has at last braced himself.

The promise of his Call is fulfilled. Sceptical, fluid and shrinking as he is by nature, he stands for this hour at least, *a strong wall and a fortress*, by his clear conscience, his simple courage, and his full surrender to whatever be in store for him. How bravely he refuses to conciliate them !—*I am in your hand, do to me as is right in your eyes*.

Again, there is proof of a popular tradition and conscience in Israel more sound than those of the religious authorities of the nation. The people remembered what their priests and prophets forgot or ignored, and through their elders gave

utterance to it on the side of justice.   In agreement with them were the princes, the lay leaders
of the nation.   To ecclesiastics of every age and
race this is a lesson, to give heed to 'the common
sense' and to the public instinct for justice.   And
on that day in Jerusalem these were called forth
by the ability of the people, commoners and
nobles alike, to recognise a real Prophet, an
authentic Speaker-for-God at once when they
heard him.

The danger that Jeremiah faced and the source
from which it sprang are revealed by the fate
which befell another denouncer of the land in the
Name of the Lord.   Of him, the narrator uses a
form of the verb *to prophesy* different from that
which he uses of Jeremiah, thus guarding himself from expressing an opinion as to whether the
man was a genuine prophet.   This is a further
tribute to the moral effect of Jeremiah's person
and word.

XXVI. 20 There was also a man who took upon
him to prophesy in the Name of the Lord,
Urijahu, son of Shemajahu, from Kiriath-
jearim, and he prophesied [1] against this land,
21 according to all the words of Jeremiah.   And
king Jehoiakim [2] and all the princes heard of
his words and they sought [3] to put him to

[1] Hebrew adds *against this city and.*
[2] Hebrew adds *and all his mighty men.*
[3] So Greek ; Hebrew *the king sought.*

death ; and Urijahu heard and fearing fled
22 and went into Egypt, and the king sent men
23 to Egypt.[1] And they took forth Urijah thence
and brought him to the king, and slew him
with the sword, and cast his corpse into the
graves of the sons of the people.

24 But the hand of Ahikam, the son of Shaphan, was with Jeremiah so as not to give him
into the hand of the people to put him to
death.

The one shall be taken and the other left !
We are not told why, after the verdict of the
princes and the people, Ahikam's intervention
was needed. Yet the people were always fickle,
and the king who is not mentioned in connection
with Jeremiah's case, but as we see from Urijah's
watched cruelly from the background, was not
the man to be turned by a popular verdict from
taking vengeance on the Prophet who had attacked
him. Ahikam, however, had influence at court,
and proved friendly to Jeremiah on other occa·
sions.[2]

All this was *in the beginning of the reign of Jehoiakim.* Before we follow Jeremiah himself through
the rest of that malignant and disastrous reign,
during which the steadfastness that his personality
had achieved was again to be shaken, we must

---

[1] Hebrew adds a name (*El-nathan, son of Achbor*) and repeats
[2] II. Kings xxii. 12 ff. ; Jer. xxxix. 14, xl. 5, 6.

understand the progress of the great events which directed his own conduct and gradually determined the fate of his people.

In 625 B.C. the successor of Asshurbanipal upon the tottering throne of Assyria had found himself compelled to acknowledge Nabopolassar the Chaldean as nominally viceroy, but virtually king, of Babylon.[1] The able chief of a vigorous race, Nabopolassar bided his time for a vaster sovereignty, and steadily this came to him. The Medes, twice baffled in their attempts on Nineveh,[2] made terms with him for a united assault on the Assyrian capital and for the division of its empire. To that assault Nineveh fell in 612 or 606,[3] and with her fall Assyria disappeared from among the Northern Powers. Whatever part of the derelict empire the Medes may have secured, Mesopotamia remained with the Chaldeans who doubtless claimed as well all its provinces south of the Euphrates. But, as we have seen, Necoh of Egypt had already overrun these and battle between him and the Chaldeans became imminent. Their armies met in 605-4 at Carchemish on The River. Necoh was defeated by Nebuchadrezzar, son of Nabopolassar, and driven south to

[1] The designations of the title differ ; what is stated above was probably the fact.

[2] See Appendix I.

[3] As vividly described, or predicted, by Nahum ; see the writer's ' Twelve Prophets,' vol. ii. ; on the date see Appendix I.

his own land. Egypt had failed ; and the northern caldrons, as Jeremiah from the first predicted, again boiled with the fate of Judah and her neighbours. *The Foe*, though no longer the Scythian of his early expectations, was still *out of the North.*

By 602, if not before, Nebuchadrezzar, having succeeded his father as King of Babylon, carried his power to the coasts of the Levant and the Egyptian border. Judah was his vassal, and for three years Jehoiakim paid him tribute, but then defaulted, probably because of promises from Egypt after the fashion of that restless power. As if not yet ready to invade Judah in force, Nebuchadrezzar let loose upon her, along with some of his own Chaldeans, troops of Moabites, Ammonites and Arameans. Soon afterwards Jehoiakim died and was succeeded by his son Jehoiachin, a youth of eighteen, who appears to have maintained his father's policy ; for in 598, if not 597, Nebuchadrezzar came up against Jeru-salem, which forthwith surrendered, and the king, his mother and wives, his courtiers and statesmen were carried into exile, with the craftsmen and smiths and all who were *apt for war ; none remained save the poorest of the people of the land.*[1]

---

[1] II. Kings xxiv. 1-16. The chronology of the end of Jehoiakim's reign is uncertain. Most have held that the three years of his tribute were his last years, 600-598. But Winckler ('A I. Untersuchungen,' 81 ff.) gives good reasons for preferring 605-3.

Throughout these convulsions of her world, this crisis in the history of Judah herself, Jeremiah remains the one constant, rational, and far-seeing power in the national life. But at what terrible cost to himself! His experience is a throng of tragic paradoxes. Faithful to his mission, every effort he makes to rouse his people to its meaning is baffled. His word is signally vindicated by the great events of the time, yet each of these but tears his heart the more as he feels it bringing nearer the ruin of his people His word is confirmed, but he is shaken by doubts of himself, his utterance of which is in poignant contrast to his steadfast delivery of his messages of judgment. No prophet was at once more sure of his word and less sure of himself; none save Christ more sternly denounced his people or upon the edge of their doom more closely knit himself to them.

It is a staggering world, and the one man who has its secret is shaken to despair about himself. Yet the Word with which he is charged not only fulfils itself in event after event but holds its distracted prophet fast to the end of his abhorred task of proclaiming it.

The cardinal event was Nebuchadrezzar's victory over Necoh at Carchemish in 605 or 604 with its assurance of Babylonian, not Egyptian, supremacy throughout Western Asia. Such confirmation of the substance of Jeremiah's prophecies

12

of the past twenty-three years was that Divine
signal which flashed on him to reduce those
prophecies to writing and have them recited to
the people by Baruch. We have already followed the story in Ch. XXXVI of how this was
done[1] and of the consequences—the communication of the Roll to the princes and by them to
the king, the king's burning of the Roll piece by
piece as he heard it read, his order for the arrest
of Jeremiah and Baruch, their escape into hiding,
and their preparation of a Second Roll containing
all the words of the First with many others like
them. We may now, in addition, note the following.

First there is the Divine Peradventure at the
beginning of the story.[2] *It may be,* God says,
that the people will hear and turn from their evil
ways that I may forgive their iniquity—a very
significant *perhaps* when taken with the Parable
of the Potter to which we are coming. Again,
the king at least understands the evil predicted

[1] See above, pp. 22 ff. Our versions render the Hebrew
correctly, but the following emendations may be made from the
Greek: Verse 1, for *this word . . . from the Lord* read *the
word of the Lord came unto me;* 2, for *Israel* read *Jerusalem;*
22, omit *in the ninth month,* unnecessary after 9; 31, omit
their iniquity, for *upon them* read *upon him,* and for *men* read
land, of Judah; 32, for *Jeremiah took* read *Baruch took* and
omit *and gave it to Baruch the scribe the son of Neriah,* and
also the words *king of Judah* and *in the fire.*

[2] xxxvi. 3.

by Jeremiah to be the destruction of his land and
people by the King of Babylon.[1]   And again,
though some of the princes encourage the
Prophet's escape, and urge the king not to burn
the Roll, none are shocked by the burning.[2]
Evidently in 605-4 they were not so impressed
with the divinity of Jeremiah's word as they had
been in 608.   Then they did not speak of telling
the king; now they say that they *must tell*[3] him.
Jehoiakim's malignant influence has grown, and
Jeremiah discovers the inconstancy of the princes,
even of some friendly to himself.

To the same decisive year, 605-4, *the fourth of
Jehoiakim*, is referred an address by Jeremiah reported in XXV. 1-11 (with perhaps 13*a*).   This
repeats the Prophet's charge that his people have
refused — now for three-and-twenty years — to
listen to his call for repentance and reaffirms
the certainty, at last made clear by the Battle of
Carchemish, that their deserved doom lies in the
hands of a Northern Power, which shall waste
their land and carry them into foreign servi-
tude for seventy years.   The suggestion that this
address formed the conclusion of the Second
Roll dictated by Jeremiah to Baruch is suitable
to the contents of the address and becomes more

---

[1] xxxvi. 29 ; cp. xxv. 9 f.   [2] xxxvi. 19, 24.

[3] Such is the force of the Hebrew idiom in the last clause of
xxxvi. 16 ; for the different attitude of the princes in 608 see
pp. 170 ff.

probable **if we** take as genuine the words in 13a.
*Thus will I bring upon that land all My words which
I have spoken against her, all that is written in this
Book.* But a curious question rises from the fact
that we have two differing reports of the address.[1] Very significantly the shorter Greek
Version contains neither the addition to the date,
*that was the first year of Nebuchadrezzar, king of
Babylon,* nor the two statements that his was the
Northern Power which would waste Judah and
which she should serve for seventy years (verses
1, 9, 11, as also the similar reference in verse 12),
all of which are inserted in the Hebrew text but
not without a sign of their being later intrusions
upon it.[2] And indeed it is inconceivable that the
Greek translator could have omitted the four
references to Nebuchadrezzar (including that in

[1] The Hebrew text is accurately rendered by our English
Versions; the following are the principal points on which the
Greek differs from it : Verse 1, both Greek and Latin lack *that
was the first year of Nebuchadrezzar, king of Babylon;* in
verse 2 Greek lacks *Jeremiah the prophet* and *all*, and in
verse 3 *the word of the Lord hath come to me* and *but ye have
not hearkened.* In verse 6 for *I will do you no hurt* Greek
reads *to your hurt.* Again, Greek lacks in 7 *saith the Lord,* in
8 *of Hosts,* in 9 *saith the Lord and to Nebuchadrezzar the
king of Babylon My servant,* and for *all the families* it reads
a family; and in 11 lacks *this, a desolation, these* and *the
king of Babylon,* substituting for the last two *shall serve
among the nations.*

[2] E.g. the preposition *to* before *Nebuchadrezzar* in verse 9
which does not construe.

verse 12) had he found them in the Hebrew text
from which he worked. Probably, therefore,
Jeremiah did not include them in the first version
of his address; and for this he had reason. His
purpose in the address was to declare the fulfilment of the substance of all his previous prophesying, and this had been not that the Chaldeans,
but that *a northern power*, would prove to be
the executioner of God's judgment upon Judah.
The references to Nebuchadrezzar were added,
possibly by Jeremiah himself or by Baruch, as
the Chaldean doom steadily drew nearer. The
interesting thing is that the earlier version of
the address survived and was used by the Greek
translator.[1]

Verses 12-14, indicating the destruction of
Babylon in her turn after seventy years, are, in
whole or in part, generally taken as a post-exilic
addition.[2] Omitting verse 14, the Greek inserts
between 13 and 15 the Oracles on Foreign
Nations, which the Hebrew postpones to Chs.
XLVI. ff.[3] In the uncertain state of the text of
12-14 it is impossible to decide whether this was
or was not the original position of those Oracles.

[1] xxv. 1-14 has been denied to Jeremiah by Schwally
('Z.A.T.W.,' viii. 177 ff.) and Duhm, but their arguments are
answered by Giesebrecht and Cornill *in loco;* see, too, Gillies,
195-8, 202, and Skinner, 240 f.

[2] See Davidson in Hastings' 'D.B.,' ii. 574, Driver and Gillies
in loco.

[3] See above, p. 14.

The rest of the chapter, verses 15-38, is so full
of expansions and repetitions, which we may
partly see from a comparison of it with the
Greek, as well as of inconsistencies with some
earlier Oracles by Jeremiah,[1] of traces of the later
prophetic style and of echoes of other prophets,
that many deny any part of the miscellany to
be Jeremiah's own. Yet we must remember that
his commission was not to Judah alone[2] but to
the nations as well, against many of which XXV.
15-38 is directed; and the figure of the Lord
handing to the Prophet the cup of the wine of
His wrath is not one which we have any reason
to doubt to be Jeremiah's. Sifting, by help of
the Greek, the Hebrew list of nations who are to
drink of the cup, we get Judah and Egypt;
Askalon, Gaza, Ekron, and the remnant of Ashdod; Dedan, Tema, Buz, and their *clipt* neighbours in Arabia; all of whom were shaken in
Jeremiah's day by the Chaldean terror. Indeed
the reference to Ashdod suits the condition of
that Philistine city in the Prophet's time better
than its restored prosperity in the post-exilic
age. The substance of verses 15-23 may therefore be reasonably left to Jeremiah. Verses
24-38 are more doubtful.[3]

[1] E.g. cp. 26 with 9 and both with i. 15.

[2] As Duhm asserts; see above, pp. 79 ff.

[3] The above paragraph on xxv. 15-38 is based on Giesebrecht's
careful analysis of the passage.

2. PARABLES.

(XIII, XVIII-XX, XXXV).

To the reign of Jehoiakim are usually referred a number of symbolic actions by Jeremiah, the narratives of which carry no dates. So far as they imply that the Prophet was still able to move openly about Jerusalem and the country they might be regarded as earlier than 604, when he was under restraint and had to hide himself.[1] But this is not certain. We are left to take them in the order in which they occur in the Book.

The first is that of the waist-cloth, XIII. 1-11. Jeremiah was charged to buy a linen waist-cloth [2] and after wearing it, but keeping it from damp, to bury it in the cleft of a rock, and after many days to dig it up, when he found it rotting. So had the Lord taken Israel to cleave to Him as such a cloth *cleaves to the loins of a man ;* but separated from Him they had likewise rotted and were good for nothing. Separated by what— God's action or their own ? As it stands the interpretation is complicated. God spoils Israel because of their pride (verse 9) and Israel spoil themselves by disobedience and idolatry (verse 10). The complication may be due to a later addition to the text. But this question is not serious.

[1] xxxvi. 5, 19, 26.

[2] Worn next the skin ; not *girdle* which came over the other garments. See ' Enc. Bibl.,' article ' Girdle.'

Neither is that of the place where Jeremiah is said to have buried the cloth. *Pĕrath*, the spelling in the text, is the Hebrew name for the Euphrates and so the Greek and our own versions render it. But the name has not its usual addition of The River. If the Euphrates be intended the story is hardly one of fact, but rather a vivid parable of the saturation of the national life by heathen, corruptive influences from Mesopotamia.[1] Yet within an hour from Anathoth lies the Wady Farah, a name which corresponds to the Hebrew *Pĕrath* or (by a slight change) *Parah;* and the Wady, familiar as it must have been to Jeremiah, suits the picture, having a lavish fountain, a broad pool and a stream, all of which soak into the sand and fissured rock of the surrounding desert.[2] That the Wady Farah was the scene of the parable is therefore possible, though not certain.[3]

[1] So virtually Cornill, who, indifferent as to whether the story is one of fact or of imagination, emphasises the choice of the Euphrates as its essential point, compares ii. 18, *to drink of the waters of the River*, and dates the story in the earliest years of Jeremiah's ministry. On the other hand Erbt, who also reads *Euphrates*, interprets the story as one of actual journeys thither by Jeremiah.

[2] I visited it in 1901 and 1904, a most surprising oasis !

[3] Pĕrath or Parah = Farah was first suggested by Ewald ('Prophets of the O. T.,' Eng. trans. iii. 152), quoting Schick ('Ausland,' 1867, 572-4), by Birch ('P.E.F.Q.,' 1880, 235), and by Marti ('Z.D.P.V.,' 1880, 11), and has been accepted by many—Cheyne, Ball, McFadyen, Peake, etc.

But the ambiguity of these details does not interfere with the moral of the whole.

This parable is immediately followed by the ironic metaphor of the Jars Full of Wine, XIII. 12-14, which I have already quoted.[1]

Next comes the Parable of the Potter, Ch. XVIII, that might be from any part of the Prophet's ministry, during which he was free to move in public. This parable is instructive first by disclosing one of the ways along which Revelation reached, and spelt itself out in, the mind of the Prophet. He felt a Divine impulse to go down to the house of the Potter,[2] *and there I will cause thee to hear My Words*, obviously not words spoken to the outward ear. For, as Jeremiah watched the potter at work on *his two stones*,[3] and saw that when the vessel he first attempted was marred he would remould the clay into another vessel as seemed good to him, a fresh conception of the Divine Method with men broke

[1] See above, p. 55.

[2] In the valley of Hinnom, where were potteries and above them a city-gate *Harsith* = (probably) *Potsherds;* in the upper valley broken pottery is still crushed for cement; lower down traces of ancient potteries appear, and there is the traditional site of the Potter's Field, Matt. xxvii. 7.

[3] So literally the term rendered *wheel*, A.V. It was of two discs, originally of stone, but later of wood, of which in earlier times the upper alone revolved and the lower and larger was stationary, but later both revolved by the potter's foot. See 'Enc. Bibl.,' article 'Pottery.'

upon Jeremiah and became articulate. A word
from the Lord flashed through his eyes upon his
mind, just as in his first visions of the almond-
blossom and the caldron.[1]

XVIII. 5. Then the Word of the Lord came unto
6 me, saying, O House of Israel, cannot I do
with you as this potter ?[2] Behold, as the clay
in the hand of the potter, so are ye in My
hand.[3]

Thus by figure and by word the Divine
Sovereignty was proclaimed as absolutely as
possible. But the Sovereignty is a real Sovereignty and therefore includes Freedom. It is
not fettered by its own previous decrees, as some
rigorous doctrines of predestination insist, but is
free to recall and alter these, should the human
characters and wills with which it works in
history themselves change. There is a Divine
as well as a human Free-will. 'God's dealing
with men is moral; He treats them as their
moral conduct permits Him to do.'[4]

The Predestination of men or nations, which
the Prophet sees figured in the work of the potter,
is to Service. This is clear from the comparison
between Israel and a vessel designed for a definite
use. It recalls Jeremiah's similar conception of

[1] See above, pp. 84 f.
[2] Hebrew adds *Rede of the Lord.*
[3] Hebrew adds *House of Israel.*
[4] A. B. Davidson.

his own predestination, which was not to a certain state, of life or death, but to the office of speaker for God to the nations. Yet because the acceptance or rejection by a nation or an individual of the particular service, for which God has destined them, naturally determines their ultimate fate, therefore this wider sense, which predestination came to have in Christian doctrine, is so far also involved in the parable.[1]

To the truths of the Divine Sovereignty and the Divine Freedom the parable adds that of the Divine Patience. The potter of Hinnom does not impatiently cast upon the rubbish which abounds there the lump of clay that has proved refractory to his design for it. He gives the lump another trial upon another design. If, as many think, the verses which follow the parable, 7-10, are not by Jeremiah himself (though this is far from proved, as we shall see) then he does not explicitly draw from the potter's patience with the clay the inference of the Divine patience with men. But the inference is implicit in the parable. Did Jeremiah intend it? If he did, this is proof that in spite of his people's obstinacy under the hand of God, he cherished, though he dared not yet utter, the hope that God would have some fresh purpose for their service beyond the wreck

[1] To this we return in dealing with Jeremiah's experience. See below, lecture vii.

they were making of His former designs for them
and the ruin they were thereby bringing on
themselves—that He would grant them still
another chance of rising to His will. But if
Jeremiah did not intend this inference from his
parable then we may claim the parable as one
more example of that of which we have already
had several, the power of this wonderful man's
experience and doctrine to start in other minds
ideas and beliefs of which he himself was not
conscious, or which at least he did not articulate
—that power which is one of his highest distinctions as a prophet. I do not think, however,
that we can deny to Jeremiah all consciousness
of what his parable implies in regard to the
Patience of the Divine Potter with the perverse
human clay in His hands. For we have already
seen from another of the Prophet's metaphors
that under the abused and rank surface of a
nation's or an individual's life he was sure of soil
which by deeper ploughing would yet yield fruits
meet for repentance.[1]

In either case the parable is rich in Gospel for
ourselves. If we have failed our God upon His
first designs for us and for our service do not let
us despair. He is patient and ready to give us
another trial under His hand. And this not only
is the lesson of more than one of our Lord's
parables, for instance that of the fig-tree found

See above, p. 109 on iv. 3.

fruitless, but nevertheless given the chance of another year,[1] and the motive of His hopes for the publicans and harlots, but is implied by all the Gospel of His life and death for sinners. In these He saw still possibilities worth His dying for.

But as Christ Himself taught, there are, and ethically must be, limits to the Divine Patience with men. Of these the men of Judah and Jerusalem are warned in the verses which follow the parable. While it is true (verse 7 ff.) that if a nation, which God has said He will destroy, turn from its evil, He will relent, the converse is equally true of a nation which He has promised to plant and build, that if it do wrong and obey not He will surely repent of the good He had planned for it. For this refractory people of Judah He is already *framing* or *moulding evil*—the verb used is that of which the Hebrew name for *potter* is the participle. Though chosen of God and shaped by His hands for high service Israel's destiny is not irrevocable; nay, their doom is already being shaped. Yet He makes still another appeal to them to repent and amend their ways. To this they answer : *No use ! we will walk after our own devices and carry out every one the stubbornness*

---

[1] Luke xiii. 6 ff. Other parables or actual incidents illustrating either the possibilities of characters commonly deemed hopeless or the fresh chances given them by God's grace, are found in Matt. xviii. 23 f., Luke vii. 39 f. (the woman who was a sinner) and xix. (Zacchæus).

of his evil heart. At least that is how Jeremiah interprets their temper; his people had hardened since Megiddo and the accession of Jehoiakim.

Some moderns have denied these verses to Jeremiah and taken them as the addition of a later hand and without relevance to the parable. With all respect to the authority of those critics,[1] I find myself unable to agree with them. They differ as to where the authentic words of the Prophet cease, some concluding these with verse 4 others with verse 6. In either case the parable is left in the air, without such practical application of his truths as Jeremiah usually makes to Judah or other nations. Nor can the relevance of the verses be denied, as Cornill, one of their rejectors, admits. Nor does the language bear traces of a later date. They seem to me to stand as Jeremiah's own.

The Prophet's threat of evil is still so vague, that, with due acknowledgment of the uncertainty of such points, we may suppose it, along with the Parable of the Potter, to have been uttered before the Battle of Carchemish, when the Babylonian sovereignty over Western Asia became assured.[2]

---

[1] Cornill *in loco*, Skinner, pp. 162 f., both of them in fine passages on the teaching of the parable, the former exposing the superficiality of Duhm's impulsive judgment upon it. Cornill finds that the genuine words of Jeremiah close with verse 4; Skinner, Erbt and Gillies (p. 158) continue them to 6.

[2] But see next page.

The next in order of Jeremiah's symbols, Ch.
XIX, the breaking of a potter's jar past restoration, with his repetition of doom upon Judah, led
to his arrest, Ch. XX, and this at last to his
definite statement that the doom would be captivity to the King of Babylon. Some therefore
date the episode after Carchemish, but this is
uncertain; Jeremiah is still not under restraint
nor in hiding.

He is charged to buy an earthen jar and take
with him some of the elders of the people and of
the priests to the Potsherd Gate in the Valley of
Hinnom.[1] There, after predicting the evils which
the Lord shall bring on the city because of her
idolatry and her sacrifice of children in that Valley
down which they were looking from this gate, he
broke the jar and flung it upon the heaps of
shattered earthenware from which the gate
derived its name;[2] and returning to the Temple
repeated the Lord's doom upon Judah and
Jerusalem. He was heard by Pashhur of the
priestly guild of Immer, who appears to have

[1] xix. 1 ff. The Greek connects this incident with the preceding
by reading *then* for the Hebrew *thus*, and with many Hebrew MSS.
adds to *saith the Lord* the phrase *to me*, making Jeremiah himself the narrator. In xix. 4 read with Greek *whom neither they
nor their fathers knew, and the kings of Judah have filled*, etc.
Throughout Greek lacks phrases which are probably later ad-
tions to Hebrew; but these are not important.

[2] See p. 185, n. 2.

been chief of the Temple police, and after being *smitten* was put in the stocks, but the next day released, probably rather because his friends among the princes had prevailed in his favour than because the mind of Pashḥur had meantime changed. For Jeremiah on his release immediately faced his captor with these words :—

XX. 3 The Lord hath called thy name not Pashḥur but Magor-Missabib, Terror-all-
4 round. For thus saith the Lord, Lo, I will make thee a terror to thyself and all thy friends, and they shall fall by the sword of their foes, and thine own eyes shall be seeing it ; and all Judah shall I give into the hand of the king of Babylon, and he shall carry them to exile and smite them with
6 the sword . . . and thou Pashḥur and all that dwell in thy house shall go into captivity and in Babylon thou shalt die.[1]

At last Jeremiah definitely states what Judah's doom from the North is to be. We wish that we knew the date of this utterance.

Assigned by its title to *the days of Jehoiakim* is

[1] The above is mainly from the Greek. The following is a significant instance of how the knowledge of the Bible still holds among some at least of the Scottish peasantry. A woman in a rural parish calling on her minister to complain about the harshness of the factor of the landlord said that he was a very Magor-Missabib. And it is no less significant that the minister had to consult his concordance to the Bible to know what she meant

another action of the Prophet, which is the
exhibition rather of an example than of a symbol,
Ch. XXXV. The story was probably dictated by
Jeremiah to Baruch, for while the Hebrew text
opens it in the first person (2-5), the Greek version
carries the first person throughout and the later
change by the Hebrew to the third person (12
and 18) may easily have been due to a copyist
mistaking the first personal suffix for the initial
letter of the name Jeremiah.[1]

The Rechabites, a tent-dwelling tribe sojourn-
ing within the borders, and worshipping the God,
of Israel, had taken refuge from the Chaldean
invasion within the walls of Jerusalem. Knowing
their fidelity to their ancestral habits Jeremiah
invited some of them to one of the Temple
chambers and offered them wine. They refused,
for they said that their ancestor Jehonadab ben-
Rechab[2] had charged them to drink no wine,

---

[1] In xxxv the differences between Greek and Hebrew continue
to be those generally found in the Book, i.e. Greek omits the
expansive formulas, including the Divine titles, redundant words
(like *all*) and phrases, and corrects the wrong preposition *to* by
the right *upon* (17). Further, it spells differently some of the
proper names, reads *house* for *chamber* (4 *bis*), *a bowl* for *bowls*
(5), *to me* for *to Jeremiah* (12), and in 18 does not address the
promise to the Rechabites, but utters it of them in the third
person, also omitting the name of Jeremiah, and in 19 for *for
ever*, lit. *all the days*, reads *all the days of the land*.

[2] The ally of Jehu, II. Kings x. 15, 23. The tribe was Kenite,
I. Chron. ii. 55. The Kenites, according to Jud. i. 16, I.

13

neither to build houses, nor sow seed nor plant vineyards. Whereupon Jeremiah went forth and held them up as an example to the men of Judah, not because of any of the particular forms of their abstinence, but because of their constancy. Here were people who remembered, and through centuries had remained loyal to, the precepts of an ancestor; while Israel had fallen from their ancient faithfulness to their God and ignored His commandments. The steadfast loyalty of these simple nomads to the institutions of a far-away human father, how it put to shame Judah's delinquency from the commands of her Divine Father! This contrast is in line with the others, which we have seen Jeremiah emphasising, between his people's fickleness towards God and the obdurate adherence of the Gentiles to their national gods, or the constancy of the processes of nature : the birds that know the seasons of their coming, the unfailing snows of Lebanon and the streams of the hills. The whole story is characteristic of Jeremiah's teaching.[1]

Sam. xv. 6, settled in the South of Judah, but Jonadab is found in North Israel and apparently his descendants, as fugitives before an invasion from the North, came from the same quarter. Heber the Kenite also dwelt on Esdraelon, Jud. iv. 17, v. 24.

[1] Duhm's criticisms of it, and rejection of some of its parts are, even for him, unusually arbitrary, especially his objection to the words in verse 13, *Go and say to the men of Judah and the inhabitants of Jerusalem*, for obviously these people were not gathered in, nor could be addressed from, the Temple chamber.

3. Oracles on the Edge of Doom.

(VII. 16—XVIII *passim,* XXII, XLV).

From the seventh to the tenth chapters of the
Book of Jeremiah there are a number of undated
passages in prose and in verse, which are generally
held to have been included in the collection of
the Prophet's Oracles written out by Baruch in
604-3, and of which some may have been delivered during the reign of Josiah, but the most of
them more probably either upon its tragic close
at Megiddo in 608, or under Jehoiakim.   We have
already considered the addresses reported in
VII. 1-15, 21-27,[1] as well as the metrical fragments
VII. 28, 29, and VIII. 8, 9.[2]   There are other
prose passages describing (1) VII. 16-20, the
worship of the Queen, or the Host, of Heaven,
which had been imposed upon Jerusalem by the
Assyrians, and either survived the decay of their
power from 625 onwards, or if suppressed by
Josiah in obedience to Deuteronomy,[3] had been
revived under Jehoiakim ; (2) VII. 30-34, the high-
places in Topheth, upon which children were
sacrificed, also condemned by Deuteronomy and

It was the people as a whole, whose fickleness from age to age
he was about to condemn ; on this verse Duhm's remarks are,
besides being arbitrary, inconsistent.

[1] Above, pp. 147 ff.   [2] Above, pp. 50, 153 f.

[3] Deut. iv. 19, xvii. 3 ; II. Kings xxiii. 5, 13.   See the present
writer's ' Jerusalem,' ii., pp. 186 ff., 260, 263.

recorded as destroyed by Josiah;[1] (3) VIII. 1-3, the desecration of the graves of Jerusalem.   It is not necessary to reproduce these prose passages, whether they be Jeremiah's or not; our versions of them, Authorised and Revised, are sufficiently clear.

But there follow, from VIII. 4 onwards, after the usual introduction, a series of metrical Oracles of which the following translation is offered in observance of the irregularity of the measures of the original.   Note how throughout the Prophet is, as before, testing his false people—*heeding* and *listening* are his words—finding no proof of a genuine repentance and bewailing the doom that therefore must fall upon them.   Some of his earlier verses are repeated, and there is the reference to the Law, VIII. 8 f., which we have discussed.[2]   There is also a hint of exile—which, however, is still future.

In Ch. VIII, verses 4-12 (including the repetitions they contain) seem a unity; verse 13 stands by itself (unless it goes with the preceding); 14, 15 echo one of the Scythian songs, but the fear they reflect may be that either of an Egyptian invasion after Megiddo or of a Chaldean; 16 and 17 are certainly of a northern invasion, but whether the same as the preceding is doubt-

[1] Deut. xii. 31, II. Kings xxiii. 10.   See 'Jerusalem,' ii., pp. 263 f.

[2] Pp. 153 f.

ful; and doubtful too is the connection of both with the incomparable elegy which follows—VIII. 18-IX. 1. For IX. 1 undoubtedly belongs to this, as the different division of the chapters in the Hebrew text properly shows. In Ch. IX. 2-9 the Prophet is in another mood than that of the preceding songs. There the miseries of his people had oppressed him; here it is their sins. There his heart had been with them and he had made their sufferings his own; here he would flee from them to a lodge in the desert.[1] IX. 10-12, is another separate dirge on the land, burned up but whether by invaders or by drought is not clear. Then 13-16 is a passage of prose. In 17-22 we have still another elegy with some of the most haunting lines Jeremiah has given us, on war or pestilence, or both. And there follow eight lines, verses 23-24, on a very different, a spiritual, theme, and then 25-26 another prose passage, on the futility of physical circumcision if the heart be not circumcised. If these be Jeremiah's, and there is no sign in them to the contrary, they form further evidence of his originality as a prophet.

The two Chs. VIII and IX are thus a collection both of prose passages and poems out of different circumstances and different moods, with

---

[1] The only apparent reason for the compiler putting the two songs together is that the last verse of the one and the first verse of the other open in the same way, *O that I had* (Hebrew *O who would give me*).

little order or visible connection. Are we to see
in them a number of those *many like words* which
Jeremiah, when he dictated his Second Roll to
Baruch, added to his Oracles on the First Roll?[1]

The first verses are in curious parallel to
Tchekov's remarkable plaint about his own people
and 'the Russian disease' as he calls their failing :
'Why do we tire so soon?   And when we fall
how is it that we never try to rise again?'

VIII.   4 And thou shalt say to them,[2] Thus saith
the Lord :

'Does any one fall and not get up,
    Or turn and not return?'[3]
5 Why then are this people turning
    Persistently turning[4]?
They take fast hold of deceit,
    Refuse to return.
6 I have been heeding, been listening—
    They speak but untruth !
Not a man repents of his evil,
    Saying, 'What have I done?'
All of them swerve in their courses
    Like a plunging horse in the battle.
7 Even the stork in the heavens
    Knoweth her seasons,

[1] xxxvi. 32.   [2] Greek omits this clause.
[3] Apparently a common proverb.
[4] Hebrew adds *Jerusalem* with no sense and a disturbance to
the metre.

And dove and swift and swallow
  Keep time of their coming—
Only my people, they know not
  The Rule[1] of the Lord.

8 How say ye, 'We are the wise,
  With us is the Law[2] of the Lord.'
But, lo, into falsehood hath wrought it[3]
  False pen of the scribes.

9 Put to shame are the wise,
  Dismayed and taken,
The Word of the Lord have they spurned—
  What wisdom is theirs?

10 So to others I give their wives,
  Their fields to who may take them,
For all from the least to the greatest
  On plunder are bent;
From the prophet on to the priest
  Everyone worketh lies.

11 They would heal the breach of my people
  As though it were trifling,
Saying 'It is well, it is well!'—
  And well it is not!

12 Were they shamed of the foulness they
    wrought?
  Nay, shamed not at all,
  Nor knew their dishonour!
So shall they fall with the falling,

---

[1] *Mishpaṭ = rule, order, ordinance.*
[2] *Torah = law*, see p. 154.
[3] Reading עָשָׂה for עָשׂוּ.

Reel in the time of their reckoning,
Sayeth the Lord.[1]

13 Would I harvest them ?—Rede of the Lord—
No grapes on the vine,
And never a fig on the fig-tree,
Withered the leaves.[2]

14 For what sit we still ?
Sweep together
And into the fortified cities,
To perish.
For the Lord our own God
Hath doomed us to perish,
Hath drugged us with waters of bale—
To Him[3] have we sinned.

15   Hoping for peace ?
'Twas no good,
For a season of healing ?
Lo, panic.[4]

16 From Dan the bruit[5] has been heard,
Hinnying of his horses,
With the noise of the neighing of his steeds
The land is aquake.

[1] With 10-12, cp. vi. 13-15 ; 11, 12 are wanting in Greek.
[2] Hebrew adds a line of corrupt text.
[3] Hebrew, *the Lord*.
[4] So Greek.   The verse is another instance of the two-stresses to-a-line metre ; see p. 46.
[5] So Greek.

He[1] comes,[1] he devours the land and her fulness
 The city and her dwellers.
17 For behold, I am sending upon you
 Basilisk-serpents,
Against whom availeth no charm,
 But they shall bite you.[2]

18 Ah! That my grief is past comfort[3]
 Faints on me my heart,
Lo, hark to the cry of my people
 Wide o'er the land.[4]
19 'Is the Lord not in Ṣion,
 Is there no king?[5]
[Why have they vexed Me with idols,
 Foreigners' fancies?][6]
20 'Harvest is past, summer is ended,
 And we are not saved!'
21 For the breaking of the daughter of my people
 I break, I blacken!
Horror hath fastened upon me
 Pangs as of her that beareth.[7]
22 Is there no balm in Gilead,
 Is there no healer?

---

[1] So Greek.   [2] Hebrew adds *Rede of the Lord.*
[3] After the Greek, Hebrew is hopeless.
[4] Lit., *from a land of distances,* usually taken as meaning exile. But exile is not yet. Duhm as above.
[5] So Greek.
[6] *Bubbles,* ii. 5. The couplet seems an intrusion breaking between the two parts of the people's cry.
[7] So Greek.

Why do the wounds never close[1]
Of the daughter of my people?
IX. 1 Oh that my head were waters,
Mine eyes a fountain of tears,
That day and night I might weep
For the slain of my people!

There follows an Oracle in a very different mood. In the previous one the Prophet has taken his people to his heart, in spite of their sin and its havoc; in this he repels and would be quit of them.

2 O that I had in the desert
A wayfarers'[2] lodge!
Then would I leave my people,
And get away from them,
For adulterers all they be,
A bundle[3] of traitors!

3 Their tongue they stretch
Like a treacherous bow, (?)
And never for truth
Use their power in the land,
But from evil to evil go forth
And Me they know not.[4]

[1] Lit., *why cometh not up the fresh skin on.*

[2] Greek, *an uttermost.*

[3] The Hebrew word seems to me to be taken here rather in its primitive sense of *bundle* than in the later, official meaning of *assembly.*

[4] Hebrew adds *Rede of the Lord* for till now the Prophet has spoken. Verse 3 is difficult. Duhm omits most, Cornill all, as breaking the metrical schemes which they think Jeremiah invari-

4 Be on guard with your friends,
   Trust not your[1] brothers,
   For brothers are all very Jacobs,
   And friends gad about to defame.

5 Every one cheateth his neighbour,
   They cannot speak truth.
   Their tongues they have trained to falsehood,
   They strain to be naughty—

6 Wrong upon wrong, deceit on deceit (?)
   Refusing to know Me.[2]

7   Therefore thus saith the Lord:[3]
   Lo, I will smelt them, will test them.
   How else should I do
   In face of the evil . . .[4] (?)
   Of the Daughter of My people?

8 A deadly[5] shaft is their tongue
   The words of their mouth[6] deceit;
   If peace any speak to his friend
   In his heart he lays ambush.

ably used.   But the form of the Hebrew text—short lines of two
beats each, with one longer line—is one into which Jeremiah sometimes falls (see pp. 46 f.).   *Like a bow* so Greek ; Hebrew, *their
bow.* Cp. our *draw a long bow* (Ball).
   [1] So Syriac.
   [2] Again Hebrew adds *Rede of the Lord.*   The text is uncertain.
Hebrew, *thy dwelling is in the midst of deceit, they refuse to know
Me.*
   [3] Hebrew adds *of Hosts.*
   [4] So Greek, Hebrew omits ; more seems to have dropped out.
   [5] So Hebrew text ; Hebrew margin and Greek *polished.*
   [6] So Greek,

9 Shall I not visit for such—
    Rede of the Lord—
Nor on a nation like this
    Myself take vengeance?

10 Raise for the mountains a wail,[1]
    For the meads of the pasture a dirge!
They are waste, with never a man[2]
    Nor hear the lowing of cattle.
From the birds of heaven to the beasts
    They have fled, they are gone.

11 I will make Jerusalem heaps,
    Of jackals the lair,
And the townships of Judah lay waste,
    With never a dweller.

12 Who is the man that is wise
    To lay this to mind,
As the mouth of the Lord hath told him,
    So to declare—
The wherefore the country is perished,
    And waste as the desert,
    With none to pass over!

13   And the Lord said unto me,[3] Because they
forsook My Law which I set before them,
14 and hearkened not to My Voice,[4] but have

---

[1] So Greek. Hebrew, *I will raise* and adds *lamentation.*

[2] Hebrew adds *passing over*, probably a mistaken transference from verse 12. Greek and Latin omit.

[3] So Greek.

[4] Hebrew uselessly adds *nor walked therein.*

walked after the stubbornness of their heart,
and after the Baals, as their fathers taught
15 them, therefore thus saith the Lord[1] the God
of Israel, Behold I will give them wormwood
16 to eat and the waters of poison to drink. And
I will scatter them among the nations, whom
neither they nor their fathers knew, and send
after them the sword till I have consumed
them.

17   Thus saith the Lord:
Call the keening women to come,
And send for the wise ones,
18 That they come and make haste
To lift us a dirge,
Till with tears our eyes run down,
Our eyelids with water.
19 For hark! from Sion the voice of wailing,
'How we are undone!
'Sore abashed we, land who have left,
Our homes overthrown!'[3]

20 Hear, O women, the saying of the Lord,
Your ears take in the word of His mouth,
Teach the lament to your daughters
Each to her comrade the dirge:

[1] Hebrew adds *of Hosts;* and *this people* for *them.*

[2] Hebrew adds *of Hosts* and *consider ye* which Greek omits as
well as *hasten* in 18; the text of the four lines is uncertain. For
us and *our* Greek has *you* and *your.*

[3] So Vulgate.

21 'For Death has come up by our windows
    And into our palaces,
  Cutting off from the streets the children
    The youths from the places; [1]
22 And the corpses of men are fallen
    As dung on the field,
  As sheaves left after the reaper
    And nobody gathers!'

23   Thus saith the Lord:
  Boast not the wise in his wisdom,
  Boast not the strong in his strength,
  Boast not the rich in his riches,
24 But he that would boast in this let him boast,
  Insight and knowledge of Me,
  That I am the Lord, who work troth,
  Judgment and justice on earth,
    For in these I delight.

25   Behold, the days are coming—Rede of the
  Lord—that I shall visit on everyone circum-
26 cised as to the foreskin: Egypt and Judah and
  Edom, the sons of Ammon and Moab, and
  all with the corner [2] clipt, who dwell in the
  desert; for all the nations are uncircumcised
  in their heart and all the house of Israel.

[1] Hebrew has the obvious intrusion, *Speak thus, Rede of the Lord*, which Greek lacks.

[2] I.e. of their hair; see xxv. 23, xlix. 32. Herodotus says (iii. 8) that some Arabs shaved the hair above their temples; forbidden to Jews, Lev. xix. 27.

Which just means that Israel, circumcised in the flesh but not in the spirit, are as bad as the heathen who share with them bodily circumcision.

Ch. X. 1-16 is a spirited, ironic poem on the follies of idolatry which bears both in style and substance marks of the later exile.

On the other hand X. 17-23 is a small collection of short Oracles in metre, which there is no reason to deny to Jeremiah. The text of the first, verses 17-18, is uncertain. If with the help of the Greek we render it as follows it implies not an actual, but an inevitable and possibly imminent, siege of Jerusalem. The couplet in 17 may alone be original and 18, the text of which is reducible neither to metre nor wholly to sense, a prose note upon it.

X. 17 Sweep in thy wares from beyond,[1]
In siege that shalt sit!

18 For thus saith the Lord, Behold, I will sling out them that dwell in this land,[2] and will distress them in order that they may find . . . (?)

Such is the most to be made of the fragment of which there are many interpretations. The next piece, 19-22, is generally acknowledged to be Jeremiah's. It has the ring of his earlier Oracles.

[1] So Greek; Hebrew, *the land*. The Hebrew part. *sitting* may like that in v. 18 be future.
[2] So Greek; Hebrew, *in the land at this time*.

The Hebrew and Greek texts differ as to the speaker in 19a. Probably the Greek is correct—the Prophet or the Deity addresses the city or nation and the Prophet replies for the latter identifying himself with her sufferings. It is possible, however, that the words *But I said* are misplaced and should begin the verse, in which case the Hebrew *my* is to be preferred to the Greek *thy* adopted below. If so the stoicism of 19 is remarkable.

19 Woe is me for thy[1] ruin,
    Sore is thy[1] stroke!
    But I said,
    Well, this sickness is mine[2]
    And I must bear it!
20 Undone is my tent and perished,[3]
    Snapped all my cords!
    My sons—they went out from me
    And they are not!
    None now to stretch me my tent
    Or hang up my curtains.
21 For that the shepherds[4] are brutish
    Nor seek of the Lord,
    Therefore prosper they shall not,
    All scattered their flock.[5]

[1] So Greek, Hebrew *my*.
[2] So some Greek and Latin versions, Syriac and Targ.
[3] Greek ; Hebrew omits.
[4] I.e. Rulers.   [5] Hebrew, *pastures*.

X. 22 Hark the bruit,
      Behold it comes,
      And uproar great
      From land of the North,
   To lay the cities of Judah waste,
      A lair of jackals.

As we have seen, Jeremiah in the excitement of
alarm falls on short lines, ejaculations of two
stresses each, sometimes as here with one longer
line.[1]

A quatrain follows of longer, equal lines as is
usual with Jeremiah when expressing spiritual
truths :—

23 Lord I know! Not to man is his way,
      Not man's to walk or settle his steps.
24 Chasten me, Lord, but with judgment,
      Not in wrath, lest Thou bring me to little!

The last verse of the chapter is of a temper
unlike that of Jeremiah elsewhere towards other
nations, and so like the temper against them felt
by later generations in Israel, that most probably
it is not his.

25 [Pour out Thy rage on the nations,
      Who do not own Thee,
   And out on the kingdoms
      Who call not Thy Name!

---

[1] See above, pp. 46 f., 93, 202 f.

14

For Jacob they devoured and consumed,
And wasted his homestead][1]

Another series of Oracles, as reasonably referred
to the reign of Jehoiakim as to any other stage of
Jeremiah's career, is scattered over Chs. XI-XX.
I reserve to a later lecture upon his spiritual conflict and growth those which disclose his debates
with his God, his people and himself—XI. 18-
XII. 6, XV. 10-XVI. 9, XVII. 14-18, XVIII. 18-
23, XX. 7-18, and I take now only such as deal
with the character and the doom of the nation.

Of these the first in the order in which they
appear in the Book is XI. 15, 16, with which we
have already dealt,[2] and the second is XII. 7-13,
generally acknowledged to be Jeremiah's own.
It is undated, but of the invasions of this time the
one it most clearly reflects is that of the mixed
hordes let loose by Nebuchadrezzar on Judah in
602 or in 598.[3] The invasion is more probably described as actual than imagined as
imminent. God Himself is the speaker : His *House*,
as the parallel *Heritage* shows, is not the Temple

[1] So, following some Greek MSS., Targ., and the parallel Ps.
lxxix. 6, 7.

[2] Above, pp. 152 ff.

[3] P. 176. Practically all agree to this. Admitting its possibility,
Duhm prefers to assign the lines to the Scythian invasion
against which see the reasons offered by Cornill *in loco*, who
further suggests a connection between xi. 15, 16 and xii. 7-13.
Ball, after Naegelsbach, argues for a date before Carchemish.

but the Land, His *Domain*. The sentence pronounced upon it is a final sentence, yet delivered by the Divine Judge with pain and with astonishment that He has to deliver it against His *Beloved*; and this pathos Jeremiah's poetic rendering of the sentence finely brings out by putting verse 9*a* in the form of a question. The Prophet feels the Heart of God as moved as his own by the doom of the people.

XII. 7 I have forsaken My House,
    I have left My Heritage,
  I have given the Beloved of My Soul
    To the hand of her foes.
  8 My Heritage to Me is become
    Like a lion in the jungle,
  She hath given against Me her voice,
    Therefore I hate her.
  9 Is My Heritage to Me a speckled wild-bird
    With wild-birds round and against her?
  Go, gather all beasts of the field,
    Bring them on to devour.
10 Shepherds so many My Vineyard have spoiled
    Have trampled My Lot—
  My pleasant Lot they have turned
    To a desolate desert.
11 They make it a waste, it mourns,
    On Me is the waste!
  All the land is made desolate,
    None lays it to heart!

12 Over the bare desert heights
    Come in the destroyers!
    [For the sword of the Lord is devouring
    From the end of the land,
    And on to the end of the land,
    No peace to all flesh.¹
13 Wheat have they sown and reaped thorns,
    Have travailed for nought,
    Ashamed of their crop shall they be
    In the heat of God's wrath.]

The last eight lines are doubtfully original:
the speaker is no longer God Himself.   There
follows, in verses 14-17, a paragraph in prose,
which is hardly relevant—a later addition,
whether from the Prophet or an editor.

The next metrical Oracles are appended to the
Parables of the Waist-cloth and of the Jars in
Ch. XIII.²   We have already quoted, in proof of
Jeremiah's poetic power, the most solemn warn-
ing he gave to his people, XIII. 15, 16.³   At
some time these lines were added to it :—

XIII. 17 But if ye will not hear it :
    In secret my soul shall weep
        Because of your pride,
    And mine eyes run down with tears
        For the flock of the Lord led captive.⁴

¹ The text of these four lines is hardly metrical.
² Above, pp. 183-185.   ³ Above, p. 59.
⁴ In this quatrain Greek reads *your soul*, and Hebrew *my eye*
and precedes this line by *shall weep indeed* which Greek omits.

The next Oracle in metre is an elegy, probably prospective, on the fate of Jehoiachin and his mother Nehushta.[1]

18 Say to the King and Her Highness,
　　Low be ye seated!
　　For from your heads is come down
　　The crown of your splendour.
19 The towns of the Southland are blocked
　　With none to open.
　　All Judah is gone into exile,
　　Exile entire.[2]

The flock of the Lord, verse 17, comes again into the next poem, addressed to Jerusalem as appears from the singular form of the verbs and pronouns preserved throughout by the Greek (but only in 20*b* by the Hebrew) which to the disturbance of the metre adds the name of the city—probably a marginal note that by the hand of some copyist has been drawn into the text. In verse 21 the people, whom Judah has wooed to be her ally but who are about to become her tyrant, are, of course, the Babylonians.[3]

The last line is one of those longer ones with which verses or strophes often conclude (see p. 35).

[1] II. Kings xxiv. 8, 15 ; Jer. xxii. 26.
[2] So Greek.
[3] See ii. 36, iv. 30 ; Ezek. xxiii. 22.

XIII. 20 Lift up thine eyes and look,
    They come from the North!
  Where is the flock that was given thee,
    Thy beautiful flock?
21 What wilt thou say when they set
    O'er thee as heads,[1]
  Those whom thyself wast training
    To be to thee friends?
  Shall pangs not fasten upon thee,
    Like a woman's in travail?
22 And if thou say in thine heart,
    Why fall on me these?
  For the mass of thy guilt stripped are thy
    skirts,
    Ravished thy limbs!
23 Can the Ethiop change his skin,
    Or the leopard his spots?
  Then also may ye do good
    Who are wont to do evil.
24 As the passing chaff I strew them
    To the wind of the desert.
25 This is thy lot, the share I mete thee—
    Rede of the Lord—
  Because Me thou hast wholly forgotten
    And trusted in fraud.
26 So thy skirts I draw over thy face,
    Thy shame is exposed.

[1] *As heads* obviously belongs to this second line of the quatrain, from which some copyist has removed it to the fourth.

27 Thine adulteries, thy neighings,
   Thy whorish intrigues;
On the heights, in the field have I seen
   Thy detestable deeds.
Jerusalem! Woe unto thee!
   Thou wilt not be clean—
   After how long yet?[1]

Ch. XIV. 1-10 is the fine poem on the Drought
which was rendered in a previous lecture.[2]   It is
followed by a passage in prose, 11-16, that implies
a wilder 'sea of troubles,' not drought only but
war, famine and pestilence.   Forbidden to pray for
the people Jeremiah pleads that they have been
misled by the prophets who promised that there
would be neither famine nor war; and the Lord
condemns the prophets for uttering lies in His
Name.   Through war and famine prophets and
people alike shall perish.

XIV. 17 And thou shalt say this word to them:
   Let your eyes run down with tears
      Day and night without ceasing,
For broken, broken is the Daughter of my
      people,
   With the direst of strokes!
18 If forth to the field I fare,
   Lo the slain of the sword!

---

[1] So Hebrew literally.
[2] Pp. 56 f.   The date is quite uncertain.

> Or come I into the city
>   Lo anguish of famine!
> Yea, prophet and priest go a-begging
>   In a land they know not.[1]

Some see reflected in these lines the situation after Megiddo, when Egyptian troops may have worked such evils on Judah; but more probably it is the still worse situation after the surrender of Jerusalem to Nebuchadrezzar. There follows, 19-22, another prayer of the people (akin to that following the drought, 7-9) which some take to be later than Jeremiah. The metre is unusual, if indeed it be metre and not rhythmical prose.

19 [Hast Thou utterly cast off Judah,
      Loathes Sion Thy soul?
    Why hast Thou smitten us so
      That for us is no healing?
    Hoped we for peace—no good!
    For a season of healing—lo panic!
20 We acknowledge, O Lord, our wickedness,
      The guilt of our fathers; to Thee have we sinned.
21 For the sake of Thy Name, do not spurn us,
      Debase not the Throne of Thy Glory,
    Remember, break not Thy Covenant with us!

---

[1] The text of the first four lines is uncertain. I have mainly followed the Greek. *Begging,* if we borrow the sense of the verb in Syriac, otherwise *huckstering, peddling.*

22 'Mongst the bubbles of the nations are makers
    of rain,
  Or do the heavens give the showers?
  Art Thou not He for whom we must wait?
  Yea, Thou hast created all these.]

As the Book now runs this prayer receives from
God a repulse, XV. 1-4, similar to that which was
received by the people's prayer after the drought
XIV. 10-12, and to that which Hosea heard to the
prayer of his generation.[1]   Intercession for such
a people is useless, were it made even by Moses
and Samuel; they are doomed to perish by the
sword, famine and exile.   This passage is in prose
and of doubtful origin.   But the next lines are in
Jeremiah's favourite metre and certainly his own.
They either describe or (less probably) anticipate
the disaster of 598.   God Himself again is the
speaker as in XII. 7-11.   His Patience which the
Parable of the Potter illustrated has its limits,[2]
and these have now been reached.   It is not God
who is to blame, but Jerusalem and Judah who
have failed Him.

XV. 5 Jerusalem, who shall pity,
    Who shall bemoan thee,
  Who will but turn him to ask
    After thy welfare?
 6 'Tis thou that hast left Me—Rede of the Lord—
    Still going backward.

----

[1] Hos. vi. 1-4.   [2] P. 189.

So I stretched my hand[1] and destroyed thee
Tired of relenting.

7 With a winnowing fork I winnowed them
In the gates of the land.
I bereaved and destroyed my people
Because of their evil.[2]

8 I saw their widows outnumber
The sand of the seas.
I brought on the mother of youths (?)
Destruction at noonday,
And let fall sudden upon them
Anguish and terrors.[3]

9 She that bare seven hath fainted,
Breathes out her life,
Set is her sun in the daytime
Shamed and abashed!
And their remnant I give to the sword
In face of their foes![4]

Through the rest of Ch. XV and through
XVI and XVII are a number of those personal
passages, which I have postponed to a subsequent
lecture upon Jeremiah's spiritual struggles,[5] and
also several passages which by outlook and
phrasing belong to a later age. The impression
left by this miscellany is that of a collection of

---

[1] Hebrew and some Greek MSS. add *against thee.*

[2] Hebrew, *they turned not from their ways.*

[3] The text of verse 8 is uncertain. I have mainly followed the Greek.

[4] Hebrew adds *Rede of the Lord.*   [5] Lecture vii.

sayings put together by an editor out of some
Oracles by our Prophet himself and deliverances
by other prophets on the same or similar themes.
In pursuance of the plan I proposed I take now only
those passages in which Jeremiah deals with the
character of his people and their deserved doom.

XVI. 5 Thus saith the Lord—
  Come not to the home of mourning,
  Nor go about to lament,[1]
  For my Peace I have swept away—
  Away from this people.[2]
 8 Nor enter the house of feasting,
  To sit with them eating and drinking
 9 For thus saith the Lord, the God of Israel:
  Lo, I make to cease from this place,
  To your eyes, in your days,
  The voices of joy and rejoicing,
  The voices of bridegroom and bride.

There follows a passage in prose, 10-13, which in
terms familiar to us, recites the nation's doom,
their exile. Verses 14, 15 break the connection
with 16 ff., and find their proper place in XXIII.
7-8, where they recur. Verses 16-18 predict,
under the figures of fishers and hunters, the
arrival of bands of invaders, who shall sweep the
country of its inhabitants, because of the idolatries
with which these have polluted it. There is no

---

[1] Hebrew adds *nor bemoan them*, an expansion.

[2] Hebrew adds *Rede of the Lord, even kindness and compassion*; verses 6 and 7 are expansion.

reason to deny these verses to Jeremiah. In 19, 20 we come to another metrical piece, singing of the conversion of the heathen from their idols— the only piece of its kind from Jeremiah—which we may more suitably consider later. Verse 21 seems more in place after 18.

XVII. 1. The sin of Judah is writ
  With pen of iron,
  With the point of a diamond graven
   On the plate of their heart—
  And eke on the horns of their altars,[1]
   And each spreading tree,
 2 Upon all the lofty heights
   And hills of the wild.
 3 Thy substance and all thy treasures
   For spoil I give,
  Because of sin thy high places
   Throughout thy borders.
 4 Thine heritage thou shalt surrender[2]
   Which I have given thee,
  And thy foes I shall make thee to serve
   In a land thou knowest not.
  Ye have kindled a fire in my wrath
   That for ever shall burn.[3]

[1] Hebrew adds *when their children remember their altars and Asherim* rightly taken by Duhm and Cornill as a gloss.

[2] Hebrew adds *in thee* for which some read *thy hand*.

[3] These four verses along with the phrase *Thus saith the Lord* which follows them are lacking in Greek. This is clearly due to the oversight of a copyist, his eye passing inadvertently from *the Lord* of xvi. 21 to *the Lord* of xvii. 5.

These verses, characteristic of Jeremiah, are more so of his earliest period than of his work in the reign of Jehoiakim, and may have been among those which he added to his Second Roll. They are succeeded by the beautiful reflections on the man who does not trust the Lord and on the man who does, verses 5-8, quoted in a previous lecture.[1] The rest of the chapter consists of passages personal to himself, to be considered later, and of an exhortation to keep the Sabbath, verses 19-27, which is probably post-exilic.[2]

In Ch. XVIII the Parable of the Potter is followed by a metrical Oracle which has all the marks of Jeremiah's style and repeats the finality of the doom, to which the nation's forgetfulness of God and idolatry have brought it. Once more the poet contrasts the constancy of nature with his people's inconstancy. Neither the metre nor the sense of the text is so mutilated as some have supposed.

> XVIII. 13 Therefore thus saith the Lord:
> Ask ye now of the nations,
> Who heard of the like ?
> The horror she hath grossly wrought,
> Virgin of Israel.
> 14 Fails from the mountain rock
> The snow of Lebánon ?

---

[1] See pp. 53, 54.
[2] Cp. 'Isaiah,' lvi. 2-7, lviii. 13, 14 ; Neh. xiii. 15-22.

Or the streams from the hills dry up,
The cold flowing streams ? [1]
15 Yet Me have My people forgotten,
And burned [2] to vanity,
Stumbling from off their ways,
The tracks of yore,
To straggle along the by-paths,
An unwrought road ;
16 Turning their land to a waste,
A perpetual hissing.
All who pass by are appalled,
And shake their heads.
17 With [3] an east wind strew them I shall,
In face of the foe.
My back not my face shall I show them
In their day of disaster.

[1] A much manipulated verse ! *Mountain*, taking *sadai* in its archaic sense as in Assyrian and some Hebrew poems, Jud. v. 4, Deut. xxxii. 13 (see the writer's ' Deut. ' in the ' Camb. Bible for Schools') where it is parallel to *highlands*, *rock* and *flinty rock*. The following emendations of the text are therefore unnecessary, and are more or less forced. *Sirion* (Duhm, Cornill, Peake, McFadyen, Skinner) ; *missurim = from the rocks* (Rothstein). The Greek takes *sadai* as *breasts* and nominative to the verb : *Do the breasts of the rock give out ?*—not a bad figure. *Hill-streams* reading *mēmē harîm* (Rothstein) for the Hebrew *maim zarîm = strange* (? far off) *streams*. Ewald takes *zarîm* from *zarar = to rush, press*. Duhm reads *mĕzarîm = Northstar*. Cornill turns the couplet to *Or do dry up from the western sea the flowing waters ?* Gillies, *the wet winds from the sea*, etc., for which there is a suggestion in the Greek ὰ μῷ.

[2] See p. 149, n. 1.   [3] So some MSS. ; the text has *like*.

Personal passages follow in verses 18-23, and in XIX-XX. 6, the Symbol of the Earthen Jar and the episode of the Prophet's arrest with its consequences, which we have already considered,[1] and then other personal passages in XX. 7-18. Ch. XXI. 1-10 is from the reign of Ṣedekiah ; 11 12 are a warning to the royal house of unknown date, and 13, 14 a sentence upon a certain stronghold, which in this connection ought to be Jerusalem, but cannot be because of the epithets *Inhabitress of the Vale* and *Rock of the Plain*, that are quite inappropriate to Jerusalem. This is another proof of how the editors of the Book have swept into it a number of separate Oracles, whether relevant to each other or not, and whether Jeremiah's own or from some one else.

From Chs. XXII-XXIII. 8, a series of Oracles on the kings of Judah, we have had before us the elegy on Jehoahaz, XXII. 10 (with a prose note on 11. 12) and the denunciation of Jehoiakim 13-19.[2] There remain the warning (in prose) to do judgment and justice with the threat on the king's house, XXII. 1-5, and the following Oracles :—

XXII. 6 For thus saith the Lord concerning the house of the king of Judah [3]—

---

[1] Pp. 191 ff.   [2] Pp. 164-167.

[3] Duhm's objection to this title as a mistake by an editor is groundless ; for though the following lines are addressed to the land or people as a whole, their climax is upon the fate of the royal house, *the choice of thy cedars*

A Gilead art thou to Me,
　Or head of Lebánon,
Yet shall I make thee a desert
　Of tenantless cities.
7 I will hallow against thee destroyers,
　Each with his weapons,
They shall cut down the choice of thy cedars
And fell them for fuel.

8　[And [1] nations shall pass by this city and
　shall say each to his mate, For what hath
9　the Lord done thus to this great city? And
　they shall answer, Because they forsook the
　Covenant of the Lord their God, and bowed
　themselves to other gods and served them.]

Whether this piece of prose be from Jeremiah
himself or from another is uncertain and of no
importance. It is a true statement of his own
interpretation of the cause of his people's doom.
The next Oracle addressed to the nation is upon
King Jeconiah, or Koniyahu. I follow mainly the
Greek.

XXII. 20 Up to Lebánon and cry,
　Give forth thy voice in Bashán,
And cry from Abarîm [2] that broken
　Be all thy lovers.
21 I spake to thee in thy prosperity,
　Thou saidst, I hear not!
This was thy way from thy youth,
　Not to hark to My Voice.

[1] Hebrew adds *many*.　　[2] Greek *from over the sea.*

22 All thy shepherds the wind shall shepherd,
   Thy lovers go captive.
   Then shamed shalt thou be and confounded
   For all thine ill-doing.

23 Thou in Lebánon that dwellest,
   Nested on cedars,
   How shalt thou groan[1] when come on thee
      pangs,
   Anguish as hers that beareth.

24 As I live — 't is the Rede of the Lord—
   Though Konyahu were
   Upon My right hand the signet,
   Thence would I tear him.[2]

25 And I shall give thee into the hand of them
   that seek thy life and into the hand of them
   thou dreadest, even into the hand of Nebuchadrezzar, king of Babylon, and into the

26 hand of the Chaldeans; and I will hurl thee
   out, and thy mother who bare thee, upon
   another land, where ye were not born, and

27 there shall ye die.   And to the land, towards
   which they shall be lifting their soul,[3] they
   shall not return.

28 Is Konyahu then despised,
   Like a nauseous vessel?
   Why is he flung and cast out
   On a land he knows not?

[1] Greek, Syriac, Vulgate.   [2] Hebrew *thee*.
[3] Hebrew adds *to return thither;* Greek lacks.

15

29 Land, Land, Land,
　　Hear the Word of the Lord!
30 Write this man down as childless,
　　A fellow . . . (?)
　　For none of his seed shall flourish
　　Seated on David's throne,
　　Or ruling still in Judah.[1]

We can reasonably deny to Jeremiah nothing
of all this passage, not even the prose by which
the metre is interrupted. We have seen how
natural it was for the rhapsodists of his race to
pass from verse to prose and again from prose to
verse. Nor are the repetitions superfluous, not
even that four-fold *into the hand of* in the prose
section, for at each recurrence of the phrase we
feel the grip of their captor closing more fast
upon the doomed king and people. Nor are we
required to take the pathetic words, *the land to
which they shall be lifting up their soul*, as true only
of those who have been long banished. For the
exiles to Babylon felt this home-sickness from the
very first, as Jeremiah well knew.

If we are to trust the date given by its title—
and no sufficient reason exists against our doing
so—there is still an Oracle of Jeremiah, which,
though now standing far down in our Book,
Ch. XLV, belongs to the reign of Jehoiakim, and

[1] In 28-30 the Greek, mainly followed above in accordance
with the metre, is far shorter than the Hebrew text.

is properly a supplement to the story of the writing of the Rolls by Baruch in 605.[1] The text has suffered, probably more than we can now detect.

XLV. 1 The Word, which Jeremiah the prophet spake to Baruch, the son of Neriah, while he was writing these words in a book at the mouth of Jeremiah,[2] in the fourth year of Jehoiakim, son of Josiah, king of Judah.[3]

2   Thus saith the Lord[4] concerning thee, O
3 Baruch, for thou didst say :—

Woe is me! Woe is me![5]
How hath the Lord on my pain heaped sorrow!
   I am worn with my groaning,
   Rest I find none!

4 [Thus shalt thou say to him[6]] thus sayeth the Lord :
   Lo, what I built I have to destroy,

---

[1] The reasons given by Giesebrecht and Duhm *in loco*, by Skinner, p. 346, and (more fancifully) by Erbt, p. 86, for impugning the date given in xlv. 1, and relegating the Oracle to the close of Jeremiah's life in exile as his last words to Baruch, have been answered in great detail, and to my mind conclusively, by Cornill, who points out how much more suited the Oracle is to conditions in 605 than to those of Baruch and Jeremiah after 586.

[2] Cornill : *the words of Jeremiah in a book.*

[3] Hebrew adds *saying*.

[4] Hebrew adds *the God of Israel.*

[5] So Greek.

[6] Superfluous after, not to say inconsistent with, verse 2 ; probably editorial.

And what I planted I have to root up.[1]
5 Thou, dost thou seek thee great things ?
  Seek thou them not,
For behold, on all flesh I bring evil—
  Rede of the Lord—
But I give thee thy life as a prey,
  Wheresoever thou goest.

The younger man, with youth's high hopes for his people and ambitions for himself in their service—ambitions which he could honestly cherish by right both of his station in life [2] and the firmness of his character—felt his spirit spent beneath the long-drawn weight of all the Oracles of Doom, which it was his fate to inscribe as final.   Now to Baruch in such a mood the older man, the Prophet, might have appealed from his own example, for none in that day was more stripped than Jeremiah himself, of family, friends, affections, or hopes of positive results from his ministry ; nor was there any whose life had been more often snatched from the jaws of death.   But instead of quoting his own case Jeremiah brought to his despairing servant and friend a still higher example.   The Lord Himself had been forced to relinquish His designs and to destroy what He

---

[1] *I have to* or *am about to.*   The Hebrew addition to this couplet, *and that is the whole earth,* is probably a gloss ; it is not found in all Greek versions.

[2] His brother Seraiah was a high officer of the king, ch. li 59 ; see also Josephus X. 'Antt.,' ix. 1.

had built and to uproot what He had planted. In face of such Divine surrender, both of purpose and achievement, what was the resignation by a mere man, or even by a whole nation, of their hopes or ambitions? Let Baruch be content to expect nothing beyond bare life : *thy life shall I give thee for a prey.* This stern phrase is found four times in the Oracles of Jeremiah,[1] and nowhere else. It is not more due to the Prophet than to the conditions of his generation. Jeremiah only put into words what must have been felt by all the men of his time—those terrible years in which, through the Oracles quoted in this lecture, he has shown us War, Drought, Famine and Pestilence fatally passing over his land; when *Death came up by the windows,* children were cut off from their playgrounds and youths from the squares where they gathered, and the corpses of men were scattered like dung on the fields. It was indeed a time when each survivor must have felt that his life had been *given* him *for a prey.*

To the hearts of us who have lived through the Great War, with its heavy toll on the lives both of the young and of the old, this phrase of Jeremiah brings the Prophet and his contemporaries very near.

Yet more awful than the physical calamities which the prophet unveils throughout these

---

[1] Here and xxi. 9, xxxviii. 2, xxxix. 18.

terrible years are his bitter portraits of the character of his people, whom no word of their God nor any of His heavy judgments could move to repentance. He paints a hopeless picture of society in Jerusalem and Judah under Jehoiakim, rotten with dishonesty and vice. Members of the same family are unable to trust each other; all are bent on their own gain by methods unjust and cruel—from top to bottom so hopelessly false as even to be blind to the meaning of the disasters which rapidly befal them and to the final doom that steadily draws near. Yet, for all the wrath he pours upon his generation and the Divine vengeance of which he is sure, how the man still loves and clings to them, and takes their doom as his own! And, greatest of all, how he reads in the heart that was in him the Heart of God Himself—the same astonishment that the people are so callous, the same horror of their ruin, nay the same sense of failure and of suffering under the burden of such a waste—*on Me is the waste!*[1] *What I built I have to destroy!*

Except that he does not share these secrets of the Heart of God, it is of Victor Hugo among moderns that I have been most reminded when working through Jeremiah's charges against the king, the priests, the prophets and the whole people of Judah—Victor Hugo in his *Châtiments* of

---

[1] ix. 3, 7 (*How else can I do?*), xii. 9, 11, see p. 211.

the monarch, the church, the journalists, the
courtiers and other creatures of the Third French
Empire. There is the same mordant frankness
and satiric rage combined with the same desire to
share the miseries of the critic's people in spite
of their faults. I have already quoted Hugo's
lines on Napoleon III as parallel to Jeremiah's on
Jehoiakim.[1]

Here are two other parallels.

To Jeremiah's description of his people being
persuaded that all was well, when well it was not,
and refusing to own their dishonour, VIII. 11, 12,
take Hugo's ' on est infâme et content ' and

Et tu chantais, en proie aux éclatants mensonges
        Du succès.

And to Jeremiah's acceptance of the miseries
of his people as his own and refusal to the end
to part from them take these lines to France :—

Je te demanderai ma part de tes misères,
    Moi ton fils.
France, tu verras bien qu'humble tête éclipsée
    J'avais foi,
Et que je n'eus jamais dans l'âme une pensée
    Que pour toi.
France, être sur ta claie à l'heure où l'on te traine
    Aux cheveux,
O ma mère, et porter mon anneau de ta chaine
    Je le veux!

[1] See p. 167.

LECTURE VI

TO THE END AND AFTER

597— ? B.C.

THE few remaining years of the Jewish kingdom ran rapidly down and their story is soon told.

When Nebuchadrezzar deported King Jehoiachin in 597, he set up in his place his uncle Mattaniah, a son of Josiah by that Hamutal, who was also the mother of the miserable Jehoahaz.[1] The name of the new king Nebuchadrezzar changed to Ṣedekiah, *Righteousness* or *Truth of Yahweh*,[2] intending thus to bind the Jew by the name of his own God to the oath of allegiance which he had exacted from him. When Ezekiel afterwards denounced Ṣedekiah on his revolt it was for *despising the Lord's oath and breaking the Lord's covenant*[3]—a signal instance of the sanctity attached in the ancient world to an oath sworn by one nation to another, even though it was to the humiliation of the swearer.[4] So far as we see,

[1] 2 Kings xxiii. 31, xxiv. 17 ; see above, p. 164.
[2] The exact transliteration of the Hebrew is *Ṣidkiyahu*.
[3] Ezek. xvi. 59, xvii. 11-21 ; especially 15-19.
[4] Ps. xv., *who sweareth to his own hurt and changeth not.*

(232)

Sedekiah was of a temper [1] to have been content
with the peace, which the observance of his oath
would have secured to him.   But he was a weak
man, master no more of himself than of his
throne,[2] distracted between a half-superstitious
respect for the one high influence left to him in
Jeremiah and the opposite pressure, first from a
set of upstarts who had succeeded to the estates
and the posts about court of their banished
betters, and second, from those prophets whose
personal insignificance can have been the only
reason of their escape from deportation.   It is one
of the notable ironies of history that, while Nebuchadrezzar had planned to render Judah powerless
to rebel again, by withdrawing from her all the
wisest and most skilful and soldierly of her popu
lation, he should have left to her her fanatics!

There remained in Jerusalem the elements—
sincerely patriotic but rash and in politics inex-
perienced—of a 'war-party,' restless to revolt
from Babylon and blindly confident of the strength
of their walls and of their men to resist the arms
of the great Empire.   Of their nation they and
their fellows alone had been spared the judgment
of the Lord and prided themselves on being the
Remnant to which Isaiah had promised survival
and security on their own land: for they said to

---

[1] Josephus imputes to him Χρεστότης καὶ δικαιοσύνη, X. 'Antt.'
vii. 5.

[2] *No strong rod, no sceptre to rule*, Ezek. xix. 14.

the Exiles, *Get ye far from the Lord, for unto us is this land given in possession.*[1] Through the early uneventful years of Sedekiah, this stupid and self-righteous party found time to gather strength, and in his fourth year must have been stirred towards action by the arrival in Jerusalem of messengers from the kings of Edom, Moab, Ammon, Tyre and Sidon, all of them states within the scope of Egyptian intrigues against Babylon.[2] For the time the movement came to nothing largely because of Jeremiah's influence, and Sedekiah is said to have journeyed to Babylon to protest in person his continued fidelity.[3] Either then or previously Nebuchadrezzar imposed on Jerusalem the Babylonian idolatry which Ezekiel describes as invading even the Temple.[4]

The intrigues of Egypt persisted, however, and, in 589 or 588, after the accession of Pharaoh Hophra,[5] at last prevailed upon Judah. Sedekiah yielded to the party of revolt and Nebuchadrezzar swiftly invested Jerusalem. Roused to realities *the king and all the people of Jerusalem* offered their repentance by a solemn covenant before God to

---

[1] Or *ye are far*, etc., Ezek. xi. 15.

[2] Jer. xxvii. ; in verse 1 for *Jehoiakim* read *Sedekiah.*

[3] Jer. li. 59 ; though some doubt this.

[4] Ezek. viii ; Jer. xliv. 17-19 and his other references to the worship of the *Queen* or *Host of Heaven* may also refer to this.

[5] Jer. xliv. 30, *Pharaoh* of xxxvii. 5, 7, 11, Ezek. xxix. 3; *Apries*, Herodotus ii. 161.

enfranchise, in obedience to the Law, those slaves
who had reached a seventh year of service.   But
when on the news of an Egyptian advance the
Chaldeans raised their siege, the Jewish slave-
owners broke faith and pressed back their
liberated slaves into bondage.[1] This proved the
last link in the long chain of lies and frauds by
which the hopelessly dishonest people fastened
upon them their doom.   Egypt again failed her
dupes.   The Chaldeans, either by the terror they
inspired or by an actual victory on the field, compelled her army to retire, and resumed the siege
of Jerusalem.   Though Jeremiah counselled surrender and though the city was sapped by famine
and pestilence, the fanatics—to whom, however
reluctantly, some admiration is due—held out
against the forces of Babylon for a year and a
half.   Then came the end.   The walls on the
north were breached.   Ṣedekiah fled by a southern gate, upon an effort to reach the East of
Jordan.   He was overtaken on the plains of
Jericho, his escort scattered and himself carried
to Nebuchadrezzar's head-quarters at Riblah on
the Orontes.   Thence, after his sons were slain
before his eyes, and his eyes put out, he was taken
in fetters to Babylon.   Nebuṣaradan, a high
Babylonian officer, was dispatched to Jerusalem
to burn the Temple, the Palace and the greater

[1] Jer. xxxiv. 8-22 ; cp. Exod. xxi. 1-6, Deut. xv. 12-18.

houses, and to transport to Babylon a second
multitude of Jews, leaving only *the poorest of
the land to be vine-dressers and husbandmen.*[1] This
was in 586.

1. The Release of Hope
(XXIV, XXIX)

From these rapidly descending years a number
of prophecies by Jeremiah have come to us, as
well as narratives of the trials which he endured
because of his faithfulness to the Word of the
Lord, and his sane views of the facts of the time.
As we read these prophecies and narratives
several changes become clear in the position and
circumstances of the Prophet, and in his temper
and outlook. Signally vindicated as his words
have been, we are not surprised that to his contemporaries he has grown to be a personage of
greater impressiveness and authority than before.
He has still his enemies but these are not found
in exactly the same quarters as under Jehoiakim.
Instead of an implacable king, and princes more
or less respectful and friendly, in the king he has
now a friend, though a timid and ineffective one,
while the new and inferior princes appear almost
wholly against him. Formerly both priests and
prophets had been his foes, but now only the
prophets are mentioned as such, and at least one

[1] 2 Kings xxv. 21.

priest is loyal to him.[1] Inwardly again, he has
no more of those debates with God and his own
soul, which had rent him during the previous
years ; only once does doubt escape from his
lips in prayer.[2] Clearest of all, his hope has
been released, and in contrast with his prophesying up to the surrender of Jerusalem in 597, but
in full agreement with his enduring faith in God's
Freedom and Patience,[3] he utters not a few predictions of a future upon their own land for both
Israel and Judah. This greatest of the changes
which appear is due partly to the fact that while
the man's reluctant duty had been to pronounce
the doom of exile upon his people, that doom has
been fulfilled, and his spirit, which never desired
it,[4] is free to range beyond its shadows. To the
clearness into which he rises he is helped, under
belief in the Divine Grace, by the truth obvious
to all but fanatics that peace and order were
possible for that shaken world only through
submission to Nebuchadrezzar's firm government, including as this did a policy comparatively lenient to the Jewish exiles. But there
was another and stronger reason why Jeremiah
should at last turn himself to a ministry of hope,
however sternly he must continue to denounce
the Jews left in Jerusalem and Judah. The

---

[1] xxix. 29 ; Skinner, p. 253, doubts this.
[2] xxxii. 16-25.   [3] See above, pp. 186-188.   [4] xvii. 16.

catastrophe of 597 largely separated the better elements of the nation, which were swept into exile, from the worse which remained in the land.

It is this drastic sifting, ethically one of the most momentous events in the history of Israel, with which Jeremiah's earliest Oracle under Ṣedekiah is concerned, Ch. XXIV. Once more the Word of the Lord starts to him from a vision, this time of two baskets, one of good the other of bad figs, which the Lord, he says, *caused me to see :* a vision which I take to be as physical and actual as those of the almond-rod and the caldron upon his call, or of the potter at his wheel, though others interpret it as imaginative like the visions of Amos.[1] Note how easily again the Prophet passes from verse to prose. The verse is slightly irregular. The stresses of the four couplets are these—3 + 3 ; 4 + 3 ; 4 + 3 ; 3 + 3—to which the following version only approximates.

XXIV. 3 And the Lord said to me, What art thou seeing, Jeremiah ? And I said, Figs, the good figs very good, and the bad very bad, which for their [2] badness cannot be eaten.
4 And the Word of the Lord came unto me,
5 saying, Thus saith the Lord, the God of Israel—

[1] So Driver ; Amos vii. 1, 4, 7, viii. 1.
[2] So Greek.

Like unto these good figs
I look on the exiles of Judah,
Whom away from this place I have sent
To the Chaldeans' land for (their) good.

6 For good will I fix Mine eye upon them,
And bring them back to this land,
And build them and not pull them down,
And plant them and not pluck up.

7 And I will give them a heart to know Me, that I am the Lord, and they shall be for a people unto Me, and I will be to them for God, when they turn to me with all their heart.

8 But like the bad figs which cannot be eaten for their [1] badness—thus saith the Lord—so I give up Ṣedekiah, king of Judah, and his princes and the remnant of Jerusalem, the left in this land,[2] with them that dwell in the land of Egypt.[3]

9 And I will set them for consternation [4] to all kingdoms of the earth, a reproach and a proverb, a taunt and a curse, in all places whither I drive them. And I will send among them the sword, the famine and the pestilence, till

---

[1] So Greek and other versions.

[2] Greek *city*.

[3] Jews who may have stirred up Egypt against Babylon.

[4] So Greek; Hebrew adds *for an evil*, 'a corrupt repetition of the preceding word' (Driver).

they be consumed from off the ground which
I gave to them.[1]

We cannot overestimate the effect upon Jeremiah
himself, and through him and Ezekiel upon the
subsequent history of Israel's religion, of this
drastic separation in 597 of the exiles of Judah
from the remnant left in the land. After suffering for years the hopelessness of converting his
people, the Prophet at last saw an Israel of whom
hope might be dared. It was not their distance
which lent enchantment to his view for he gives
proof that he can descry the dross still among
them, despite the furnace through which they have
passed.[2] But the banished were without doubt
the best of the nation, and now they had 'dreed
their weird,' gone through the fire, been lifted out
of the habits and passions of the past, and
chastened by banishment—pensive and wistful as
exile alone can bring men to be.

We also have come out of the Great War with
the best of us gone, and feel the contrast between
their distant purity, *out of great tribulation*, and the
unworthiness of those who are left. But neither
to Jeremiah nor to any of his time was such inspiration possible as we draw from our brave,
self-sacrificing dead. No confidence then existed
in a life beyond the grave. Jeremiah himself can
only *weep for the slain of his people*. His last vision

---

[1] Hebrew adds *and to their fathers*.

[2] xxix. 20, 15, 21-32, see pp. 245-247.

of them is of *corpses strewn on the field like sheaves left after the reaper which nobody gathers,* barren of future harvests; and the last word he has for them is, *they went forth and are not.*[1]   But that separated and distant Israel has for the Prophet something at least of what the cloud of witnesses by which we are encompassed means for us.   There was quality in them, quality purified by suffering and sacrifice, more than enough to rally the conscience of the nation from which they had been torn.   For the Prophet himself they released hope, they awoke the sense of a future, they revived the faith that God had still a will for His people, and that by His patient Grace a pure Israel might be re-born.

If the vision of the Figs reveals the ethical grounds of Jeremiah's new hope for Israel, his Letter to the Exiles, XXIX. 1-23, discloses still another ground on which that hope was based— his clear and sane appreciation of the politics of his time. And it adds a pronouncement of profound significance for the future of Israel's religion, that the sense of the presence of God, faith in His Providence and Grace, and prayer to Him were independent of Land and Temple.

From the subsequent fortunes of the exiles we know what liberal treatment they must have received from Nebuchadrezzar.   They were settled by themselves; they were not, as in Egypt of old,

---

[1] ix. 22 ; x. 20.

16

hindered from multiplying; they were granted
freedom to cultivate and to trade, by which many
them gradually rose to considerable influence of
among their captors.   All this was given to
Jeremiah to foresee and to impress upon the first
exiles.   But it meant that their exile would be
long.

It is proof of the change in the Prophet's position
among his people[1] that his Letter was carried to
Babylon by two ambassadors from the King of
Judah to Nebuchadrezzar, and evidently with the
consent of Ṣedekiah himself.   The text of the
Letter and of its title, originally no doubt from
Baruch's memoirs, has been considerably expanded, as is clear not only from the brevity of
the Greek version, but from the superfluous
formulas and premature insertions which the
Hebrew and the Greek have in common.   Following others I have taken verses 5-7 as metre; and
if this is right we have a fresh instance of
Jeremiah's passing from metre to prose in the
same discourse.   The metrical character of 5-7 is
not certain.   Its couplets run on the following
irregular scheme of stresses : 3 + 4, 2 + 3, 3 + 3,
3 + 2 (?), 3 + 4, 3 + 4—the last line as so often
in a strophe being a long one.[2]

XXIX. 1 These are the words of the Letter
which Jeremiah sent from Jerusalem unto [the

---

[1] See above, p. 236.   [2] See above, p. 35.

3 remnant of] the elders of the exiles, by the
hand of Eleasah, son of Shaphan, and
Gemariah, son of Hilkiah, whom Ṣedekiah,
king of Judah, sent to Babylon unto the king
4 of Babylon saying, Thus saith the Lord, the
God of Israel, unto the exiles whom I have
exiled from Jerusalem :[1]

   5 Build houses and settle ye down,
     Plant gardens and eat of their fruit,
   6 Take ye wives,
     And beget sons and daughters.
     Take wives to your sons,
     Give your daughters to husbands,
     To beget sons and daughters,[2]
     And increase [3] and do not diminish.
   7 And seek ye the peace of the land,[4]
     To the which I have banished you,
     And pray for it unto the Lord,
     For in her peace your peace shall be.

[1] This title has been much expanded, as the briefer Greek shows,
and indeed much more than it shows. In 1 the addition of
priests and prophets is in view of 8 and 15 evidently wrong.
The Hebrew *remnant of* (before *the elders*) which Greek lacks
is difficult. It seems a later addition to the text when many of
the elders had died. Duhm's suggestion of a revolt of the early
exiles and the execution of many of the elders by Nebuchadrezzar is imaginary. In verse 2 we have such a needless gloss
or expansion as later scribes were fond of making.

[2] Greek omits this line.   [3] Hebrew adds *there*.
[4] Greek ; Hebrew *city*.

8 [For thus saith the Lord, Let not the prophets
in your midst deceive you, nor your diviners,
nor hearken to the dreams they (?) dream.

9 For falsehood are they prophesying unto you
in My Name; I have not sent them.][1]

10 For thus saith the Lord, So soon as seventy
years be fulfilled for Babylon, I will visit you
and establish My Word toward you by bringing you[2] back to this place.

11 For I am thinking about you—
Rede of the Lord—
Thoughts not of evil but peace
To give you a Future and Hope.

12 Ye shall pray Me, and I will hear you,

13 Seek Me and find;
If ye ask Me with all your heart

14 I shall be found of you.

By omitting all of verses 12-14 that is not given
by the Greek we get these eight lines in approxi-
mately Jeremiah's favourite Qinah-measure. The
Greek also lacks verses 16-20, which irrelevantly
digress from the exiles to the guilt and doom of
the Jews in Jerusalem, and which it is difficult to
think that Jeremiah would have put into a letter
to be carried by two of these same Jews.[3] Verse

---

[1] 8 and 9 strike one as a premature reference to the prophets.

[2] Greek perhaps better *your people*, for in seventy years the
elders addressed must have died out.

[3] Duhm.

15 goes with 21-23,[1] a separate message to the exiles which we shall treat in the following section.

2. Prophets and Prophets.

(XXIII. 9-32, XXVII-XXIX, etc.)

Jeremiah's Letter to the Exiles had its consequences. *First*, there was their claim to have prophets of the Lord among themselves, which in our text immediately follows the Letter as if part of it, XXIX. 15, 21-23, but which is probably of a somewhat later date.

XXIX. 15 Because ye have said, The Lord
21 hath raised us up prophets in Babylon, thus saith the Lord concerning Ahab son of Kolaiah and concerning Ṣedekiah son of Maaseiah,[2] Behold I am to give them into the hand of the king of Babylon and to your eyes shall he
22 slay them. And of them shall a curse be taken up by all the exiles of Judah who are in Babylon saying, 'The Lord set thee like Ṣedekiah and like Ahab, whom the king of
23 Babylon roasted[3] in the fire!' Because they have wrought folly in Israel and committed adultery with their neighbours' wives, and in My Name have spoken words which I

---

[1] As even Lucian's version shows in spite of its retaining 16-20.

[2] Greek lacks the names of both the fathers, and also the last clause of Hebrew, 21, *which prophesy a lie to you in My Name.*

[3] This verb is a play on the name of Ahab's father.

commanded them not. I am He who knoweth
and am witness—Rede of the Lord.

And, *second*, another of the 'prophets' among
the exiles sent to Jerusalem a protest against
Jeremiah's Letter, XXIX. 24-29.

This passage, especially in its concise Greek
form, which as usual is devoid of the repetitions
of titles and other redundant phrases in the
Hebrew text, bears the stamp of genuineness.

XXIX. 24 And unto Shemaiah the Nehemalite
thou shalt say :[1]

25*b* Because thou hast sent in thine own name
a letter to Sephaniah, son of Maaseiah, the
26 priest,[2] saying, The Lord hath appointed
thee priest, instead of Jehoiada the priest,
to be overseer in the House of the Lord for
every man that is raving and takes on himself
to be a prophet, that thou shouldest put him
27 in the stocks and in the collar. Now therefore why hast thou not curbed Jeremiah of
Anathoth, who takes on himself to prophesy
28 unto you? Hath he not sent to us in Babylon
saying, 'It[3] is long! Build ye houses and
settle down, and plant gardens and eat their
fruit.'

[1] In Hebrew follows in 25*a* a useless editorial addition.

[2] Hebrew precedes this with *to all the people which are in
Jerusalem and*, and follows it with *and to all the priests*, ad-
ditions very doubtful in view of verse 29. In II. Kings xxv. 18
Sephaniah is *second priest*.

[3] The time of the captivity.

29   And Ṣephaniah read this letter in the ears
30   of Jeremiah ; and the Word of the Lord came
31   to Jeremiah saying, Send to the exiles saying : Thus saith the Lord concerning Shemaiah the Nehemalite, Because Shemaiah hath
prophesied unto you, although I did not send
32   him, and hath led you to trust in a lie ; therefore thus saith the Lord, Behold I am about
to visit upon Shemaiah and upon his seed ;
there shall not be a man to them in your
midst to see the good which I am going to
do you.[1]

In one respect Jeremiah has not changed.   His
denunciation of individuals who oppose the Word
of the Lord by himself is as strong as ever, and
still more dramatically than in the case of Shemaiah it appears in his treatment of the prophets
within Jerusalem, who flouted his counsels of
subjection to Nebuchadrezzar, Chs. XXVII-
XXVIII.   In this narrative or narratives (for the
whole seems compounded of several, perhaps
not all referring to the same occasion) the differences between the Greek and Hebrew texts are
even more than usually great.   The Greek again
attracts our preference by its freedom from superfluous titles, repetitions and redundances, and is
probably nearer than the Hebrew to the original
of Baruch's Memoirs of the Prophet.   But it is

---

[1] Greek lacks the unnecessary remainder.

obviously not complete, missing out clauses, the presence of which is implied by subsequent ones.[1] The following is the substance of what Baruch reports.

It was the fourth year of Sedekiah, 593, when messengers from the neighbouring nations came to Jerusalem to intrigue under Egyptian influence for revolt against Babylon. Jeremiah was commanded to make a yoke of bars and thongs, and having put it on his neck to charge the messengers to tell their masters—

XXVII. 4 Thus saith the Lord of Hosts, the
5 God of Israel: I have made the Earth by
My great power and Mine outstretched arm,
and I give it unto whom it seems right to
6 Me. So now I have given all these lands[2]
into the hand of Nebuchadrezzar, king of
Babylon, to serve him,[3] and even the beasts
8 of the field to serve him. And it shall be
that the nation and kingdom, which will not
put their neck into the yoke of the king of
Babylon, with the sword and with the famine[4]

---

[1] The following are some details as to xxvii. The Hebrew verse 1 is not given by Greek; *Jehoiakim* is of course a copyist's error for *Sedekiah*, as 3, 12, 20 and xxviii. 1 show. Greek lacks the second clause of verse 5, all 7, several clauses of 8, one of 10, from *under* onwards in 12, all 13, the first of 14, *now shortly* in 16 (but adds *I have not sent them*), all 17, the last half of 18, most of 19, much of 20, all 21, and two clauses of 22.

[2] Greek *the earth*.　　　　[3] Hebrew *my servant*.

[4] Hebrew adds *pestilence*.

shall I visit them—Rede of the Lord—till they
9 be consumed at his hand (?).   But ye, hearken
ye not to your prophets, nor to your diviners
nor to your dreamers,[1] nor to your sooth-
sayers, nor to your sorcerers, who say, ' Ye
10 shall not serve the king of Babylon '; for
they prophesy a lie unto you, to the result
of removing you far from your own soil.
11 But the nation which brings its neck into the
yoke of the king of Babylon and serves him,
I will let it rest on its own soil and it shall
till this and abide within it.

This is followed by a similar Oracle to Ṣedekiah
himself, 12-15, and by another, 16-22, to the priests
concerning a matter of peculiar anxiety to them.

16 Thus saith the Lord, Hearken ye not to the
words of the [2] prophets, who prophesy to you
saying, Behold, the vessels of the Lord's
House shall be brought back from Babylon ;
for a lie are they prophesying to you.   I have
18 not sent them.[3]   But if prophets they be,
and if the Word of the Lord is with them,
let them now plead with Me [that the vessels
left in the House of the Lord come not to
19 Babylon].   Yet thus saith the Lord concern-
20 ing the residue of the vessels, which the
king of Babylon did not take when he carried

[1] Greek ; Hebrew *dreams.*
[2] Greek ; Hebrew *your.*   [3] So adds Greek.

22 Jeconiah into exile from Jerusalem, unto
Babylon shall they be brought—Rede of the
Lord.

The Hebrew text concludes with a prophecy of
the restoration of the vessels, which had it been
in the original the Greek translators could hardly
have omitted, and which is therefore probably a
post factum insertion. Not only, then, were the
sacred vessels taken away in 597 to remain in
Babylon, but such as were still left in Jerusalem
would also be carried thither. It is possible that
this address is now out of place and should follow
the next chapter, XXVIII, which deals only with
the vessels carried off in 597. Like the Hebrew
the Greek text gives XXVIII a separate introduction which dates it in the fifth month of the fourth
year of Ṣedekiah, but omits the Hebrew statement that the year was the same as that of the events
and words recorded in XXVII. The extent of
the differences between the Hebrew and Greek
continues to be at least as great as before,[1] as
a comparison will show between the Authorised
Version and the following rendering which ad-
heres to the Greek.

[1] The general differences in xxviii are : after *the Lord* Hebrew
adds *of Hosts the God of Israel* verses 2, 14 ; in 11 and 14 the
name *Nebuchadnezzar* as in xxvii ; in 3, 4, 14, 16, 17 unnecessary explanatory clauses or expansions ; and throughout the
title *the prophet* to the names *Jeremiah* and *Hananiah* respectively. Of all these the Greek is devoid ; other differences are
marked in the notes to the translation.

Jeremiah was still wearing his symbolic yoke
of wood and thongs in the Temple, when his prediction that the sacred vessels would not be restored was flatly contradicted and with as much
assurance that the contradiction was from the
God of Israel, as Jeremiah's assurance about his
own words. The speaker was like himself from
the country of Benjamin, from Gibeon near Anathoth, Hananiah son of Azzur, who said—

XXVIII. 2 Thus saith the Lord, I have broken [1]
  3 the yoke of the king of Babylon ! Within two
    years I will bring back to this place the vessels
  4 of the House of the Lord, and Jeconiah and all
    the exiles of Judah that went to Babylon ; for I
    will break the yoke of the king of Babylon.
  5   Then said Jeremiah to Hananiah, before
    the priests and all the people [2] standing in
  6 the House of the Lord—yes Jeremiah said, [3]
    Amen ! The Lord do so ! The Lord establish
    the words thou hast prophesied, by bringing
    back the vessels of the Lord's House and all
  7 the exiles from Babylon to this place ! Only
    hear, I pray thee, the Word of the Lord
    which I am about to speak in thine ears and in
  8 the ears of all the people. The prophets who
    have been before me and thee from of old,

[1] The prophetic perfect = *I will break*, verse 4.
[2] As in xxvii. 16 Greek puts the priests after the people.
[3] Baruch is not well accustomed to long sentences, therefore
repeats this clause (Duhm).

they prophesied against many lands and against great kingdoms of war [and of

9 famine (?) and pestilence].[1] The prophet who prophesies of peace (it is only) when the word[2] comes to pass that the prophet is known[3] whom in truth the Lord hath sent.

10 Then Hananiah[4] took the bars off the neck
11 of Jeremiah and brake them. And Hananiah spake before all the people saying: Thus saith the Lord, Even so will I break the yoke of the king of Babylon [within two years][5] from off the necks of all the nations.

And Jeremiah went his way.

12 Then came the Word of the Lord to Jeremiah, after Hananiah had broken the bars
13 from off his neck, saying, Go tell Hananiah, Thus saith the Lord : Thou hast broken the bars of wood but I will[6] make in their stead
14 bars of iron. For thus saith the Lord, An iron yoke have I put upon the necks of all [these] nations, that they may serve the
15 king of Babylon. And Jeremiah said to

[1] Greek lacks the bracketed words ; *famine* by changing one letter of the Hebrew for *evil*.

[2] Hebrew adds *of the prophet*.

[3] *Recognised* or *acknowledged*.

[4] Greek adds *In the sight of all the people;* also gives the plural *bars*.

[5] Greek lacks these words.

[6] So Greek ; Hebrew *thou shalt*.

Hananiah,[1] The Lord hath not sent thee, but
thou leadest this people to trust in a lie.

16 Therefore thus saith the Lord, Behold, I am
about to dispatch thee from off the face of
the ground—this year thou shalt die.

17   And he was dead[2] by the seventh month.

All praise to Baruch for his concise and vivid
report, and to the Greek translator who has re-
produced it! The editors of the Hebrew text
have diluted its strength.

With this narrative we are bound to take the
section of the Book entitled *Of the Prophets*, XXIII
9-32.   The text is in parts uncertain, and includes
obvious expansions.   These removed, we can
fairly distinguish a continuous metrical form up
to 29, with the exception perhaps of 25-27.   The
metre is sometimes irregular enough to raise
the suggestion[3] that the whole is rhetorical
prose, between which and metre proper it is
often hard, as we have seen, to draw the line.
But we have also learned how often and how
naturally irregular, when the subject requires it,
Jeremiah's metres tend to become.   So I have
ventured, with the help of the Greek, to render
the whole as metre, in which form are parts beyond doubt.   Verses 18 and 30-32 are in prose,
and both, but more probably the former, may

---

[1] Hebrew adds *Hear now Hananiah.*
[2] Hebrew adds *that year.*
[3] By Giesebrecht.

be later additions, as are 19, 20, and clauses in 9, 10.

There is no reason against taking the remainder as Oracles by Jeremiah himself. No dates are given them; they probably come from various stages of his ministry, for he early found out the false prophets, and his experience of them and their errors lasted to the end. But probably this collection of the Oracles was made under Ṣedekiah; that Baruch gathered it still later is not so likely.

XXIII. 9 Of the prophets :—

> Broken my heart within me,
>   All pithless my bones.
> I'm become like a drunken man
>   Like a wight overcome with wine.[1]
> 10 Of adulterers the land is full
>
> .   .   .   .   .   .   (?)[2]
>
> Their course it is evil,
>   Their might not right.
> 11 For prophet and priest alike
>   Are utterly godless.[3]

[1] Hebrew adds *Before the Lord, yea before His holy words* (Greek *before His glorious majesty*). Both break the connection and are unmetrical.

[2] The couplet here given by Hebrew and Greek is too long for the verse, breaks the connection, and is apparently a copyist's dittography expanded by quotation from ix. 2 (Duhm). But a single line is needed. Helped by Greek, we might read *and because of these mourns.*

[3] After Duhm.

E'en in My House their evil I find—
　　Rede of the Lord.

12 Therefore their way shall they have
　　In slippery places,
Thrust shall they be into darkness[1]
　　And fall therein,
When I bring calamity on them,
　　The year of their visitation.

13 In Samaria's prophets I saw the unseemly,
　　By Baal they prophesied.[2]

14 In Jerusalem's prophets I see the horrible—
　　Adultery, walking in lies.
They strengthen the hands of ill-doers,
　　That none from his wickedness turns.
To Me they are all like Sodom,
　　Like Gomorra her[3] dwellers!

15 Therefore thus saith the Lord:[4]
Behold, I will feed them with wormwood,
　　And drug them with poison.[5]
For forth from Jerusalem's prophets
　　Godlessness starts o'er the land.

16 Thus saith the Lord of Hosts
Hearken not to the words of the prophets
　　They make them bubbles,[6]

---

[1] So Syriac, alone yielding a sound division of the lines.
[2] Hebrew and Greek add a line breaking metre and parallel
[3] Jerusalem's (?).
[4] Greek adds *of Hosts concerning the prophets*.
[5] Cornill rejects this couplet, I think needlessly.
[6] So Greek, cp. ii. 5, p. 92.

From their hearts a vision they speak,
Not from the mouth of the Lord.

17 Saying to the scorners of His[1] Word
'Peace shall be yours;'
To all who follow their stubborn hearts
'No evil shall reach you!'

18 [For who hath stood in the council of the
Lord and hath seen His Word? Who hath
attended and heard?][2]

21 I have not sent the prophets,
Of themselves they run.
I have not spoken to them,
They do the prophesying.

22 If they had stood in My Council,
And heard My Words,
My people they would have been turning[3]
From[4] the wrong of their doings.

23 I am a God who is near
Not a God who is far.[5]

24 Can any man hide him in secret
And I not see him?

[1] Or *My*, Erbt and Cornill.

[2] So Greek. Hebrew *feared and heard His word.* These
clauses are not metrical and may be a later intrusion; which 19,
20 certainly are, for they find their proper place in xxx. 23, 24.

[3] So Greek.

[4] Hebrew expands, *from their evil way and.*

[5] So Greek affirmatively. Hebrew, by putting the couplet as
a question, confuses the meaning. To *near* it adds *Rede of the
Lord.*

Is it not heaven and earth that I fill ?—
 Rede of the Lord.
25 I have heard what the prophets say
 Who preach in My Name,
Falsely saying, 'I have dreamed,
 'I have dreamed, I have dreamed.'[1]
26 Will the heart of the prophets turn,[2]
 Who prophesy lies ?
And in their prophesying . . . (?)[3]
 The deceit of their heart,
27 Who plan that My people forget My Name[4]
 Through the dreams they tell,
Just as their fathers forgot
 My Name through Baal.
28 The prophet with whom is a dream
 Let him tell his[5] dream ;
But he with whom is My Word
 My Word let him speak in truth.
What has the straw with the wheat ?[6]
 —Rede of the Lord—
29 My Word, is it not[7] like fire
 And the hammer that shatters the rock ?
30 Therefore, Behold, I am against the prophets
 —Rede of the Lord—who steal My Words

---

[1] So Duhm happily takes a third repetition (for other cases of this kind, see vii. 4 ; xxii. 29) instead of the senseless *how long* at the beginning of the next verse.

[2] Giesebrecht's happy emendation.

[3] So Greek. [4] Greek *Law*. [5] So Greek

[6] Greek adds *so My words*. [7] Hebrew adds *thus*

17

31 each from his mate. Behold, I am against the
prophets who fling out their tongues and rede
32 a Rede.[1] Behold, I am against the prophets
of false dreams who tell them and lead My
people astray by their falsehood and extravagance [2]—not I have sent them or charged
them, nor of any profit whatsoever are they
to this people.[3]

We have now all the material available for
judgment upon Jeremiah's life-long controversy
with the other prophets. His message and theirs
were diametrically opposite. But both he and
they spoke in the name of the same God, the God
of their nation. Both were convinced that they
had His Mind. Both were sure that their respective predictions would be fulfilled. Each repudi-
ated the other's claim to speak in the name of
their nation's God. With each it was an affair of
strong, personal convictions, which we may grant,
in the case of some at least of Jeremiah's opponents,
to have been as honest as his. At first sight it
may seem hopeless to analyse such equal assurances, based apparently on identical grounds, with
the view of discovering psychological differences
between them ; and as if we must leave the issue

---

[1] So lit. or *call it a Rede ; fling out* so two Greek versions,
Hebrew *take*.

[2] Zeph. iii. 4.

[3] In 31 and 32 Hebrew repeats *Rede of the Lord.* The section
which follows can hardly be Jeremiah's.

to the course of events to which both parties confidently appealed.   Even here the decision is not
wholly in favour of the one as against the others.
For Jeremiah's predictions in the Name of the
Lord were not always fulfilled as he had shaped
them.   The northern executioners of the Divine
Judgment upon Judah were not the Scythians as
he at first expected ; and—a smaller matter—
Jehoiakim was not *buried with the burial of an ass,
dragged and flung out from the gates of Jerusalem,* but
slept with his fathers.[1] Yet these are only exceptions.
Jeremiah's prophesying was in substance vindicated by history, while the predictions of the other
prophets were utterly belied.   This is part of
Jeremiah's meaning when he says, *Of no profit
whatsoever are they to this people.*[2]

What were the grounds of the undoubted difference?   On penetrating the similar surfaces of
Jeremiah's and the prophets' assurances we find
two deep distinctions between them—one moral
and one intellectual.

We take the moral first for it is the deeper.
Both Jeremiah and the prophets based their predictions on convictions of the character of their
God.   But while the prophets thought of Him
and of His relations to Israel from the level of that

[1] xxii. 19 ; II. Kings xxiv. 6 ; just as conversely Huldah's
prophecy that Josiah would *be gathered to his fathers in peace,*
II. Kings xxii. 20, was belied at Megiddo.

[2] xxiii. 32, repeating what he has frequently said already.

tribal system of religion which prevailed throughout their world, and upon that low level concluded that Yahweh of Israel could not for any reason forsake His own people but must avert from them every disaster however imminent; Jeremiah was compelled by his faith in the holiness and absolute justice of God to proclaim that, however close and dear His age-long relations to Israel had been and however high His designs for them, He was by His Nature bound to break from a generation which had spurned His Love and His Law and proved unworthy of His designs, and to deliver them for the punishment of their sins into the hands of their enemies.[1] *What else can I do?* Jeremiah hears God say. The opposing prophets reply, *Not He!* This is the ground of his charge against them, that they plan to make the *people forget the Name*, the revealed Nature and Character, of God, just as *their fathers forgat Him through Baal*,[2] confusing His Nature with that of the lower, local god.[3] This ethical difference between Jeremiah and the prophets is clear beyond doubt; it was profound and fundamental. There went with it of course the difference between their respective attitudes to the society of their time—on the one

[1] As Amos had more strongly put it, *You only have I known of all the families of the earth, therefore I will visit upon you all your iniquities*, iii. 2.

[2] xxiii. 27.

[3] As we have seen ; above, pp. 76, 104 f., 137.

side his acute conscience of the vices that corrupted
the people, on the other their careless temper
towards those vices. They would *heal the hurt of
the daughter of my people lightly*, saying *it is well, it
is well when well it is not*, and in their prophesying
there was no call to repentance.[1]   Moreover,
though this may not have been true of all of them,
some both in Jerusalem and among the exiles were
partakers of other men's sins ; for Jeremiah charges
them with the prevailing immoralities of the day
—adultery and untruth.   Instead of turning Judah
from her sins, they were the promoters of the
godlessness that spread through the land.[2]
Though we have only Jeremiah's—or Baruch's—
word for this, we know how natural it has ever
been for the adherents, and for even some of the
leaders, of a school devoid of the fundamental
pieties to slide into open vice.   Jeremiah's charges
are therefore not incredible.

But the grounds of the difference between
Jeremiah and the other prophets were also intellectual. Jeremiah had the right eye for events
and throughout he was true to it.   Just as he tells
us how the will of God was sometimes suggested
to him by the sight of certain physical objects—
the almond-blossom that broke the winter of
Anathoth, the boiling caldron, or the potter at his
wheel—so the sight of that in which the physical

[1] viii. 11 ; xxiii. 14, 17, 22, etc., etc.   [2] xxix. 23, xxiii. 14.

and spiritual mingled, the disposition and progress of the political forces of his world, made clear to him the particular lines upon which the ethically certain doom of Judah would arrive. He had the open eye for events and allowed neither that horror of his people's ruin, of which he tells us his heart was full, nor any other motive of patriotism, nor temptations to the easier life that had surely been his by flattery and the promise of peace to his contemporaries, to blind him to the clear and just reading of his times, to which God's Word and his faith in the Divine character had opened his vision. On the contrary the other prophets, to take them at their best, were blinded by their patriotism, blinded by it even after Carchemish and when the grasp of Babylon was sensibly closing upon Judah—even after the first captivity and when the siege of Jerusalem could only end in her downfall and destruction. Nothing proved sufficient to open such eyes to the signs of the times.

Making allowance, then, for the fact that we depend for our knowledge of the controversy upon the record of only one of the parties to it, and imputing to the other prophets the best possible, we are left with these results : that as proved by events the truth was with Jeremiah's word and not with that of his opponents, and that the causes of this were his profoundly deeper ethical conceptions of God working in concert with his unwarped understanding of the political and military movements of his time.

To this were allied other differences between Jeremiah and the prophets who were against him.

Along with the priests they clung to tradition, to dogma, to things that had been true and vital for past generations but were no longer so for this one, which turned exhausted truths into fetishes. To all these he opposed *the Word of the Living God*, Who spoke to the times and freely acted according to the character and the needs of the present generation.

Again, the other prophets do not appear to have attached any conditions to their predictions; these they delivered as absolute and final. In contrast, not merely were Jeremiah's prophecies conditional but the conditions were in harmony with their fundamentally moral spirit. His doctrine of Predestination was (as we have seen) subject to faith in the Freedom of the Divine Sovereignty, and therefore up to the hopeless last he repeated his calls to repentance, so that God might relent of the doom He had decreed, and save His people and His land to each other.

Further, despite his natural outbursts of rage Jeremiah showed patience with his opponents, the patience which is proof of the soundness of a man's own convictions. He believed in 'the liberty of prophesying,'

The prophet with whom is a dream
Let him tell his dream,
And he with whom is My Word
My Word let him speak in truth!

Jeremiah had no fear of the issue being threshed out between them. The wheat would be surely cleared from the straw.[1] That is a confidence which attracts our trust. In the strength of it Jeremiah was enabled to pause and reflect on the apparently equal confidence which he encountered in his opponents, and to give this every opportunity to prove itself to him before he repeated his own convictions. I cannot think, as many do, that his words to Hananiah were sarcastic; and when Hananiah broke the yoke on Jeremiah's shoulders, and it is said, *But Jeremiah went his way*, this was not in contempt but to think out the issue between them.[2] Nor do I feel sarcasm in his wish that his opponents' predictions of the return of the sacred vessels from Babylon might be fulfilled.[3] His brave calm words to the prophets and priests who sought his life in the Temple in 604[4] bear similar testimony. All these are the marks of an honest, patient and reflective mind which weighs opinions opposite to its own.

Further still, Jeremiah had to his credit that of which his opponents appear to have been

[1] xxiii. 28, above, p. 257 ; cp. xxvii. 18.
[2] xxviii. 11, cp. xlii. 1-7. [3] xxviii. 6; above, p. 251
[4] xxvi. 14, 15.

devoid. As we have seen no prophet was less
sure of himself, or more reluctant to discharge the
duties of a prophet. Everywhere he gives evidence of being impelled by a force not his own
and against his will.[1] But the other prophets
show no sign of this accrediting reluctance. They
eagerly launch forth on their mission; *fling about
their tongues, and rede a Rede* of the Lord.[2] They
give no impression of a force behind them.
Jeremiah says that *they run of themselves* and *prophesy
of themselves*, they have not been sent.[3] We still
keep in mind that we owe the accounts of them to
Jeremiah and Baruch, their opponents. But our
own experience of life enables us to recognise
the portraits presented to us, as of characters
found in every age : pushful men, who have no
doubts of their omniscience, but, however patriotic
or religious or learned, leave upon their contemporaries no impression of their being driven
by another force than themselves, and whose
opinions either are belied by events, or melt into
the air.

One point remains. In answering Hananiah
Jeremiah adduced the example of the acknowledged prophets of the past as being always
prophets of doom, so that the presumption was in
favour of those who still preached doom; yet he
allowed that if any prophet promised peace, and
peace came to pass, he also might be known as

[1] See further, Lecture vii.   [2] xxiii. 31, p. 258.   **xxiii. 21**

genuine. That was sound history, and in the circumstances of the day it was also sound sense.

3. THE SIEGE.
(XXI, XXXII-XXXIV, XXXVII, XXXVIII)

History has no harder test for the character and doctrine of a great teacher than the siege of his city. Instances beyond the Bible are those of Archimedes in the siege of Syracuse, 212 B.C., Pope Innocent the First in that of Rome by Alaric, 417 A.D., and John Knox in that of St. Andrews by the French, 1547. A siege brings the prophet's feet as low as the feet of the crowd. He shares the dangers, the duties of defence, the last crusts. His hunger, and, what is still keener, his pity for those who suffer it with him, may break his faith into cowardice and superstition. But if faith stands, and common-sense with it, his opportunities are high. His powers of spiritual vision may prove to be also those of political and even of military foresight, and either inspire the besieged to a victorious resistance, or compel himself, alone in a cityful of fanatics, to counsel surrender. A siege can turn a prophet or quiet thinker into a hero.

The Old Testament gives us three instances—Elisha's brave visions during the Syrian blockade of Dothan and siege of Samaria; Isaiah, upon the solitary strength of his faith, carrying Jerusalem inviolate through her siege by the Assyrians ; and now a century later Jeremiah, with a more costly courage, counselling her surrender to the Babylonians.

The records of the Prophet's activity and sufferings during the siege are so curiously scattered through the Book and furnished with such headlines as to leave it clear that they were added at different times and possibly from different sources. Some of them raise the question whether or not they are doublets.

Three, XXI. 1-10, XXXIV. 1-7, XXXVII. 3-10, bear pronouncements by Jeremiah that the city must surrender or be stormed and burned. Of these the first and third each gives, as the occasion of the pronouncement it quotes, Ṣedekiah's mission of two men to the Prophet. Several critics regard these missions as identical. But can we doubt that during that crisis of two years the distracted king would send more than once for a Divine word ? And for this what moments were so natural as when the Chaldeans were beginning the siege, XXI. 4, and when they raised it, XXXVII. 5 ? That one of the two messengers is on each occasion the same affords an inadequate reason—and no other exists—for arguing that both passages are but differently telling the same story.[1] Nor have any

---

[1] Stade's combination (*ZATW* 1892, 277 ff.) of xxi. 1, 2 ; xxxvii. 4-10 ; xxi. 3-10 ; xxxvii. 11 ff. yields a contradiction—a prayer for the raising of the siege (xxi. 1, 2) already raised (xxxvii.

grounds been offered for identifying the occasion of either passage with that of XXXIV. 1-7. Thus we have three separate deliverances from Jeremiah to the king, each with its own vivid phrases and distinctive edge.

The first, XXI. 1-10, was given as the Chaldeans closed upon Jerusalem but the Jews were not yet driven within the walls.[1] Ṣedekiah sent Pashḥur and Ṣephaniah to inquire if by a miracle the Lord would raise the siege. The grim answer came that the Lord Himself would fight the besieged, till they died of pestilence and the survivors were slaughtered by Nebuchadrezzar—*I*[2] *shall not spare nor pity them*—which is proof that this Oracle was uttered before the end of the siege, when the survivors were not slain but deported. The people are advised to desert to the enemy—counsel which we shall consider later.

The second, XXXIV. 1-7, records a pronouncement unsought by the king but evoked from

5). Erbt avoids this by combining only xxi. 1, 2a; xxxvii. 6-10; similarly Gillies (p. 309). But, as Cornill says, one cannot explain how from this form the two accounts have risen. Older critics (except Ewald) and Davidson, Giesebrecht, Peake, Thomson, (196, 198) and Cornill refer the passages to different occasions. Skinner leaves the question in suspense (259 n.). Duhm disposes of xxxvii. 3-10 as a Midrash legend and xxi. 1-10 as 'a free composition' upon it by another hand !

[1] Probably the original tenor of verse 4, but the text 's confused by additions.

[2] Greek; Hebrew *he*.

Jeremiah by the progress of the Chaldean arms, which had overrun all Judah save the fortresses of Jerusalem, Lachish and 'Azekah. Its vivid genuineness is further certified by its unfulfilled promise of a peaceful death for Sedekiah. The following is mainly after the Greek.

XXXIV 2*b*. Thus saith the Lord : This city shall certainly be given into the hand of the king of Babylon, and he shall take it and burn it

3 with fire. And thou shalt not escape but surely be taken and delivered into his hand ; and thine eyes shall look into his eyes, and his mouth speak with thy mouth,[1] and to

4 Babylon shalt thou come. Yet hear the Lord's Word, O Sedekiah, king of Judah !

5 Thus saith the Lord,[2] In peace shalt thou die, and as the burnings[3] for thy fathers who reigned before thee so shall they burn for thee, and with 'Ah lord!' lament thee. 1 have spoken the Word—Rede of the Lord.

The miserable king, how much worse was in store for him than even Jeremiah was given to foresee ! Duhm (to our surprise, as Cornill remarks) agrees

---

[1] Greek omits this clause inadvertently. The proposed reversal to *thy mouth speak with his mouth* (Giesebrecht, etc.) misses the point ; surely the captor would speak first.

[2] Hebrew adds *concerning thee, thou shalt not die by the sword*.

[3] Of spices. Some Greek versions read *mournings*, and *so shall they mourn for thee.*

that the passage is from Baruch ; but only in order
to support the precarious thesis that Baruch knew
nothing of Ṣedekiah's being afterwards blinded
and that the reports of this [1] sprang from un-
founded rumour.

The third pronouncement to Ṣedekiah, XXXVII.
3-10, [2] was made when the king sent Jehucal and
Ṣephaniah to seek the Prophet's prayers, after the
Chaldeans had raised the siege in order to meet
the reported Egyptian advance to the relief of
Jerusalem.

XXXVII. 7. Thus saith the Lord : Thus say ye to
the king of Judah who sent you to inquire of
Me, [3] Behold, Pharaoh's army, which is coming
forth to help you, shall return to the land of
8 Egypt. And the Chaldeans shall come back
and fight against this city and take it and burn
9 it with fire.   For [4] thus saith the Lord : Deceive not yourselves saying, The Chaldeans
shall surely go off from us ; they shall not go.
10 Even though ye smote the whole host of the
Chaldeans that are fighting with you, and
but wounded men were left, yet should these

[1] xxxix. 7 ; II. Kings xxv. 7.

[2] Verses 1, 2 either belonged originally to this section, and
mark it as from another source than, or different edition of,
Baruch's memoirs, or more probably were added by an editor as
necessary after the preceding sections (xxxv, xxxvi) from
Jehoiakim's reign.

[3] Greek reads *say thou* and *thee* for *me*, and omits *you*.

[4] So Greek.

rise, each in his tent,[1] and burn this city with
fire.

It is very remarkable how the spiritual powers of
the Prophet endowed him with these sound views
of the facts of his time, and of their eventualities
whether in the political or in the military sphere.
For nearly forty years he had foretold judgment
on his people out of the North : for eighteen at
least he had been sure that its instrument would
be Nebuchadrezzar and he had foreseen the first
deportation of the Jews to Babylonia. Now step
by step through the siege he is clear as to what
must happen—clear that the Chaldeans will invest
the city, clear when they raise the investment that
they will beat off the Egyptian army of relief and
return, clear that resistance to them is hopeless,
and will but add thousands of deaths by famine
and pestilence before the city is taken and burned
and its survivors carried into exile—all of which
comes to pass. But this political sagacity and
military foresight have their source in moral and
spiritual convictions—the Prophet's assurance of
the character and will of God, his faith in the
Divine Government not of a single nation but of
all the powers of the world, and his belief that a
people is saved and will endure for the service of
mankind, neither because of past privileges nor by
the traditions in which it trusts, nor by adherence

[1] Greek *place.*

to dogmas however vital these have been to its fathers, nor even by its passionate patriotism and its stubborn gallantry in defence of land and homes, but only by its justice, its purity, and its obedience to God's will. These are the spiritual convictions which alone keep the Prophet's eyes open and his heart steadfast through the fluctuations of policy and of military fortune that shake his world, and under the agony of appearing to be a traitor to his country and of preaching the doom of a people whom he loves with all his soul.

The case of John Knox affords a parallel to that of the Hebrew prophet. He told the garrison and citizens of St. Andrews, when besieged by the French, that 'their corrupt life could not escape punishment of God and that was his continued advertisement from the time he was called to preach' among them. 'When they triumphed of their victory (the first twenty days they had many prosperous chances) he lamented and ever said "They saw not what he saw!" When they bragged of the force and thickness of their walls, he said, "They should be but egg-shells!" When they vaunted "England will rescue us!" he said, "Ye shall not see them, but ye shall be delivered into your enemies' hands and shall be carried to a strange country!"' that is France. All of which came to pass, as with Jeremiah's main predictions.[1]

[1] Knox's 'History of the Reformation in Scotland,' Bk. i.

The second of Jeremiah's pronouncements given above is followed by the story of the besieged's despicable treatment of their slaves, XXXIV. 8-22 ; based on a memoir by Baruch, but expanded. Both the Hebrew and the shorter Greek offer in parts an uncertain text, and add this problem that their story begins with a covenant to *proclaim a Liberty*[1] for the Hebrew slaves in general, while the words which they attribute to Jeremiah limit it to the emancipation, in terms of a particular law, of those slaves who had completed six years of service (verse 14).[2] But neither this nor the other and smaller uncertainties touch the substance of the story.[3] As the siege began the king and other masters of

[1] Cp. 'declare a Liberty of Tender Consciences,' Declaration of Breda by Charles II.

[2] A possible solution is ' that the emancipation was undertaken in obedience to the neglected law, and that to make their action even more effective. . . . they decided to emancipate all their slaves without waiting till the legal term had expired ' (Peake). Yet it is also possible that the reference in verses 13, 14 to the law, Deut. xv. 12, is due to an editor.

[3] The chief differences between Hebrew and Greek are : 8, Greek la ks *all* and the senseless *unto them ;* 9, Greek reads *so that no Jew should be a slave;* 10, 11, for Hebrew *heard* (R.V. *obeyed*), Greek reads *turned,* omits the last two clauses of 10, all of 11 save the last and in 12, 13 *from the Lord* and *God of Israel;* 14 reads *six* for Hebrew *seven* and 15 *they* for *ye* (twice) ; 16 omits *and brought them into subjection,* 17, *to his brother and every man,* 18 all reference to the calf and its parts, 20, 21 *and into the hand of them that seek their life* (twice).

18

slaves in Jerusalem entered into solemn covenant
to free their Hebrew slaves, obviously in order
to propitiate their God, and also some would
assert (though unsupported by the text) in order
to increase their fighting ranks; but when the
siege was raised they forced their freedmen back
to bondage: 'a deathbed repentance with the
usual sequel on recovery.'[1] This is the barest
exposure among many we have of the character
of the people with whom Jeremiah had to deal,
and justifies the hardest he has said of their
shamelessness.

XXXIV. 17. Therefore thus saith the Lord: Ye
have not obeyed Me by proclaiming a Liberty
each for his countryman. Behold I am about
to proclaim for you a Liberty—to the sword,
to the famine and to the pestilence, and I will
set you a consternation to all kingdoms of the
21 earth. . . . . And Ṣedekiah, king of Judah,
and his princes will I give into the hands of
their foes, the king of Babylon's host that
22 are gone up from you. Behold, I am about
to command—Rede of the Lord—and bring
them back to this city and they shall storm
and take it and burn it with fire, and the
townships of Judah will I make desolate and
tenantless.

Are we not in danger of the guilt of a similar
perjury to the men who fought for us in the Great

[1] Peake.

War, and for whom we have not yet fulfilled all the promises made to them by our governors?

About this time the ill-treatment of Jeremiah, which had ceased on Ṣedekiah's accession, was resumed. The narrative, or succession of narratives, of this begins at XXXVII. 11, and continues to XXXIX. 14, with interruptions in XXXIX. 1, 2, 4-13. Save for a few expansions, the whole must have been taken from Baruch's memoirs. Except for the omission of XXXIX. 4-13, the differences of the Greek from the Hebrew are unimportant, consisting in the usual absence of repetitions of titles, epithets and names.

The siege being raised, Jeremiah was going out by the North gate of the city to Anathoth to claim or to manage[1] some property there, when he was arrested by the captain of the watch, and charged with deserting. He denied this, but was taken to the princes, who flogged him and flung him into a vault in the house of Jonathan, the Secretary. After many days he was sent for by the king who asked, *Is there Word from the Lord?* *There is*, he replied, and, as if drumming a lesson into a stupid child's head, repeated his message, *Thou shalt be delivered into the hand of the King of Babylon.* He asked what he had done to be treated as he had been, and, by contrast, where

---

[1] xxxvii. 12 ; the phrase is obscure.

were the prophets who had said that the Babylonians would not come to Judah—his irony was
not yet starved out of him!—and begged not to
be sent back to the vault. The king committed
him to the Court of the Guard, where at least he
was above ground, could receive visitors, and
was granted daily a loaf from the Bakers' Bazaar
while bread lasted in the city.[1]

Yet through his bars he still defied his foes and
they were at him again, quoting to the king two
Oracles which he had uttered before and apparently was repeating to those who resorted to
him in the Guard-Court.

XXXVIII. 1 And Shephatiah, Mattan's son,
    Gedaliah Pashhur's son, Jucal Shelamiah's
    son, and Pashhur Malchiah's son,[2] heard the
    words Jeremiah was speaking about the
  2 people:[3] 'Thus saith the Lord, He that
    abides in this city shall die by the sword, the
    famine or the pestilence, but he that goes
    forth to the Chaldeans shall live—his life
    shall be to him for a prey but he shall live.'[4]
  3 'Thus [5] saith the Lord: This city shall surely
    be given into the hand of the king of Babylon's
    host and they shall take it.'

Verse 2 is rejected by Duhm and Cornill partly

---

[1] xxxvii. 11-21.   [2] Greek omits this last named.
[3] So Greek: Hebrew *unto all the people.*
[4] Greek lacks *to him* and Syriac the last clause.
[5] Greek *For thus.*

on the insufficient ground that verses 2 and 3 have
separate introductions and therefore could have
had originally no connection. But in quoting
two utterances of the Prophet for their cumulative
effect it was natural to prefix to each his usual
formula.   Duhm's and Cornill's real motive,
however, is their repugnance to admitting that
Jeremiah could have advised desertion from the
city.   So Duhm equally rejects XXI. 9, of which
XXXVIII. 2 is but an abbreviation; while
Cornill seeks to save XXI. 9 by reading it as a
summons to the *whole* people to surrender and
so distinguishes it from XXXVIII. 2, advice *to
individuals* to desert.   I fail to follow this distinction. The terms used are as individual in
the one verse as in the other ; if the one goes the
other must also. But need either go ? Duhm's
view is that both are from a later period, when
there was no longer a native government in
Judah, reverence for the monarchy was dead,
and the common conscience of Jewry was not
civic but ecclesiastical ! This is ingenious, but
far from convincing.   There are no grounds
either for denying these verses to Jeremiah, or
for reading his advice *to go forth to the Chaldeans*
as meant otherwise than for the individual
citizens.

Was such advice right or wrong ? The question
is much debated. The two German scholars just
quoted find it so wrong that they cannot think of

it as Jeremiah's. But in that situation and under
the convictions which held him, the Prophet could
not have spoken differently. He knew, and
soundly knew, not only that the city was doomed
and that her rulers who persisted in defend-
ing her were senseless, if gallant, fanatics, but
also that they had forfeited their technical legitimacy. To talk to-day of duty, civil or military,
to such a perjured Government does not even
deserve to be called constitutional pedantry, for
it has not a splinter of constitutionalism to support it. Ṣedekiah held his vassal throne only by
his oath to his suzerain of Babylon and when he
broke that oath his legitimacy crumbled.[1] Of
right Divine or human there was none in a
government so forsworn and self-disentitled,
besides being so insane, as that of the feeble king
and his frantic masters, the princes. For Jeremiah the only Divine right was Nebuchadrezzar's.
But to the conviction that Ṣedekiah and the
princes were not the lawful lords of Judah, we
must add the pity of the Prophet as he foresaw
the men, women and childen of his people done
to useless death by the cruel illusions of their
illegitimate governors. Calvin is right, when,
after a careful reservation of the duties of private
citizens to their government at war, he pronounces
that 'Jeremiah could not have brought better

---

[1] See above, p. 232.

counsel' to the civilians and soldiers of Jerusalem.[1] And it is no paradox to say that the Prophet's sincerity in giving such advice is sealed by his heroic refusal to accept it for himself and resolution to share to the end what sufferings the obstinacy of her lords was to bring on the city. Nor, be it observed, did he bribe his fellow citizens to desert to the enemy by any rich promise. He plainly told them that this would leave a man nothing but bare life—*his life for a prey*.

It would, however, be most irrelevant to deduce from so peculiar a situation, and from the Divine counsels applicable to this alone, any sanction for 'pacificism' in general, or to set up Jeremiah as an example of the duty of deserting one's government when at war, in all circumstances and whatever were the issues at stake. We might as well affirm that the example of the man, who rouses his family to flee when he finds their home hopelessly on fire, is valid for him whose house is threatened by burglars. Isaiah inspired resistance to the Assyrian besiegers of Jerusalem in his day with as Divine authority as Jeremiah denounced resistance to the Chaldean besiegers in his. Nor can we doubt that our Prophet would have appreciated the just, the inevitable revolt of the Maccabees against their pagan

[1] Calvin's discriminating remarks on xxxviii. 2, in No. cxlvii of his prelections on the Book of Jeremiah, are well worth reading. See, too, Peake (p. 24) and Skinner (261 ff.).

tyrants, which is divinely praised in the Epistle to the Hebrews as a high example of faith. It is one thing to deny allegiance, as Jeremiah did, to a government that had broken the oath on which alone its rights were founded, and the keeping of which was the sole security for 'the stability of the times.' It is another and very different thing to refuse, on alleged grounds of conscience, to follow one's government when it lifts the sword against a people who have broken *their* oath, and mobilises its subjects in defence of justice and of the freedom of weaker nations, imperilled by that perjury.

But the princes seem to have honestly believed that Jeremiah was guilty of treason, and said to the king—

XXXVIII. 4 Let this man, we pray, be put to death forasmuch as he weakens the hands of the men of war left to the city and the hands of all the people by speaking such words to them, for this man is seeking not the welfare of this people but the hurt.

5 And the king said, Behold he is in your hand; for the king was not able to do anything against them.[1]

6 So they took Jeremiah and cast him into the cistern of Malchiah the king's son, in the Court of the Guard; and they let down Jere-

[1] So Greek. Hebrew takes this clause as part of Ṣedekiah's reply : *the king is not able to do anything against you.*

miah with cords. In the cistern there was
no water, only mire, and Jeremiah sank in
the mire.

The story which follows is one of the fairest in
the Old Testament, XXXVIII. 7-13.[1] When no
others seem to have stirred to rescue the Prophet
—unless Baruch had a hand in what he tells
and is characteristically silent about it—Ebed-
melech, a negro eunuch of the palace, sought the
king where he then was[2] and charged the princes
with starving Jeremiah to death.[3] The king at
once ordered him to take three[4] men and rescue
the Prophet. The thoughtful negro, perhaps
prompted by the women of the palace, procured
some rags and old clouts from a lumber room,
told Jeremiah to put them under his arm-pits to
soften the roughness of the ropes, and so drew
him gently from the mire and he was restored to
the Guard-Court. Ebed-melech had his reward
in the Lord's promise to save him from the men

[1] Greek again is devoid of the repetitions, etc., that overload
the Hebrew.

[2] Hebrew adds *sitting*, an obvious intrusion (not in Greek),
for in the siege the king would hardly hold council in the
Benjamin-Gate.

[3] Greek reads that he charged not *the princes* but *the king*.
The text of 9 is uncertain. Duhm thinks the original meant
that the princes wished Jeremiah's death so as to save bread.

[4] Hebrew and versions *thirty*, differing little from the Hebrew
for *three*, which is now generally read.

whom he had made his foes by his brave rescue of their prey.[1]

Once more, as we might expect, the restless king sent for Jeremiah.[2] Shaken by his terrible experiences the Prophet, before he would answer, asked if the king would put him to death for his answer or act on his advice. The king swore not to hand him over to the princes; so Jeremiah promised that if Ṣedekiah would give himself up to the Chaldeans he and his house would be spared and the city saved. The king—it is another credible trait in this weak character—feared that the Chaldeans would deliver him to the mockery of those Jews who had already deserted to them. Jeremiah sought to reassure him, again urged him to surrender, and then burst out with the vision—an extraordinarily interesting phase of prophetic ecstasy—of another mockery which the king would suffer from his own women if he did not yield but waited to be taken captive.

XXXVIII. 21 But if thou refuse to go forth this
    is the thing the Lord has given me to see:
22 Behold all the women, that are left in the

---

[1] xxxix. 15-18.

[2] xxxviii. 14-28 ; Greek agrees with Hebrew save for its usual omissions as well as *secretly*, 16. Both read *the third entry of the Lord's House*, which some, by adding a letter, would change to *entry of the Shalishim* or *guards ;* unnecessarily, as Haupt shows.

king of Judah's house,[1] brought forth to the
princes of the king of Babylon and saying,

They set thee on and compelled thee,
  The men of thy peace;
Now they have plunged thy feet in the swamp
  They turn back from thee![2]

The verse is in Jeremiah's favourite measure,
and its figures spring immediately from his experience. The mire can hardly have dried on
him, into which he had been dropped, but at
least his friends had pulled him out of it; the
king had been forced into far deeper mire by
his own counsellors, and they were leaving him
in it!

The nervous king jibbed from the vision without
remark and begged Jeremiah not to tell what had
passed between them, but, if asked, to say that
he had been supplicating Ṣedekiah not to send
him back to the house of Jonathan; which answer
the Prophet obediently gave to the inquisitive
princes and so quieted them: *the matter was not
perceived*. He has been blamed for prevaricating.
On this point Calvin is as usual candid and sane.
'It was indeed not a falsehood, but this evasion
cannot wholly be excused. The Prophet had an
honest fear; he was perplexed and anxious—it

---

[1] After the deportation of 597.

[2] So Greek; Hebrew reads *thy feet are plunged*, and omits
from thee; 23 is a late expansion.

would be better to die at once than be thus
buried alive in the earth. . . . Yet it was a kind
of falsehood. He confesses that he did as the
king charged him and there is no doubt that he
had before him the king's timidity. . . . He cannot
be wholly exempted from blame. In short, we
see how even the servants of God have spoken
evasively when under extreme fear.' The prophets
were *men of like passions with ourselves.* By now
Jeremiah had aged, and was strained by the
flogging, the darkness, the filth and the hunger
he had suffered. Can we wonder at or blame
him? But with what authenticity does its frankness stamp the whole story !

With most commentators I have treated Ch.
XXXVIII as the account of a fresh arrest of
Jeremiah and a fresh interview between him and
Ṣedekiah. I see, however, that Dr. Skinner takes
the whole chapter to be 'a duplication.'[1] He con-
siders it a general improbability that two such
interviews, as XXXVII. 17-21 and XXXVIII.
14-27 relate, 'should have taken place in similar
circumstances within so short a time.' Yet the
king was just the man to appeal to the Prophet
time after time during the siege. The similarities
in the two stories are natural because circumstances were more or less similar at the various
stages of such a siege ; but the differences are

[1] Pp. 258-9 n., thus exceeding Steuernagel's and Butten-
wieser's readings of parts of it as a variant of xxxvii.

more significant. The vivid details of XXXVIII attest it as the account of an event and of sayings subsequent to those related in XXXVII. The Prophet's precaution, before he would answer, in getting a pledge that he would not be put to death nor handed over to the princes, as he had already been, and his consent for Ṣedekiah's sake, as well as for his own, to prevaricate to the princes are features not found in the other reports of such interviews, but intelligible and natural after the terrible treatment he had suffered. Dr. Skinner, too, admits that the two accounts may be read as of different experiences of the Prophet, 'if we can suppose that the offence with which he is charged in XXXVIII. 1 ff. could have been committed while he was a prisoner in the court of the guard;' but this appears to Dr. Skinner as 'hardly credible.' Yet the incidents related in XXXII. 6-15 show not only that it is credible but that it actually happened. In the East such imprisonment does not prevent a prisoner, though shackled, from communicating with his friends and even with the gaping crowd outside his bars, as I have seen more than once.

In the Court of the Guard Jeremiah remained till the city was taken.[1] He regained communication with his friends; and it is not surprising

---

[1] xxxviii. 28

to have as from this time several sayings by him, or to discover from them that his heart, no longer confined to reiterating the certain doom of the city, was once more released to the hope of a future for his people, hope across which the shadow of doubt appears to have fallen but once. His guard-court prophecies form part of that separate collection, Chs. XXX-XXXIII, to which the name The Book of Hope has been fitly given. Of these chapters XXX and XXXI, without date, imply that the city has already fallen and the exile of her people is complete. But XXXII and XXXIII are assigned to the last year of the siege and to the Prophet's confinement to the guard-court. There is now general agreement that XXXII. 1-5 (or at least 3-5) are from a later hand, which correctly dates the story it introduces but attributes Jeremiah's imprisonment to Ṣedekiah instead of to the princes, and even seems to confound Ṣedekiah with Jehoiachin; and *second* that the story itself, of a transaction between Jeremiah and his cousin regarding some family property, is genuine, dictated by the Prophet to Baruch before or after the end of the siege. Some reject as later all the rest of the chapter: a long prayer by Jeremiah and the Lord's answer to it, both of which are full of deuteronomic phrases. Yet that an editor should have made so large an addition to the book without genuine material to work from is hardly

credible; while it is characteristic of Jeremiah
to have fallen into the doubt his prayer reveals,
and this doubt would naturally be followed by a
Divine answer.   But such original elements it is
not possible to discriminate exactly from the expansions by which they have been overlaid.[1]

XXXII. 6 And Jeremiah said, The Word of
7 the Lord came to me saying, Behold, Hanamel
    son of Shallum thine uncle is coming to thee
    to say, Buy thee my field in Anathoth, for
    thine is the right of redemption to buy it.
8 And Hanamel son of my uncle came to me in
    the guard-court and said, Buy my field that is

[1] Duhm and Cornill take as original only 6-15; Giesebrecht
reasonably adds 16, *Ah Lord Yahweh* in 17, 24, 25, and in the
main 26-44, from which probably more deductions should be
made than he makes.   Gillies (270 ff.) takes 16-25 as later reflections on a prayer by Jeremiah, 24-41 as editorial, 42-44 as
bringing us back to the actual situation.   This is safer than
Peake's distinction of 16, 24-26, 36-44 as genuine (slightly
qualified by his notes).   Hebrew and Greek throughout are the
same, save for the usual Greek omissions, and these are more
in the narrative 1-15 (especially 5*b*, 11*b*, 14 *these deeds* with *it*
for *them* and *they*, while in 8 for Hebrew *the redemption is
thine* it has *thou art the elder*) than in the prayer and the
divine answer (30*b*, 36 *captivity* for *pestilence*, 41 *visit* for
rejoice over).   In 6 for Hebrew *me* Greek has *Jeremiah*,
but confirms the 1st person in 8, 9-13, 16, 25, and in 26 has
me for Hebrew *Jeremiah*.   Greek, too, has some of its unusual
surplus: 8 *Shullum*, 12 *son of*, 19 ὁ θεος ὁ μέγας ὁ παντοκράτωρ
καὶ μεγαλώνυμος Κύριος, 25 *and I wrote the deed and sealed it*,
33*b still*, 43 *again*.

Anathoth, for the right of inheritance is thine
and thine the redemption; buy it for thyself.
Then I knew that it was the Lord's Word.

9 So I bought the field from Hanamel mine
uncle's son and weighed to him seventeen

10 silver shekels. And I subscribed the deed
and sealed it and took witnesses, weighing the

11 money in the balances. And I took the deed
of sale, both that which was sealed and that

12 which was open,[1] and I gave it to Baruch son
of Neriah, son of Mahseiah, in the sight of
Hanamel mine uncle's son, and in sight of

13 the Jews sitting in the guard-court. And in

14 their sight I charged Baruch, saying, Thus
saith the Lord of Hosts : Take this deed of sale
which is sealed, and this deed which is open,
and put them in an earthen vessel that they

15 may last many days. For thus saith the Lord,
Houses and fields and vineyards shall yet
again be bought in this land.

16   Now after I had given the deed of sale to
Baruch, Neriah's son, I prayed to the Lord

24 saying, Ah Lord . . . (?) behold the mounts;
they are come to the city to take it, and the
city shall be given into the hands of the
Chaldeans who are fighting against it, because
of the sword and the famine and the pestil-

[1] The custom was to have one copy open for reference, and
one sealed for confirmation if the open one should be disputed
To *sealed* Hebrew adds *th injunction and conditions.*

ence; and what Thou hast spoken is come to
25 pass, and, lo, Thou art seeing it. Yet Thou
saidst to me, Buy thee the field for money, so I
wrote the deed and sealed it and took witnesses—whereas the city is to be given into
the hands of the Chaldeans!

The tone of the expostulating Jeremiah is here
unmistakable; and (as I have said) a Divine
answer to his expostulations must have been given
him, though now perhaps irrecoverable from
among the expansions which it has undergone,
verses 26-44. Two things are of interest: the
practical carefulness of this great idealist, and the
fact that the material basis of his hope for his
country's freedom and prosperity was his own
right to a bit of property in land. Let those observe, who deny to such individual rights any
communal interest or advantage. Jeremiah at
least proves how a small property of his own may
help a prophet in his hope for his country and
people.

All this is followed in Ch. XXXIII by a series
of oracles under the heading *The Word of the Lord
came to Jeremiah a second time while he was still shut
up in the guard-court.* Because verses 14-26 are
lacking in the Greek and could not have been
omitted by the translator had they been in the
original text, and because they are composed
partly of mere echoes of Jeremiah and partly of
promises for the Monarchy and Priesthood not

19

consonant with his views of the institutions of Israel, they are very generally rejected. So are 2 and 3 because of their doubtful relevance and their style, that of the great prophet of the end of the Exile. The originality of 1 and 4-13 has also been denied. The question is difficult. But there is no reason to doubt that the editor had good material for the data in 1, or that under the Hebrew text, which as it stands in 4, 5 is impossible [1] and throughout 6-13 has been much expanded, there is something of Jeremiah's own. Verses 4 and 5 reflect the siege in progress, though if the date in verse 1 be correct we must take *torn down* as future. In 6-13 are promises of the restoration of the ruined city, of peace and stability, of the return of the exiles both of Judah and Israel and of their forgiveness; Jerusalem shall again be a joy, and the voices of joy, of the bridegroom and bride, and of worship in the Temple, shall again be heard; shepherds and their flocks shall be restored throughout Judah and the Negeb. It would be daring to deny to the Prophet the whole of this prospect. The city was about to be ruined, its houses filled with dead; the land had already been ravaged. His office of doom was discharged; it is

---

[1] The numerous emendations are purely conjectural; the least unsatisfactory being Cornill's: *The houses . . . shall be torn down against which the Chaldeans are coming to fight with mounds and sword and to fill with the corpses of men whom I have smitten in my wrath,* etc.

not unnatural to believe that his great soul broke
out with a vision of the hope beyond for which
he had taken so practical a pledge. That is all
we can say; some of the details of the prospect
can hardly be his.[1]

Jerusalem fell at last in 586 and Jeremiah's imprisonment in the guard-court was over.[2]

4. And After.

(XXX, XXXI, XXXIX-XLIV.)

There are two separated accounts of what befel
Jeremiah when the city was taken. Ch. XXXIX.
3, 14 tells us that he was fetched from the guard-
court by Babylonian officers,[3] and given to
Gedaliah, the son of his old befriender Ahikam,
to be taken home.[4] At last!—but for only a brief
interval in the life of this homeless and harried
man When a few months later Nebuṣaradan
arrived on his mission to burn the city and deport
the inhabitants Jeremiah is said by Ch. XL to
have been carried off in chains with the rest of

---

[1] One may eliminate the few words not found in Greek, and
naturally suspect the liturgical clause in 11. Some take 13 as a
late expansion of 12. [2] xxxviii. 28.

[3] Verse 14 follows directly on verse 3. The statement that
Nebuṣaradan was one of them is in verse 13 which belongs to
the very late section, 4-13, lacking in the Greek.

[4] Hebrew: lit. *to the house;* Greek omits.

the captivity as far as Ramah, where, probably on Gedaliah's motion, Nebuṣaradan released him and he joined Gedaliah at Miṣpah.[1]

It is unfortunate that we take our impressions of Nebuchadrezzar from the late Book of Daniel instead of from the contemporary accounts of his policy by Jeremiah, Baruch and Ezekiel. A proof of his wisdom and clemency is here. While deporting a second multitude to Babylonia in the interests of peace and order, he placed Judah under a native governor and chose for the post a Jew of high family traditions and personal character. All honour to Gedaliah for accepting so difficult and dangerous a task ! He attracted those Jewish captains and their bands who during the siege had maintained themselves in the country,[2] and advised them to acknowledge the Chaldean power and to cultivate their lands, which that year fortunately produced excellent crops. At last there was peace, and the like-minded Governor and Prophet must together have looked forward to organising in Judah the nucleus at least of a restored Israel.

To this quiet interval, brief as it tragically

---

[1] Either Neby Samwîl or Tell-en-Naṣb, both a few miles north of Jerusalem. The above exposition takes xxxix. 3, 14 and xl. 1-6 as supplementary. But some read them as variants of the same episode, debating which is the more reliable. For a full discussion see Skinner, pp. 272 ff.

[2] Hebrew, *the forces* (Greek, *the force*) *in the field.*

proved, we may reasonably assign those Oracles of Hope which it is possible to recognise as Jeremiah's among the series attributed to him in Chs. XXX, XXXI. No chapters of the book have been more keenly discussed or variously estimated.[1] Yet at least there is agreement that their compilation is due to a late editor who has arranged his materials progressively so that the whole is a unity[2]; that many of these materials are obviously from the end of the exile in the style then prevailing ; but that among them are genuine Oracles of Jeremiah recognisable by their style. These are admitted as his by the most drastic of critics. It is indeed incredible that after such a crisis as the destruction of the Holy City and the exile of her people, and with the new situation and prospect of Israel before him, the Prophet should have had nothing to say. And the most probable date for such utterances of hope as we have now to consider is not that of his imprisonment but the breathing-space given him after

[1] The oscillations of this controversy have been recently so fully recounted (by Cornill and Peake) that it is unnecessary to repeat them here.

[2] Whether the datum xxx. 2, that Jeremiah was commanded by the Lord to write the words spoken to him in a book, is historical, is uncertain. It is not impossible that as he had been moved to write down his Oracles of doom (xxxvi) he should now be similarly advised about these later Oracles of hope The rejection of xxx. 2, by most critics, seems to me rash.

586, when the Jewish community left in Judah made such a promising start.[1]

From its measure and vivid vision the first piece might well be Jeremiah's; but it uses Jacob, the later literature's favourite name for Israel, which Jeremiah does not use, and (in the last two verses) some phrases with an outlook reminiscent of the Second Isaiah. The verses describe a day when the world shall again be shaken, but out of the shaking Israel's deliverance shall come.

XXX. 5 [The sound of trembling we hear,
　　　　Dread without peace.

6 Enquire now and look ye,
　　If men be bearing?
　Why then do I see every man[2]
　　With his hands on his loins?
　All faces are changed, and
　　Livid become.[3]

7 For great is that day,
　　None is there like it,
　With a time of trouble for Jacob.
　　Yet out of it saved shall he be.

8 It shall come to pass on that day—
　　Rede of the Lord—

---

[1] This in answer to Rothstein (Kautzsch's ‘ Heilige Schrift des A. T.,’ 754), whose upper date for them *after* 597 is toc early, and to Gillies (p. 238) who refers them to the Prophet's imprisonment.

[2] Hebrew adds the gloss *like a bearing woman.*

[3] So Greek, reading הָיוּ for הָיוּ.

I will break their[1] yoke from their[1] neck,
  Their[1] thongs I will burst;
And strangers no more shall they serve,[2]
  9 But serve the Lord their God,
    And David their king,
  Whom I will raise up for them.]

The next piece is more probably Jeremiah's, as
even Duhm admits; verses 10 and 11 which precede it are not given in the Greek.

12 Healless to me is thy ruin,
    Sick is thy wound,
13 Not for thy sore is remede,
    No closing (of wounds) for thee!
14 Forgot thee have all thy lovers,
    Thee they seek not.
  With the stroke of a foe I have struck thee,
    A cruel correction.
15 Why criest thou over thy ruin,
    Thy healless pain?
  For the mass of thy guilt, thy sins profuse
  Have I done to thee these.

If these Qînah quatrains are not Jeremiah's,
some one else could match him to the letter and
the very breath. They would fall fitly from his
lips immediately upon the fulfilment of his people's
doom. Less probably his are the verses which
follow and abruptly add to his stern rehearsal of

---

[1] So Greek, Hebrew *thy*.   [2] After the Greek.

judgment on Judah the promise of her deliverance, even introducing this with a *therefore* as if deliverance were the certain corollary of judgment—a conclusion not to be grudged by us to the faith of a later believer ; for it is not untrue that the sinner's extremest need is the occasion for God's salvation.[1] Yet the sudden transition feels artificial, and lacks, be it observed, what we should expect from Jeremiah himself, a call to the doomed people to repent. Note, too, the breakdown of the metre under a certain redundancy, which is not characteristic of Jeremiah.

16 [Therefore thy devourers shall all be devoured,
　　And all thine oppressors.
　All shall go off to captivity ;
　　Thy spoilers for spoil shall be
　And all that upon thee do prey, I give for prey.
17 For new flesh I shall bring up upon thee,
　　From thy wounds I shall heal thee ;[2]
　Outcast they called thee, O Ṣion,
　　Whom none seeketh after.]

The rest of the chapter is even less capable of being assigned to Jeremiah.

More of Jeremiah's own Oracles are readily recognised in Ch. XXXI. I leave to a later lecture the question of the authenticity of that on The New Covenant and of the immediately pre-

---

[1] Driver.　　　[2] Hebrew adds *Rede of the Lord.*

ceding verses [1]; while the verses which close the chapter are certainly not the Prophet's. But I take now the rest of the chapter, verses 1-28. The first of these may be editorial, the link by which the compiler has connected Chs. XXX and XXXI; yet there is nothing to prevent us from hearing in it Jeremiah himself.

XXXI. 1 At that time—Rede of the Lord—I
shall be God to all the families [2] of Israel,
and they shall be a people to Me.

A poem follows which metrically and in substance bears every mark of being Jeremiah's. The measure is his favourite Qînah, and the memory of the Lord's ancient love for Israel, which had stirred the youth of the Prophet,[3] revives in his old age and is the motive of his assurance that Israel will be restored. It is of Ephraim as well as of Judah that he thinks, indeed of Ephraim especially. We have seen how the heart of this son of Anathoth-in-Benjamin was early drawn to the exiles from that province on which the northward windows of his village looked out.[4] Now once more he was in Benjamin's territory, at Ramah and at Miṣpah, with the same northward prospect. Naturally his heart went out again to Ephraim and its banished folk. Of the priestly tribe as Jeremiah's family were, their long residence in the land of Benjamin

[1] Lecture viii   [2] Greek, *family*.   [3] iii. 6 f.   [4] See p. 72.

must have infected them with Benjamin's sense
of a closer kinship to Ephraim, the son of Joseph,
the son of Rachel, than to Judah, the son of Leah.
And there was, in addition, the influence of neigh-
bourhood. If blood be thicker than water it is
equally true that watered blood is warmed to
affection by nearness of locality and closeness of
association.[1]

It is questionable whether the opening couplet
quotes the deliverance of Israel from Egypt as a
precedent for the future return of the northern
tribes from captivity, described in the lines that
follow ; or whether this return is at once predicted by the couplet, with the usual prophetic
assurance as though it had already happened. If
we take *the desert* as this is taken in Hosea II. 14,
we may decide for the latter alternative.

XXXI. 2 Grace have they found in the desert,
   The people escaped from the sword;
  While Israel makes for his rest from afar
3   The Lord appears to him[2]:
  'With a love from of old I have loved thee,
   So in troth I (now) draw thee.[3]
4 'I will rebuild thee, and built shalt thou be,
   Maiden of Israel!

[1] Cornill dates the poem, 'surely,' from the earliest stage of
Jeremiah's prophetic career ; but both its late place in the Book
and the reasons given above argue strongly for a date at Miṣpah
under Gedaliah.

[2] So Greek.   [3] Or *continue troth to thee.*

'Again thou shalt take [1] thee thy timbrels
  And forth to the merrymen's dances.
5 'Again shall vineyards be planted [2]
  On the hills of Samaria,
 'Planters shall surely plant them (?)
  And forthwith enjoy [3] (their fruit).
6 'For comes the day when watchmen are calling
  On Ephraim's mountains :
 'Rise, let us go up to Șion,
  To the Lord our God.'

The everyday happiness promised is striking. Here speaks again the man, who, while
ruin ran over the land, redeemed his ancestral
acres in pledge of the resettlement of all his
people upon their own farms and fields. He is
back in the country, upon the landscapes of his
youth, and in this fresh prospect of the restoration of Israel he puts first the common joys and
fruitful labours of rural life, and only after these
the national worship centred in Jerusalem. Cornill denies this last verse to Jeremiah, feeling it
inconsistent with the Prophet's condemnation of
the Temple and the Sacrifices.[4] But that con-

---

[1] So Greek ; Hebrew *deck thee with.*   [2] So Greek.

[3] Lit *make common,* i.e. not be obliged to wait over the first
four crops as required by the law, Lev. xix. 23-25, before having
the fruit released for their own use. Greek reads the similar
Hebrew verb *praise.*

[4] Above, pp. 149 f., 152, 155 ff.

demnation had been uttered by Jeremiah because
of his contemporaries' sinful use of the House of
God, whereas now he is looking into a new dispensation. How could he more signally clinch
the promise of that reunion of Israel and Judah,
for which all his life he had longed, than by this
call to them to worship together?

The next verses are not so recognisable as
Jeremiah's, unless it be in their last couplet.
The rest rather reflect the Return from Exile as
on the point of coming to pass, which happened
long after Jeremiah's time; and they call the
nation *Jacob*, the name favoured by prophets of
the end of the Exile.

7 [Ring out with joy for Jacob,
    Shout for (?) the head of the nations,[1]
Publish ye, praise ye and say,
    The Lord hath saved His [2] people,
      The Remnant of Israel!
8 Behold from the North I bring them,
    And gather from ends of the earth;
Their blind and their lame together,
    The mother-to-be and her who hath borne
    In concourse great back they come hither.
9 With weeping forth did they go,[3]
    With consolations [4] I bring them,

[1] Duhm emends to *on the top of the hills*.
[2] So Greek and Targ.   [3] So Greek.   [4] *Ibid.*

I lead them by [1] streams of water,
　　On an even way,
They stumble not on it] [2]

For a father I am become to Israel,
　　And my first-born is Ephraim!

This couplet may well be Jeremiah's; bu
whether it should immediately follow verse 6 is
doubtful. The next lines are hardly his, bearing
the same marks of the late exile as we have seen
in verses 7-9a.

10 [Hear, O nations, the Word of the Lord,
　　And declare on the far-away isles [3] :
Who hath scattered Israel will gather,
　　And guard as a shepherd his flock.
11 For the Lord hath ransomed Jacob
　　And redeemed from the hand of the stronger
　　　　than he.
12 They are come and ring out on Mount Sion,
　　Radiant [4] all with the wealth of the Lord,

[1] So Greek.

[2] It is singular how each of these three verses contains not
four but five lines. Cornill, by using the introduction *Thus
saith the Lord*, omitting *the remnant of Israel*, combining two
pairs of lines and including the following couplet, effects the
arrangement of octastichs to which he has throughout the book
arbitrarily committed himself. Duhm has another metrical
arrangement.

[3] Or *coasts*.

[4] Lit. *they stream upon*, A.V. *flow together;* but the verb is
to be taken in the same sense as in Ps. xxxiv. 5 *were lightened*

With the corn, the new wine, the fresh oil,
The young of the flock and the herd ;
Till their soul becomes as a garden well-
watered,
Nor again any more shall they pine.
13 Then rejoice in the dance shall the maidens,
The youths and the old make merry.[1]
When their mourning I turn to mirth[2]
And give them joy from their sorrow.
14 When I richly water the soul of the priests,[3]
And My folk with My bounty are filled—
Rede of the Lord.]

The next poems no one denies to Jeremiah ·
they are among the finest we have from him.
And how natural that he should conceive and
utter them in those quiet days when he was
at, or near, Ramah, the grave of the mother
of the people.[4] He hears her century-long
travail of mourning for the loss of the tribes
that were sprung from her Joseph, aggravated
now by the banishment of her Benjamin; but
hears too the promise that her travail shall
be rewarded by their return. The childless old

and in Is. lx. 5, R.V. It is the liquid rippling light, thrown
up on the face from water.

[1] So Greek. [2] Hebrew adds *and will comfort them.*

[3] *Richly* lit. *with fat,* which Greek omits but to *priests* adds
the sons of Levi, an instance of how ready later hands have
been to add prose glosses to the poetry.

[4] I Sam. x. 2.

man has the soul of mother and father both—now
weeping with the comfortless Rachel and now,
in human touches unmatched outside the Parable
of the Prodigal, reading into the heart of God the
same instinctive affections, to which, in spite of
himself, every earthly father is stirred by the
mere mention of the name of a rebellious and
wandered son. The most vivid details are these :
after I had been brought to know, which might also
be translated *after I had been made to know myself*
and so anticipate *when he came to himself* of our
Lord's Parable ; *I smote on my thigh*, the gesture
of despair ; and in 20*a* the very human attribution to the Deity of surprise that the mere name
of Ephraim should move Him to affection, which
recalls both in form and substance the similar
question attributed to the Lord in XII. 9.

There is no reason to try, as some do, to correct
in the poems their broken measures, for these
both suit and add to the poignancy and tenderness which throb through the whole.[1]

15 Hark, in Ramah is heard lamentation
　　And bitterest weeping,
　　Rachel beweeping her children,
　　And will not be comforted,[2]
　　For they are not.
16 Thus saith the Lord :

See above pp. 46 f.
[2] Hebrew and some versions add *for her children.*

Refrain thy voice from weeping,
  And from tears thine eyes,
For reward there is for thy travail—
  They are back from the land of the foe!

17 [And hope there is for thy future,
  Thy sons come back to their border.][1]

18 I have heard, I have heard
  Ephraim bemoaning,
' Thou hast chastened me, chastened I am,
  Like a calf untrained.
' Turn me Thyself, and return I will,
  For Thou art my God.

19 ' For after I had turned away (?)[2]
  I repented . . . (?)
' And after I was brought to know,[3]
  I smote on my thigh.
' I am shaméd, yea and confounded,
  As I bear the reproach of my youth.'[4]

20 Is Ephraim My dearest son,[5]
  A child of delights?

[1] Greek has not the first line of this couplet, and reads differently the second. The whole seems a needless variant or paraphrase of 16.

[2] Or *turned to* (?). Greek reads *after my captivity*.

[3] Some would read *was chastised*.

[4] Still have that on my conscience; there is no need to doubt this line in whole or part as some do.

[5] After all that has passed!

That as oft as against him I speak
 I must think of him still.
My bowels for him are yearning,
 Pity him I must!—Rede of the Lord.

21 Set thee up way-marks,
 Plant thyself guide-posts!
Put to the highway thy heart,
 The way that thou wentest.
22 Come back, O maiden of Israel,
 Back to thy towns here.
How long to drift hither and thither,
 Thou turn-about daughter!
[For the Lord hath created a new thing on
  earth,
 A female shall compass a man.][1]

The next small poem, when we take from it
certain marks of a later date is possibly Jeremiah's,
though this is not certain; to the previous Oracles
on Ephraim it naturally adds one upon Judah.

23 Thus saith the Lord:[2]
Once more shall they speak this word.
 In Judah's land and her towns,
When I turn again their captivity:

[1] *Compass* or *change to* (?)   This couplet has been the despair
of commentators.   Its exilic terms, *created* and *female*, relieve us
of it.

[2] Hebrew adds *of hosts, God of Israel.*

20

'The Lord thee bless, homestead of justice!'[1]

24 In Judah and all her towns shall be dwelling
   Tillers and they that roam with flocks,
25 For I have refreshed the [2] weary soul,
   And cheered every soul that was pining.
26 [On this I awoke and beheld,
   And sweet unto me was my sleep.][3]

27 Behold, are coming the days—
   Rede of the Lord—
   When Israel and Judah [4] I sow
   With the seed of man and of beast;
28 And it shall be, as I was wakeful upon them
   To tear down and do evil,[5]
   So wakeful on them will I be,
   To build and to plant—
   Rede of the Lord.

These prophecies of the physical restoration of
Israel and Judah are fitly followed by two, in what
is rather rhythmical prose than verse, which define the moral and spiritual aspects of the new
dispensation; both laying stress on individual

---

[1] Hebrew and Greek add *holy mount*, a late term and here
irrelevant, for it is *all* Judah that is described.

[2] Greek *each*.

[3] Doubtful. Jeremiah had nothing to do with dreams as
means of prophecy.

[4] Hebrew adds to each *the house of*.

[5] Hebrew adds from i. 10 (*q.v.*), *pluck up, break down and
destroy*.

responsibility, the one in ethics, 29, 30, the other in religion, 31 ff., the proclamation of The New Covenant. They are no doubt Jeremiah's: we shall take them up in the last lecture.

The time of relief and fair promise, out of which we have supposed that the Prophet conceived and uttered the preceding Oracles, came to a sudden and tragic close with the assassination of the good governor Gedaliah by the fanatic Ishmael. Had this not happened we can see from those Oracles on what favourable lines the restoration of Judah might have proceeded under the co-operation of Gedaliah and Jeremiah, and how after so long and heart-breaking a mission of doom to his people the Prophet might at last have achieved before his eyes some positive part in their social and political reconstruction; for certainly he had already proved his practical ability as well his power of far vision. But even such sunset success was denied him, and once more his people crumbled under his hand. God provided some better thing for him in the spiritual future of Israel, to which he must now pass through still deeper sacrifice and humiliation.[1]

Ishmael, against whom the noble Gedaliah would take no warning, was one of those fanatics with whom the Jewish nation have been cursed at all

---

[1] As Dr. Skinner says, 'it was only by way of the eternal world that Jeremiah could enter on the fruition of his hopes.'

crises in their history.[1] The motive for his crime was the same as had inspired the fatal defence of Jerusalem, a blind passion against the Chaldean rule. Having slain Gedaliah he attempted to remove the little remnant at Miṣpah to the other side of Jordan but was overtaken by a force under Gedaliah's lieutenant, Johanan-ben-Kareah, and his captives were recovered. Fearing the wrath of the Chaldeans for the murder of their deputy, the little flock did not return to Miṣpah but moved south to Gidroth[2]-Chimham near Bethlehem, broken, trembling, and uncertain whether to remain in their land or to flee from it.[3]

The Prophet was the one hope left to them, and like Ṣedekiah they turned to him in their perplexity for a word of guidance from the Lord. With his usual deliberation he took ten days to answer, laying the matter before the Lord in prayer ; studying, we may be sure, the actual facts of the situation (including what he already knew to be the people's hope of finding security in Egypt) and carefully sifting out his own thoughts and impulses from the convictions which his prayers brought him from God. The result was clear : the people must abide in their land and not fear

---

[1] 'That atrocious brigand' (Renan).

[2] *The folds of*, as Aquila shows that we should read Hebrew *Geruth*.

[3] For the above see ch. xli, continuing from xl what is no doubt Baruch's account.

the Chaldeans, who under God's hand would let them be; but if they set their faces for Egypt, the sword which they feared would overtake them. This was God's Word; if they broke their promise to obey it, they would surely die.[1]

With shame we read the rest of the story. Jeremiah had well discerned[2] that those of his countrymen, who had been deported in 597, were the good figs of his vision and those who remained the bad. The latter were of the breed that had turned Temple and Sacrifice into fetishes, for as such they now treated the Prophet, the greatest whom God ever sent to Israel. Covetous of having him with them they eagerly asked him for a Word of the Lord, promising to obey it, in the expectation of their kind that it would be according to their own ignorant wishes; but when it declared against these, they scolded Jeremiah as disappointed barbarians do their idols, and presuming on his age as a weakness, complained that he had been set against them by Baruch, a philo-Chaldean who would have them all carried off to Babylon! So Baruch also—all praise to him—held the same sane views of the situation as his Prophet and as

---

[1] So ch. xlii. This and xli are substantially the same in Hebrew and Greek, the Greek as usual omitting the repetitions of the Divine Titles and of the names of the fathers of the actors, and a few other expansions; and suggesting, as Syriac and Vulg. also do, some minor corrections.

[2] xxiv. 1 ff.

that wise governor Gedaliah. In spite of their promise they refused to obey the Word of the Lord, fled for Egypt carrying with them Jeremiah and Baruch, and reached the frontier town of Tahpanhes. How it must have broken the Prophet's heart![1]

But not his honesty or his courage! At Tahpanhes he set before the fugitives one of those symbols which had been characteristic of his prophesying. He laid great stones in the entry of the house of the Pharaoh and declared that Nebuchadrezzar would plant his throne and spread his tapestries upon them, when he came to smite Egypt, assuming that land as easily as a shepherd dons his garment; and after breaking the obelisks of its gods and burning their temples he would safely depart from it.[2]

[1] xliii. 1-7. Hebrew and Greek still agree in essentials, Greek as usual omitting Divine Titles (which the Hebrew copyists delight in repeating), the needless father-names and also the term *proud* (or *presumptuous*) in 2, where it reads *the others* for the senseless Hebrew participle *saying*. In 6 it reads *remainder* for *children*, and *household* for *daughters—of the king*.

[2] xliii. 8-13. In 9 for the obscure Hebrew phrase, R.V. *in mortar in the brickwork*, Greek reads ἐν προθύροις ; in 10 lacks *My servant*, for *I* and *I have* reads *he* and *thou hast;* and in 12 *he shall* for *I will*. Also in 12 for *he shall array himself with the land of Egypt as a shepherd putteth on his garment*, Greek has *he shall clear out the land as a shepherd clears his garment from lice*. Suitable and vivid as this figure is and adopted by many moderns, one hesitates to use it for lack of confirmation from other sources. The other one is sufficient.

So far the narrative runs clearly, but in Ch. XLIV, the last that is written of Jeremiah, the expander has been specially busy.[1] The chapter opens, verses 1-14, with what purports to be an Oracle by Jeremiah concerning, not the little band which had brought him down with them, but *all the Jews which were dwelling in the land of Egypt, at Migdol and Tahpanhes,*[2] on the northern frontier, *and in the land of Pathros,* or Upper Egypt. It is not said that these came to Tahpanhes to receive the Oracle. Yet the arrival of a company fresh from Judah and her recent awful experiences must have stirred the Jewish communities already in Egypt and drawn at least representatives of them to Tahpanhes to see and to hear the newcomers. If so, it would be natural for Jeremiah to expound the happenings in Judah, and the Divine reasons for them. No date is given for the Prophet's Oracle. This need not have been uttered for some time after he reached Egypt, when he was able to acquaint himself with the conditions and character

---

[1] Besides its usual *minus* Greek omits in 1 *and at Noph,* in 3 *and to serve* and *neither . . . fathers,* in 9 *and your own wickedness,* in 10 *neither have they feared, in my law nor, before you and,* in 11 *against you . . . all Judah,* at least half of 12, in 15 *unto other gods* and *that stood by,* in 18 *and to pour out . . . unto her,* in 19 *to portray her,* in 22, *without inhabitant,* in 23 *as it is this day,* in 28 *mine or theirs.* Also Greek begins 19, *And all the women answered and said,* and in 25 for *ye and your wives* reads properly *ye women.*

[2] Hebrew adds *and at Noph* (Memphis).

of his countrymen in their pagan environment, and learn in particular how they had fallen away like their fathers to the worship of other gods. Such indeed is the double theme of the words attributed to him. He is made to say that Jerusalem and Judah are now desolate because of their people's wickedness, and especially their idolatry, in stubborn disobedience to the repeated Word of their God by His prophets; surely a similar punishment must befall the Jews in Egypt, for they also have given themselves to idols. But so awkwardly and diffusely is the Oracle reported to us that we cannot doubt that, whatever its original form was, this has been considerably expanded. At least we may be sure that Jeremiah uttered some Oracle against the idolatry of the Jews in Egypt, for in what follows they give their answer.

From verse 15 the story and the words it reports become—with the help of the briefer Greek version and the elision of manifest additions in both the Hebrew and the Greek texts[1] —more definite. Either *both* the men whom Jere-

---

[1] Duhm, Rothstein, Cornill, Gillies, etc., eliminate from 15 as a later addition *all the men who knew that their wives burned to other gods* on the ground that 19 shows the women alone to be the speakers; Duhm, precariously changing besides *a great assembly* (by the alteration of one letter) to *with a great* (loud) *voice*. And these critics and Driver, Giesebrecht and Peake rightly take *even all the people . . . in Pathros* as a late gloss founded on verse 1.

miah addressed *and* their women, or, as is textua!ly more probable, the women alone answered him in the following remarkable terms. These run in rhythmical prose, that almost throughout falls into metrical lines, which the English reader may easily discriminate for himself.

XLIV. 16 The word which thou hast spoken to us in the Name of the Lord!—we will not hearken to thee!

17 But we shall surely perform every word, which has gone forth from our mouth :[1] to burn to the Queen of Heaven and pour her libations, as we and our fathers did, our kings and our princes, in the cities of Judah and streets of Jerusalem, and had fulness of bread, and were well and saw no evil.

18 But since we left off to burn to the Queen of Heaven, and to pour her libations, we have lacked everything and been by the sword and the famine consumed.

19 And [2] while we were burning to the Queen of Heaven and poured her libations, did we make her cakes [3] and pour her libations without our husbands ?

This was a straight challenge to the prophet,

---

[1] That is *solemnly sworn ;* Judg. xi. 36 ; Numb. xxx. 2, 12.

[2] Some Greek MSS. and Syriac have *and all the women answered,* an addition felt to be necessary after the mention of *both* men and women in 15.

[3] Hebrew adds *to portray her,* that is on the cakes.

returning to him the form of his own argument.
As he had traced the calamities of Judah to her
disobedience of Yahweh, they traced those which
hit themselves hardest as women to their having
ceased to worship Ashtoreth. What could Jeremiah answer to logic formally so identical with
his own? The first of the answers attributed to
him, verses 20-23, asserts that among their other
sins it was their worship of the Queen of Heaven,
and not, as they said, their desisting from it,
which had worked their doom. But this answer
is too full of deuteronomic phrasing for the
whole of it to be the Prophet's; if any of it is
genuine this can only be part of the obviously
expanded opening, 21, 22a.

The real, the characteristic answers of Jeremiah are the others: to the women reported in
verses 24, 25, and to all the Jews in Egypt 26-28,
in which respectively he treats the claim of the
women ironically, and leaves the issue between
his word and that of his opponents to be decided
by the event. These answers also have been expanded, but we may reasonably take the following
to be original.[1] Note how they connect in verse
24 with verse 19. I again follow the Greek.

XLIV. 24 And Jeremiah said [to the people

---

[1] Erbt first made clear the metrical form of these verses,
though I think too grudgingly, and has ignored the fact that
they are not one but two Oracles.

25 and] to the women, Hear the Word of the
Lord, Thus saith the Lord, Israel's God:

Ye women[1] have said with your mouths
    And fulfilled with your hands,
'We must indeed perform our vows,
    Which we have vowed,
'To burn to the Queen of Heaven,
    And to pour her libations!'
Indeed then establish your words[2]
    And perform your vows!

Jeremiah 'adds this by way of irony.'[3] Having
thus finished with the women, he adds an Oracle
to the Jews in general.

26 Therefore hear the Word of the Lord all
Judah, who are settled in the land of Egypt:

By My great Name I swear,
    Sayeth the Lord,
That My Name shall no more be called
    By the mouth of a man of Judah—
Saying, 'As liveth the Lord!'—
    In all the land of Egypt.
27 Lo, I am wakeful upon you
    For evil and not for good.[4]

[1] So Greek.

[2] Generally accepted instead of Hebrew *vows*.

[3] Calvin.

[4] The rest of 27 and 28*a*, the destruction of all the Jews in
Egypt, is a prose expansion.

28*b* And the remnant of Judah shall know,
Whose is the word that shall stand.[1]

These are the last words we have from him,
and up to these last he is still himself—broken-
hearted indeed and disappointed in the ultimate
remnant of his people—but still himself in his
honesty, his steadfastness to the truth and his
courage; still himself in his irony, his deliberate-
ness and his confident appeal to the future for
the vindication of his word.

So he disappears from our sight. How pathetic
that even after his death he is not spared from
spoiling but that the last clear streams of his
prophesying must run out, as we have seen, in
the sands of those expanders!

[1] Hebrew adds, but Greek lacks, *from me or from them.*

LECTURE VII.

THE STORY OF HIS SOUL.

In this Lecture I propose to gather up the story of the soul of the man, whose service, and the fortunes it met with, we have followed over the more than forty years of their range. The interest of many great lives lies in their natural and fair development: the growth of gift towards occasion, the beckoning of occasion when gift is ripe, the sympathy between a man and his times, the coincidence of public need with personal powers or ambition—the zest of the race and the thrill of the goal. With Jeremiah it was altogether otherwise.

1. PROTEST AND AGONY.

(I, IV. 10, 19, VI. 11, XI. 18-XII. 6, XV. 10-XVI. 9, XVII. 14-18, XVIII. 18-23, XX. 7-18.)

If, as is possible, the name Jeremiah means *Yahweh hurls* or *shoots forth*, it fitly describes the Prophet's temper, struggles and fate. For he was a projectile, fired upon a hostile world with a force not his own, and on a mission from which, from the first, his gifts and affections recoiled and against which he continued to protest. On his

(317)

passage through the turbulence of his time he reminds us of one of those fatal shells which rend the air as they shoot, distinct even through the roar of battle by their swift, shrill anguish and effecting their end by their explosion.

Jeremiah has been called The Weeping Prophet, but that is mainly because of the attribution to him of The Book of Lamentations, which does not profess to be his and is certainly later than his day. Not weeping, though he had to weep, so much as groaning or even screaming is the particular pitch of the tone of this Prophet. As he says himself,

> For as oft as I speak I must shriek,
> And cry 'Violence and Spoil!'[1]

His first word is one of shrinking, *I cannot speak, I am too young.*[2] The voice of pain and protest is in most of his Oracles. He curses the day of his birth and cries woe to his mother that she bare him. He makes us feel that he has been charged against his will and he hurtles on his career like one slung at a target who knows that in fulfilling his commission he shall be broken—as indeed he was.

> Lord, Thou beguiled'st me, and beguiled I let myself be,
> Thou wast too strong for me, Thou hast prevailed.[3]

[1] xx. 8. [2] l. 6. [3] xx. 7.

Power was pain to him; he carried God's Word as *a burning fire in his heart*.[1]   If the strength and the joy in which others rise on their gifts ever came to him they quickly fled.   Isaiah, the only other prophet comparable, accepts his mission and springs to it with freedom.   But Jeremiah, always coerced, shrinks, protests, craves leave to retire.   So that while Isaiah's answer to the call of God is *Here am I, send me*, Jeremiah's might have been 'I would be anywhere else than here, let me go.'   He spent much of himself in complaint and in debate both with God and with his fellow-men :

> Mother! Ah me!
>   As whom hast thou borne me?
>   A man of quarrel and of strife
>   To the whole of the land—
>   All of them curse me.[2]

Nor did he live to see any solid results from his work.   His call was

> To root up, pull down and destroy,
>   To build and to plant.[3]

If this represents the Prophet's earliest impression of his charge, the proportion between the destructive and constructive parts of it is ominous; if it sums up his experience it is less than the truth.   Though he sowed the most

[1] vi. 11, xx. 9   [2] xv. 10; cp. xii. 1.   [3] i. 10, p. 83

fruitful seeds in the fields of Israel's religion, none sprang in his lifetime. For his own generation he built nothing. Sympathetic with the aims and the start of the greatest reform in Israel's history, he grew sceptical of its progress and had to denounce the dogmas into which the spirit of it hardened. A king sought his counsel and refused to follow it; the professional prophets challenged him to speak in the Name of the Lord and then denied His Word; the priests were ever against him, and the overseer of the Temple put him in the stocks. Though the people came to his side at one crisis, they rejected him at others and fell back on their formalist teachers, and the prophets of a careless optimism. Though he loved his people with passion, and pled with them all his life, he failed to convince or move them to repentance—and more than once was forbidden even to pray for them. He was charged not to marry nor found a family nor share in either the griefs or the joys of society. His brethren and his father's house betrayed him, and he was stoned out of Anathoth by his fellow-villagers. Though he could count on a friend or two at court, he had to flee into hiding. King Ṣedekiah, who felt a slavish reverence for his word, was unable to save him from imprisonment in a miry pit, and he owed his deliverance, neither to friend nor countryman, but to a negro eunuch of the palace. Even after the fall of Jerusalem, when his pro-

phecies were vindicated almost to the letter, he
failed to keep a remnant of the nation in Judah;
and his word had no influence with the little
band which clung to him as a fetish and hurried
him to Egypt.   There, with his back to the brief
ministry of hope that had been allowed him, he
must take up again the task of denunciation
which he abhorred; and this is the last we hear
of him.

It was the same with individuals as with the
people as a whole.   We may say that with few
exceptions, whomever he touched he singed,
whomever he struck he broke—*a man of quarrel
and strife to the whole land, all of them curse me.*   And
he cursed them back.   When Pashhur put him in
the stocks Jeremiah called him *Magor Missabib*,
Terror-all-round, *for lo, I will make thee a terror to
thyself and to all thy friends, they shall fall by the sword
and thou behold it.*[1]   Nothing satisfied his contempt for Jehoiakim, but that dying the king
should be buried with the burial of an ass.[2]   Even
for Ṣedekiah, to whom he showed some tenderness, his last utterance was of a vision of the weak
monarch being mocked by his own women.[3]
His irony, keen to the end, proves his detachment
from all around him.   His scorn for the bulk of
the other prophets is scorching, and his words

[1] xx. 2 ff.; see p. 192.   [2] xxii. 18 f.; see p. 167.
[3] xxxviii. 19 ff.; pp. 282 f.

21

for some of them fatal. Of Shemaiah, who wrote of the captives in Babylon letters of a tenor opposite to his own, he said *he shall not have a man to dwell among this people.*[1] When the prophet Hananiah contradicted him, he foretold, after carefully deliberating between his rival's words and his own, that Hananiah would die, and Hananiah was dead within a few months.[2] He had no promise for those whom he counselled to desert to the enemy save of bare life; nor anything better even for the best of his friends: *Seekest thou great things for thyself? Seek them not! Only thy life will I give thee for a prey in all places whither thou goest.*[3]

The following are the full texts from which the foregoing summary has been drawn and most of which I have reserved for this Lecture.

IV. 10. Then said I, Ah Lord Yahweh, Verily Thou hast deceived this people and Jerusalem, saying Yours shall be peace!—whereas the sword striketh to the life!

19 O my bowels! My bowels, I writhe!
O the walls of my heart!
My heart is in storm upon me,
I cannot keep silence!

VI. 11. I am filled with the rage of the Lord,
Worn with holding it in!
Pour it out on the child in the street,
Where the youths draw together.

[1] xxix. 24-32.   [2] xxviii. 17.   [3] xlv. 5; p. 228.

The following refers to the conspiracy of his fellow-villagers against him.

XI. 18. The Lord let me know and I knew it,
    Then I saw through[1] their doings;
19 But I like a tame lamb had been,
    Unwittingly[2] led to the slaughter.
On me they had framed their devices
    'Let's destroy the tree in its sap.[3]
Cut him off from the land of the living,
    That his name be remembered no more.'
20 O Lord, Thou Who righteously judgest,
    Who triest the reins and the heart,
Let me see Thy vengeance upon them,
    For to Thee I have opened[4] my cause.
21 Therefore thus saith the Lord of the men of
Anathoth, who are seeking my[5] life, saying,
Thou shalt not prophesy in the Name of the
Lord, that thou die not by our hands:[6]
22 Lo, I am to visit upon them!
    Their[7] youths shall die by the sword,

[1] So Greek ; Hebrew *thou lettest me see.*

[2] Greek ; Hebrew takes this with the next line.

[3] So generally read since Hitzig ; Hebrew has *bread,* i.e. *fruit.*

[4] Others : *on Thee I have rolled;* cp. xx. 12.

[5] Greek ; Hebrew *thy.*

[6] Hebrew copyists senselessly repeat, *Thus saith the Lord of Hosts;* Greek omits.

[7] So Greek.

Their sons and their daughters by famine,
23   Till no remnant be left them.
For evil I bring on the men of Anathoth,
The year of their visitation.

XV. 10. Mother! Ah me!
As whom[1] hast thou borne me?
A man of strife and of quarrel
To the whole of the land.
I have not lent upon usury, nor any to me,
Yet all of them curse me.
11   Amen,[2] O Lord!   If I be to blame (?),
If I never besought Thee,
In the time of their trouble and straits,
For the good of my foes.
12   Is the arm on my shoulder iron
Or brass my brow?[3]
15   Thou hast known it,[4] O Lord.
Think on and visit me!
Avenge me on them that pursue me,
Halt not Thy wrath.
Know that for Thee I have borne reproach
16   From them who despise[5] Thy words.

[1] Greek.

[2] Greek, meaning, Thy sanction to their curses.

[3] The text of the last six lines is corrupt; the above is Duhm's reading after the Greek.   See too J. R. Gillies.   Verses 13, 14 are out of place here, see xvii. 3, 4.

[4] Greek omits.

[5] So Greek; Hebrew (with same consonants, but the first two transposed) *Found were Thy words.*

[End them![1] Thy word's my delight
    And the joy of my heart.
For Thy Name has been calléd upon me,
    Lord of Hosts!]
17 I have not sat in their company
    Jesting and merry.[2]
Because of Thy hand alone I sit,
    For with rage Thou hast filled me.
18 Why is my pain perpetual,
    My wound past healing?
Art Thou to be a false stream to me,
    As waters that fail?

This to Him on Whom he had called as The
Fountain of Living Water!

19 Therefore thus saith the Lord:
If thou wilt turn, then shall I turn thee,
    That before Me thou stand;
And if thou bring forth the dear from the vile,
    As My Mouth thou shalt be.
[Then may those turn to thee,
    But not thou to them.]
20 For to this people I set thee
    An impassable wall.[3]

---

[1] So Greek; Hebrew *I did eat them.* But all this bracketed
quatrain breaks the connection between what precedes and
verse 17.

[2] Cornill after Greek.

[3] Omit *of bronze* for the metre's sake; it is a copyist's echo
of i. 18. Cornill omits *impassable* instead.

When they fight thee they shall not prevail,
With thee am I to deliver,[1]

21 And deliver thee I shall from the power of
the wicked,
From the hand of the cruel redeem thee.

XVI. 2. [2]Thou shalt not take a wife—
Rede of the Lord—
Nor shall sons nor daughters be thine
Within this place.

3 For thus hath the Lord said:
As for the sons and the daughters
Born in this place,
[As for their mothers who bore them
And their fathers who gat them
Throughout this land.]

4 Painfullest deaths shall they die
Unmourned, unburied,
[Be for dung on the face of the ground,
Consumed by famine and sword.]
And their corpses shall be for food
To the birds of the heaven and beasts of
the earth.[3]

---

[1] Hebrew adds *Rede of the Lord*.

[2] Hebrew precedes this with And the Word of *the Lord
came unto me*, which Greek is without, thus closely connecting
XVI. 2 ff. with XV. 21.

[3] In 3, 4 the bracketed lines are probably expansions of the
original.

5 Thus saith the Lord:
> Come not to the house of mourning,
> Nor go about to lament,[1]
> Because My Peace I have swept
> Away from this people.[2]

6b For them shall none lament,
> Nor gash nor make themselves bald;

7 Neither break bread[3] to the mourner,[4]
> For the dead to console him,
> Nor pour him[5] the cup of condolement
> For his father or mother.

8 Come thou not to the house of feasting,
> To sit with them eating and drinking.

9 For thus saith the Lord of Hosts,[6]
> The God of Israel:
> Lo, I shall stay from this place,
> In your days, to your eyes,
> The voices of joy and of gladness,
> The voices of bridegroom and bride.

Follows, in 10-13, the moral reason of all this—
the people's leaving of their God—and the doom
of exile.

---

[1] Hebrew, etc., add *nor bemoan them*—expansion.
[2] 5b, 6a are not in Greek.
[3] So Greek.
[4] By a change of vowels.
[5] So Greek
[6] Greek lacks *of Hosts*.

XVII. 14. Heal me O Lord, and I shall be healed,
Save me and saved shall I be.[1]

15 Lo, there be those, who keep saying to me.
'Where is the Word of the Lord?
Pray let it come!'

16 But I have not pressed. . . . (?)
Nor for evil[2] kept at Thee,
Nor longed for the woeful day,
Thyself dost know.
Whatever came forth from my lips
To Thy face it was.

17 Be not a (cause of) dismay to me,
My Refuge in evil days.

18 Shamed be my hunters, but shamed not I,
Dismayed, but dismayed not I.
Bring Thou upon them the day of disaster
And break them twice over!

XVIII. 18. And they said, Come and let us devise
against Jeremiah devices, for the Law[3] shall
not perish from the priest, nor Counsel from
the wise, nor the Word from the prophet
Come let us smite him with the tongue and
pay no heed to any of his words.

19 O Lord, unto me give Thou heed,
And hark to the voice of my plea![4]

[1] Perhaps 14 connects with 9, 10. The line *For Thou art
my praise* is a late addition.

[2] So Aq. Symm. Syr., reading *ra'ah, evil* for *ro'eh.
shepherd.*

[3] *Torah*, see p. 154.

[4] So Greek ; Hebrew *of mine accusers.*

20 Shall evil be rendered for good,
      That they dig a pit for my life ?[1]
   O remember my standing before Thee,
      To bespeak their good—
   To turn Thy fury from off them.
21 Give therefore their sons to famine,
      And spill them out to the sword.
   Let their wives be widows and childless
      And their men be slain of death—
   And smitten their youths by the sword in
      battle.
22 May crying be heard from their homes,
      As a troop comes sudden upon them!
   For a pit have they dug to catch me,
      And hidden snares for my feet.
23 But Thou, O Lord, hast known
      Their counsels for death against me.
   Pardon Thou not their iniquities,[2]
      Nor blot from Thy Presence their sins ;[2]
   But let them be tumbled before Thee
      Deal with them in time of Thy wrath.

Verses 21-23 are rejected by Duhm and Cornill,
along with XI. 22*b*, 23, XII. 3*b*, XVII. 18 for no
textual or metrical reasons, but only because
these scholars shrink from attributing to Jeremiah such outbursts of passion : just as we have

----

[1] To this line Greek adds *have privily laid a stumbling block*.
Most regard both lines as an expansion from 22.

[2] Pl. : So Greek.

seen them for similarly sheer reasons of sentiment
refuse to consider as his the advice to desert to
the enemy.[1] Yet they admit inconsistently the
genuineness of VI. 11, XI. 20, XV. 15.[2]

XX. 7. Lord, Thou beguiledst me, and beguiled
  I let myself be,
  Too strong for me, Thou hast prevailed,
  A jest I have been all the day,
  Every one mocks me.
 8 As oft as I speak I must shriek,
  Crying 'Violence and spoil.'
  Yea, the Word of the Lord is become my
  reproach
  All day a derision.
 9 If I said, I'll not mind Him [3]
  Nor speak in His name,[4]
  Then in my heart 'tis a burning fire,
  Shut up in my bones.
  I am worn away with refraining,
  I cannot hold on.[5]
10 For I hear the whispering of many,
  Terror all round!
  'Denounce, and let us denounce him,'
  —And these my familiars!—

[1] Above, pp. 276 ff.
[2] In contrast with its boldness in textual criticism a curious
timidity of sentiment has set through recent O.T. scholarship in
Germany from which the older German scholars were free.
[3] Greek *the name of the Lord.*
[4] Greek ; Hebrew adds *any more.*   [5] So Greek.

Keep ye watch for him tripping,
 Perchance he'll be fooled,
'And we be more than enough for him,
 And get our revenge.'
11 Yet the Lord He is with me,
 Mighty and Terrible!
So they that hunt me shall stumble
 And shall not prevail.
Put to dire shame shall they be
 When they fail to succeed.
Be their confusion eternal,
 Nor ever forgotten!
12 O Lord,[1] Who triest the righteous,
 Who lookest to the reins and the heart,
Let me see Thy vengeance upon them,
 For to Thee I have opened my cause.[2]

XX. 14 Cursed be the day,
 Whereon I was born!
The day that my mother did bare me,
 Be it unblessed!
15 Cursed be the man who carried the news,
 Telling my father,
'A man child is born to thee!'
 Making him glad.
16 Be that man as the cities the Lord overthrew,
 And did not relent,
Let him hear a shriek in the morning,

[1] Hebrew adds *of Hosts*.
[2] Verse 13, a doxology, is probably a later addition.

And at noon-tide alarms;

17 That he slew me not in [1] the womb,
   So my mother had been my grave,
   And great for ever her womb!
18 For what came I forth from the womb?
   Labour and sorrow to see,
That my days in shame should consume.

Considering the passion of these lines, it is not
surprising that they are so irregular.[2]

Some have attributed the aggravations, at least,
of this rage to some fault in the man himself.
They are probably right. The prophets were
neither vegetables nor machines but men of
like passions with ourselves. Jeremiah may have
been by temper raw and hasty, with a natural
capacity for provoking his fellows. That he felt
this himself we may suspect from his cry to his
mother, that he had been born to quarrel. His
impatience, honest though it be, needs stern
rebuke from the Lord.[3] Even with God Himself he is hasty.[4] There are signs throughout,
naïvely betrayed by his own words, of a fluid
and quick temper, both for love and for hate. For
so original a poet he was at first remarkably dependent on his predecessors. The cast of his
verse is lyric and subjective; and for all its wist-
fulness and plaint is sometimes shrill with the
shrillness of a soul raw and too sensitive about

---

[1] So Greek.   [2] Cp. xviii. 20 f. p. 329.
[3] xii. 5; cp. xv. 19.   [4] iv. 10; p. 322; xv. 18

herself. His strength as a poet may have been his weakness as a man—may have made him, from a human point of view, an unlikely instrument for the work he had to do and the force with which he must drive—painfully swerving at times from his task, and at others rushing in passion before the power he hated but could not withstand.

So probable an opinion becomes a certainty when we turn to God's words to him. *Be not dismayed lest I make thee dismayed* and *I set thee this day a fenced city and wall of bronze.*[1] For these last imply that in himself Jeremiah was something different. God does not speak thus to a man unless He sees that he needs it. It was to his most impetuous and unstable disciple that Christ said, *Thou art Peter, and on this rock will I build.*

Yet while his own temper thus aggravated his solitude and his pain we must also keep in mind that neither among the priests, the prophets and the princes of his time, nor in the kings after Josiah, did Jeremiah find any of that firm material which under the hands of Isaiah rose into bulwarks against Assyria. The nation crumbling from within was suffering from without harder blows than even Assyria dealt it. These did not weld but broke a people already decadent and with nothing to resist them save the formalities of religion and a fanatic gallantry. The people lost heart and care. He makes them use more than

---

[1] i. 17 f. ; cp. xv. 19.

once a phrase about themselves in answer to his call to repent : *No'ash, No use! All is up!* Probably this reflects his own feelings about them. He was a man perpetually baffled by what he had to work with.

Poet as he was he had the poet's heart for the beauties of nature and of domestic life : for birds and trees and streams, for the home-candle and the sound of the house-mill, for children and the happiness of the bride, and the love of husband and wife ; and he was forbidden to marry or have children of his own or to take part in any social merriment—in this last respect so different from our Lord. Was it unnatural that his heart broke out now and then in wild gusts of passion against it all ?

There is another thing which we must not forget in judging Jeremiah's excessive rage. We cannot find that he had any hope of another life. Absolutely no breath of this breaks either from his own Oracles or from those attributed to him. Here and now was his only chance of service, here and now must the visions given him by God be fulfilled or not at all. In the whole book of Jeremiah we see no hope of the resurrection, no glory to come, no gleam even of the martyr's crown. I have often thought that what seem to us the excess of impatience, the rashness to argue with Providence, the unholy wrath and indignation of prophets and psalmists under the Old

Covenant, are largely to be explained by this,
that as yet there had come to them no sense of
another life or of judgment beyond this earth.
When we are tempted to wonder at Jeremiah's
passion and cursing, let us try to realise how we
would have felt had we, like him, found our *one*
service baffled, and the *single* possible fulfilment
of our ideals rendered vain.   All of which shows
the difference that Christ has made.

2. PREDESTINATION.

(I, XVIII, etc.)

Yet though such a man in such an age Jeremiah
is sped through it with a force, which in spite of
him never fails and which indeed carries his influence to the end of his nation's history

What was the powder which launched this
grim projectile through his times ?   Part at least
was his faith in his predestination, the bare sense
that God Almighty meant him from before his
beginning for the work, and was gripping him to
it till the close.   This alone prevailed over his
reluctant nature, his protesting affections, and his
adverse circumstance.

> Before in the body I built thee, I knew
>   thee,
> Before thou wast forth from the womb,
>   I had put thee apart,
>   I have set thee a prophet to the
>   nations.

From the first and all through it was God's choice
of him, the knowledge of himself as a thought of
the Deity and a consecrated instrument of the
Divine Will, which grasped this unbraced and
sensitive creature, this alternately discouraged
and impulsive man, and turned him, as we have
seen, into the opposite of himself.

The writers of the Old Testament give full
expression to the idea of predestination, but what
they understand by it is not what much of Jewish
and Christian theology has understood. In the
Old Testament predestination is not to character
or fate, to salvation or its opposite, to eternal life
or eternal punishment, but to service, or some
particular form of service, for God and man. The
Great Evangelist of the Exile so defines it for
Israel as a whole : Israel an eternal purpose of
God for the enlightenment and blessing of mankind. And this faith is enforced on the nation, not
for their pride nor to foster the confidence that
God will never break from them, but to rouse their
conscience, and give them courage when they are
feeble or indolent or hopeless of their service.
So with Jeremiah in regard both to his own predestination and that of his people. In his Parable
of the Potter (as we have seen) it is for service as
vessels that the clay is moulded ; God is revealed
not as predestining character or quality, but as
shaping characters for ends for which under His
hand they yield suitable qualities. The parable

illustrates not arbitrariness of election nor irresistible sovereignty but a double freedom—freedom in God to change His decrees for moral reasons, freedom on man's part to thwart God's designs for him. In further illustration of this remember again the wonderful words, *Be thou not dismayed before them, lest I make thee dismayed ; if thou wilt turn, then shall I turn thee.* To work upon man God needs man's own will.

From imagining the Deity is sheer absolute will, to which the experience of the resistless force behind his own soul must sometimes have tempted him, Jeremiah was further guarded by his visions of the Divine working in Nature. He is never more clear or musical than when singing of the regularity, faithfulness and reasonableness of this. With such a Creator, such a Providence, there could be neither arbitrariness nor caprice.

Having this experience of God's ways with man it was not possible for Jeremiah to succumb to those influences of a strong unqualified faith in predestination which have often overwhelmed the personalities of its devotees. Someone has talked of 'the wine of predestination,' and history both in the East and in the West furnishes cases of men so drugged by it as to lose their powers of will, reason and heart, and become either apathetic unquestioning slaves of fate, or violent and equally unquestioning dogmatists and tyrants—the soulless instruments of a pitiless force. God overpowers them : He is all and they are nothing. It was far otherwise with Jeremiah, who realised and preserved his individuality not only as against the rest of his people but as against God Himself. His earlier career appears from the glimpses we get of it to have been, if not a constant, yet a frequent struggle with the Deity. He argues against the Divine calls to him. And even when he yields he expresses his submission in terms which almost proudly define his own will as over against that of God :

> Lord thou beguiledst me, and I let myself be beguiled,
> Thou wast stronger than I and hast conquered.

The man would not be mastered, but if mastered is not crushed. He questions each moment of his own sufferings, each moment of his people's on-coming doom. He debates with God on matters of justice. He wrestles things out with God and emerges from each wrestle not halt and limping like Jacob of old, but firm and calm, more clear in his mind and more sure of himself—as we see him at last when the full will of God breaks upon his soul with the Battle of Carchemish and he calmly surrenders to his own and his people's fate. That is how this prophet, by nature so fluid, and so shrinking stands out henceforth *a fenced city and a wall of bronze over against the whole people of the land:* the one unbreakable figure in the breaking-up of the state and the nation. We perceive the method in God's discipline of such a soul. He sees his servant's weakness and grants him the needful athletic for it, by wrestling with him Himself.

We may here take in full the remarkable passage, part of which we have already studied.[1]

XII. 1 Too Righteous art Thou, O Lord,
  That with Thee I should argue.
  Yet cases there are I must speak with Thee
    of:—
  The way of the wicked—why doth it prosper,
  And the treacherous all be at ease?
 2 Thou did'st plant them, yea they take root,
  They get on, yea they make fruit;
  Near in their mouths art Thou,
  But far from their reins.
 3 But me, O Lord, Thou hast known,[2]
  And tested my heart with Thee;
  Drag them out like sheep for the shambles,
  To the day of slaughter devote them.

 5 Thou hast run with the foot and they wore
    thee—
  How wilt thou vie with the horse?
  If in peaceful country thou can'st not trust,
  How wilt thou do in the rankness of Jordan?

[1] See above, p. 160.
[2] Hebrew adds, *Thou seest me.*

6 For even thy brothers, the house of thy father,
Even they have betrayed thee.
Even they have called after thee loudly,
Trust them not, though they speak thee fair.[1]

The rankness or *luxuriance of Jordan* is the jungle on both sides of the river, in which the lions lie. This then is all the answer that the wearied and perplexed servant gets from his Lord. The troubles of which he complains are but the training for still sorer. The only meaning of the checks and sorrows of life is to brace us for worse. It is the strain that ever brings the strength. Life is explained as a graded and progressively strenuous discipline, the result of it a stronger and more finely tempered soul. But this surely suggests the questions: Is that the whole result? Is the soul thus to be trained, braced and refined, only at last to be broken and vanish? These are natural questions to the Lord's answer, but Jeremiah does not put them. Unlike Job he makes no start, even with this stimulus, to break through to another life.

[1] See also p. 160. Verse 4 is clearly out of place here, referring to a hardly relevant subject. Verse 6 is less improbable an illustration of the harder troubles in store for the prophet. There is no reason to doubt the genuineness of the rest : *Thou can'st not trust*, so Greek ; Hebrew *thou art trusting*. Hitzig, etc., by changing one consonant read *thou art fleeing*. *Rankness* lit. *pride* or *extravagance*. If verse 6 is original, the date of the whole is early.

3. SACRIFICE.

But in thus achieving his individuality over against both his nation and his God, Jeremiah accomplished only half of the work he did for Israel and mankind. It is proof of how great a prophet we have in him that he who was the first in Israel to realise the independence of the single self in religion should also become the supreme example under the Old Covenant of the sacrifice of that self for others, that he should break from one type of religious solidarity only to illustrate another and a nobler, that the prophet of individuality should be also the symbol if not the conscious preacher of vicariousness. This further stage in Jeremiah's experience is of equally dramatic interest, though we cannot always trace the order of his utterances which bear witness to it.

There must often have come to him the temptation to break loose from a people who deserved nothing of him, but cruelly entreated him, and who themselves were so manifestly doomed. Once at least he confesses this.

IX. 2 O that I had in the wilderness
A wayfarers' lodge !
Then would I leave my people,
And get away from them ;
For adulterers all of them be,
A bundle of traitors.

3 They stretch their tongues
Like a falsing bow,
And never for truth
Use their power in the land.
But from evil to evil go forth
And Me they know not![1]

Well might the Prophet wish to escape from
such a people—worn out with their falsehood,
their impurity, and their senseless optimism. Yet
it is not solitude for which he prays but some inn
or caravanserai where he would have been less
lonely than in his unshared house in Jerusalem,
sitting alone because of the wrath of the Lord. His
desire is to be set where a man may see all the
interest of passing life without any responsibility
for it, where men are wayfarers only and come
and go like a river on whose bank you lie, and
help you to muse and perhaps to sing but never
touch the heart or the conscience of you. It is
the prayer of a poet sick of being a prophet and a
tester. Jeremiah was weary of having to look
below the surface of life, to know people long
enough to judge them with a keener conscience
than their own and to love them with a hopeless
and breaking heart that never got an answer to its
love or to its calls for repentance—wearied with
watching habit slowly grow from ill to ill, old
truths become lies or at the best mere formalities,

[1] See above, p. 202.

prophets who only flattered, priests to bless them, and the people loving to have it so.[1] O to have no other task in life than to watch the street from the balcony!

But our prayers often outrun themselves in the utterance and Jeremiah's too carried with it its denial. *My people—that I might leave my people—* this, it is clear from all that we have heard from him, his heart would never suffer him to do. And so gradually we find him turning with deeper devotion to the forlorn hope of his ministry, his fate to feel his judgment of his people grow ever more despairing, but his love for them deeper and more yearning.

From the year of Carchemish onward he appears not again to have tried or prayed to escape. Through the rest of the reign of Jehoiakim they persecuted him to the edge of death. Prophets and priests called for his execution. He was stoned, beaten and thrust into the stocks. The king scornfully cut up the roll of his prophecies; and the people following their formalist leaders rejected his word. With the first captivity under Jehoiachin all the better classes left Jerusalem, but he elected to remain with the refuse. When in the reign of Ṣedekiah the Chaldeans came down on the city and Jeremiah counselled its surrender he was again beaten and was flung into a pit to starve to death. When he was freed and the

[1] v. 31; p. 125.

besiegers gave him the opportunity, he would not
go over to them. Even when the city had fallen
and her captors hearing of his counsel offered him
security and a position in Babylonia, he chose instead to share the fortunes of the little remnant
left in their ruined land. When they broke up it
was the worst of them who took possession of his
person and disregarding his appeals hurried him
down to Egypt. There, on alien soil and among
countrymen who had given themselves to an alien
religion, the one great personality of his time, who
had served the highest interests of his nation for
forty years, reluctant but unfaltering, and whose
scorned words, every one, had been vindicated by
events, is with the dregs of his people swept from
our sight. *He had given his back to the smiters and
his cheeks to them who plucked out the hair; he had not
hidden his face from the shame and the spitting.   He
was a man of sorrows and acquainted with grief.   He
was taken from prison and from judgment and cut off
from the land of the living; and they made his grave
with the wicked, though he had done no violence
neither was deceit in his mouth.*   It is the second
greatest sacrifice that Israel has offered for mankind.

If Jeremiah thus of his own will suffered *with*
his people, and to the bitter end with the worst of
them, was he also conscious of suffering *for* them?
After his death, when the full tragedy of his life
came home to his people's heart, the sense of the
few suffering for the many, the righteous for the

sinners, began to be articulate in Israel—remarkably enough, let us remember, in the very period when owing to the break-up of the nation the single soul came to its own and belief in the responsibility of every man for his own sins also emerged and prevailed. Of the influence of the example of Jeremiah's spiritual loneliness, combined with his devotion to his sinful people, in developing these doctrines of individualism and self-sacrifice for others there can be no doubt. The stamp of his sufferings is on every passage in that exilic work 'Isaiah' XL-LXVI, which presents the Suffering Servant of the Lord and declares the atoning virtues of His Agonies and Death.

But it is not clear that Jeremiah ever felt anything of this about himself; if he did so he has refrained from uttering it. Yet he must have been very near so high a consciousness. His love and his pity for his sinful people were full. He can hardly have failed to descry that his own spiritual agonies which brought him into so close a personal communion with God would show to every other man the way for his approach also to the Most High and Holy and his reconciliation with his God Again he was weighed down with his people's sins; he bore on his heart the full burden of them. He confessed them The shame which the people did not feel for them, he felt; and he painted the curse upon them in words which prove how deeply the iron had entered his own soul. He had a profound sense of the engrained quality of evil,[1] the deep saturation of sin, the enormity of the guilt of those who sinned against the light and love of God.[2] A fallacy of his day was that God could easily and would readily forgive sin, that the standard ritual might at once atone for it and comfortable preaching bring the assurance of its removal. He denied this, and affirmed that such things do not change character; that no wash of words can cleanse from sin, no sacraments, however ancient, can absolve from guilt.[3] That way only strict and painful repentance can work ; repentance following the deep searching of the heart by the Word and the Judgments of God and the agony of learning and doing His Will.[4] To its last dregs he drank the cup of the Lord's wrath upon His false and wilful nation; he suffered with them every pang of the slow death their sins had brought upon them. And yet he was most conscious of his own innocence when most certain of his fate. The more he loyally gave himself to his mission the more he suffered and the nearer was he brought to death. The tragedy perplexed him,

---

[1] ii. 22 f. ; xiii. 23 ; xvi. 12 ; xvii. 1 ; etc.
[2] ii. 11-13, 22, 25, 31 f.
[3] ii. 35 ; v. 31 ; vii. 4-11, 21 ff.; xi. 15 ; xiv. 12.
[4] iv. 3, 4 ; vii. 3 ff. etc.

Why is my pain perpetual,
My wound past healing ?[1]

The only reply he heard from heaven was the
order to stand fast, for God was with him to deliver—but that more troubles awaited him.   And
beyond this what is there to answer the staggering
Prophet save that if a man have the Divine gifts
of a keener conscience and a more loving heart
than his fellows, there inevitably comes with
such gifts the obligation of suffering for them.
Every degree in which love stands above her
brethren means pain and shame to love though
as yet she bear no thorn or nail in her flesh.
This spiritual distress Jeremiah felt for the people
long before he shared with them the physical
penalties of their sins.   Just there—in his keener
conscience, in his hot shame for sins not his as
if they were his, in his agony for his people's
estrangement from God and in his own constantly
wounded love — lay his real substitution, his
vicarious offering for his people.

Did Jeremiah ever conceive the far-off fulness
of the travail thus laid upon his soul, the truth
that this vicarious agony of a righteous man for
the sins of others is borne by God Himself?   To
that question we have only fragments of an
answer.   In his discourses, both earlier and later,
when he talks directly in the Name of the Deity

[1] xv. 18.

—when the Deity speaks in the first person—the words breathe as much effort and passion as when Jeremiah speaks in his own person. The Prophet is very sure that his God is Love, and he hears that love utter itself in tones of yearning for the love of men, and even of agony for their sin and misery. There is, too, a singular prayer of his which is tense with the instinct, that God would surely be to Israel what Jeremiah had resolved and striven to be—not a far-off God who occasionally visited or passed through His people, but One in their midst sharing their pain; not indifferent, as he fears in another place,[1] to the shame that is upon them, but bearing even this. The prayer which I mean is the one in XIV. 8, 9, which recalls not only the terms but the essence of Jeremiah's longing to escape from his people, and lodge afar with wayfaring men, aloof and irresponsible.

> O Hope of Israel, His Saviour
>   In time of trouble.
> Why be like a passenger through the land,
>   Or the wayfaring guest of a night?
> Yet Lord Thou art in our midst,
>   Do not forsake us.[2]

I may be going too far in interpreting the longing and faith that lie behind these words

---

[1] *Debase not the throne of Thy Glory*, xiv. 21.
[2] xiv. 8, 9 ; see p. 57.

But they come out very fully in later prophets
who explicitly assert that the Divine Nature does
dwell with men, shares their ethical warfare and
bears the shame of their sins.   And the truth of
it all was manifested past doubt in the Incarna-
tion, the Passion and the Cross of the Son of
God.

But whether Jeremiah had instinct of it, as I
have ventured to think from his prayer, or had
not, he foreshadowed, as far as mere man can, the
sufferings of Jesus Christ for men—and this is his
greatest glory as a prophet.

LECTURE VIII.

GOD, MAN AND THE NEW COVENANT.

W<small>E</small> have followed the career of Jeremiah from
his call onwards to the end, and we have traced
his religious experience with its doubts, struggles,
crises, and settlement at last upon the things that
are sure : his debates with God and strifes with
men, which while they roused him to outbursts
of passion also braced his will, and stilled the
wilder storms of his heart. There remains the
duty of gathering the results of this broken and
gusty, yet growing and fruitful experience : the
truths which came forth of its travail, about
God and Man and their relations. And in particular we have still to study the ideal form
which Jeremiah, or (as some questionably argue)
one of his disciples, gave to these relations: the
New Covenant, new in contrast to God's ancient
Covenant with Israel as recorded and enforced
in the Book of Deuteronomy.

1. G<small>OD</small>.

Among the surprises which Jeremiah's own
Oracles have for the student is the discovery of
how little they dwell upon the transcendent and

(350)

infinite aspects of the Divine Nature. On these
Jeremiah adds almost nothing to what his predecessors or contemporaries revealed Return
to his original visions and contrast them with
those, for example, of Isaiah and Ezekiel.

Isaiah's vision was of the Lord upon a Throne,
high and lifted up, surrounded by Seraphim
crying to one another, *Holy, Holy, Holy is the
Lord of Hosts! the whole earth is full of His Glory!*
And their voices rocked the Temple and filled
it with smoke.   Here are a Presence, Awful
Majesty, Infinite Holiness and Glory, blinding
the seer and crushing his heart contrite.   Or
take the inaugural vision of Ezekiel—the storm-
wind out of the North, the vast cloud, the fire
infolding itself, the brightness round about and
out of the midst thereof as the colour of amber;
the rush and whirl of life that followed, wheels
and wings and rings full of eyes ; and over this
the likeness of a firmament of the colour of the
terrible ice and the sound of wings like the noise
of many waters, as the Voice of the Almighty and
above the firmament a Throne and on the Throne
the Appearance of a Man, the Appearance of
the likeness of the Glory of the Lord.   *And I,
when I saw it, fell upon my face.*

In the inaugural visions of Jeremiah there is
none of this Awfulness—only *What art thou seeing
Jeremiah ? the branch of an almond tree . . . a caldron
boiling.*   That was characteristic of his encounters

and intercourse with the Deity throughout. They were constant and close, but in them all we are aware only of a Voice and an Argument. There is no Throne, no Appearance, no Majesty, no overwhelming sense of Holiness and Glory, no rush of wings nor floods of colour or of song.[1] Jeremiah takes for granted what other prophets have said of God. But the Deity whose Power and Glory they revealed is his Familiar. The Lord talks with Jeremiah as a man with his fellow.

For this there were several reasons, and first the particular quality of the Prophet's imagination. His native powers of vision were not such as soar, or at any rate easily soar, to the sublime. He was a lyric poet and his revelations of God are subjective and given to us by glimpses in scattered verses, which, however intimate and exquisite, have not the adoring wonder of his prophetic peers.

Again there were the startled recoil of his nature from the terrible office of a prophet in such times, and those born gifts of questioning and searching which fitted him for his allotted duty as Tester of his people,[2] but which he also turned upon the Providence and Judgments of the Lord Himself.[3] His religious experience, as we have seen, was largely a struggle with

[1] x. 1-16 is a later writer's ; see p. 207.
[2] vi. 27 ; see pp. 132, 133.   [3] xii. 1 ff., etc.

the Divine Will, and it left him not adoring but
amazed and perplexed. Such wrestling man's
spirit has to encounter like Jacob of old in the
dark, and if like the Patriarch it craves the Name,
which is the Nature, of That with which it
struggles, all the answer it may get is another
question, *Wherefore askest thou after My Name?*
Morning may break, as it broke on Jacob by
Jabbok with the assurance of blessing or as on
Jeremiah with a firmer impression of the Will not
his own; but no strength is left to glory in the
Nature behind the Will. There is a horrified
breathlessness about his lines—

Thou wast stronger than I and hast conquered,
The Lord is with me as a Mighty and Terrible.[1]
From his struggles he indeed issues more sure
of God and finally more trustful in Him, as is
testified by his fair song on the beauty and fruit-
fulness of faith, beginning

Blessed the wight that trusts in the Lord,
And the Lord is his trust.[2]
But even here is none of the awe and high wonder
which fall upon Israel through other prophets.
Lyrist as he is and subjective, Jeremiah dwells
not so much upon the attributes of God on which
faith rests as upon the effects of faith in man.

Again by the desperate character of the times
he was starved of hope, the hope by which the

[1] xx. 7, 11.   [2] xvii. 7 f. ; p. 54.

Apostle says *we are saved*, which not only braces
the will but clears the inner eyes of men and
liberates the imagination. As the years went
on he was ever more closely bound to the prediction of his people's ruin, and, when this came,
to the sober counsel to accept their fate and settle
down to a long exile in patience for the Lord's
time of deliverance. As we have seen, his intervals of release from so grim a ministry were
brief, and his Oracles of a bright future but few.
Even in these he does not rise, like the Evangelist
of the Exile whom he inspired, to exultation in
the Almighty Power of God or to visions of vast
spaces of the Divine Providence, or of Israel's
service wide as the world. His happy peasant-
heart is content to foresee his restored people
tending their vineyards again, enjoying their
village dances and festivals, and sharing with
their long divided tribes the common national
worship upon Ṣion.[1]

Like those of all the prophets Jeremiah's most
immediate convictions of God are that He has
done, and is always doing or about to do, things.[2]
From the first Yahweh of Israel had been to the
faith of his people a God of Deeds. He delivered
them from Egypt, led them through the desert,

---

[1] See above, p. 299.

[2] Shortly before his death, Professor A. B. Davidson said to
me, " These prophets were terribly one-idea'd men "—their one
idea being that the Lord was about to do something.

ever ready to avenge them on any who molested them, and He had brought them to a land of delight.[1] By his creative and guiding Word, always clear and potential,[2] He had planted them and built them up to be a nation. These were the proofs of Him—ever operative, effective and victorious both over their foes and over every natural obstacle which their life encountered. And being *the Living God* He still works and is ready to work, would His people only seek where![3] He is awake, watching over His Word *to perform it* and controlling the nations.[4] It is He who has made the earth and gives it to whom He will,[5] who prepares the destroyers of His people, who calls for the kingdoms of the North, even for the far Scythians beyond the edge of the world, to execute His purposes.[6] He brings the King of Babylon against Jerusalem, and recalls the Chaldeans to their interrupted siege of the city, gives it into their hands and Himself banishes its people.[7] He moulds the nations for his own ends, and if they fail Him, decrees their destruction.[8] His Word builds and plants but also pulls up and tears down.[9] He is always near to guide or to argue with nations

---

[1] ii., iii. *passim.*   [2] ii. 31.

[3] ii. 8 ; *Where is the Lord?*   [4] i. 12 ff.

[5] xxvii. 5.   [6] xxii. 7 ; i. 15 ; iv. 6 ; v. 15, etc.

[7] xxii. 25 f. ; xxiv. 8 ff. ; xxv. 9 ; xxvii. 6 ; xxxii. 3 ; xxxiv. 2, 22.

[8] xviii. 1-10.   [9] i. 9 f. ; etc.

and individuals, and to give directions and sug
gestions of practical detail to His servants for
the interpretation and fulfilment of His purposes.[1]

It was all this activity and effectiveness, with
their sure results in history, which distinguished
Him from other gods, the gods of the nations,
who were ineffective, or as Jeremiah puts it *un-
profitable—no-gods*, *nothings* and *do-nothings*, *the work
of men's hands*, *lies* or *frauds*, and mere *bubbles*.[2]
On this line Jeremiah's monotheism marks a
notable advance; for alongside of faith in the
Divine Unity and Sovereignty there had lingered
even in Deuteronomy a belief in the existence
of other gods.[3] With Jeremiah every vestige
of this superstition is gone, and other gods con-
signed to limbo once and for all.

Yet Jeremiah's monotheism, like that of all the
Hebrew prophets, is even more due to convictions
of the character of the God of Israel. We have
seen how he dwells on the Divine Love, faithful
and yearning for love in return, pleading and
patient even with its delinquent sons and
daughters;[4] but equal to this is his emphasis on

[1] ii. 9; xii. 1 ff.; xiii. 1; xviii. 1; xix. 1, xxiv. 1 f.; xxvii. 2;
xxxii. 6; xxxv. 2; xxxvi. 2, 28.

[2] ii. 5, 11; viii. 19 (?); xiv. 22; xvi. 19, 20; xviii. 15; xxxii
30 (?), etc. *Bubble*, Hebrew *hebel*, lit. *breath*, usually rendered
vanity by our versions.

[3] Deut. iv. 19 reconciles the two by saying that Yahweh
ad assigned the gods to their respective nations.

[4] Above, pp. 187 ff.; ii. 9, 31 f.; iii. 12, 19; etc.

the righteousness of the Most High, by all His deeds *working troth, justice, and judgment on the earth,* which are His delight and the knowledge of which is man's only glory.[1] He demands from His people not sacrifices, which He never commanded to their fathers, nor vows but a better life, justice between man and man, and care for the weak and the innocent.[2] To know Him is to do justice and right.[3] Because the present generation have fallen away from these, and practise and love falsehood, slander, impurity, treacherous and greedy violence, therefore God, being justice and truth, must judge and condemn them : *What else can I do ?*[4] The ethical necessity of the doom of the people is clear to the Prophet from a very early stage of his ministry,[5] and throughout, though his heart struggles against it. But, if possible, even more abhorrent to God than these sins against domestic and civic piety in themselves, is the fact that they are committed in the very face of His Love and despite all its pleading. With Jeremiah as with Hosea the sin against love is the most hopeless and unpardonable, and this people have sinned it to the utmost.

[1] ix. 24 ; cp. v. 1 ff., etc.
[2] vii. 3 ff. ; xxvi. 13. See above, pp. 155 ff.
[3] xxii. 15 f.
[4] ix. 7 ; cp. ii. 9, 35 ; v. 7-9, 25.
[5] Not from the very earliest ; ii. and iii. utter pleadings rather than condemnations.

As a woman is false to her fere,
Have ye been false to me.[1]

Hence most deeply springs the Wrath of the Lord, a Wrath on which Jeremiah broods and explodes more frequently and fiercely than any other prophet: *I am full of the rage of the Lord; the glow of His wrath; take the cup of the wine of this fury at My hand and give all nations to whom I send thee to drink of it; the fierce anger of the Lord shall not turn until He have executed it.*[2] And He does execute it. God's Wrath breaks out in His *spurning* of His nation, in the hot names He calls it, *adulteress* and *harlot*, and in *hating* it.[3] He will not relent nor pardon it, nor listen to prayer for it.[4] He says, *I must myself take vengeance upon them. I shall not spare nor pity them.*[5] They will reel in the day of their visitation. He will feed them with wormwood and drug them with poison; He will suddenly let fall on them anguish and terrors; He will take His fan and winnow them out in the gates of the land and as the passing chaff strew them on the wind of the desert; the garden-land withers to wilderness and its cities break down at His presence and before His fierce anger; He will

[1] iii. 1 ff., 20.
[2] vi. 11; iv. 8, 26; xxv. 15; xxx. 24 (also, but out of place *in* xxiii. 20); cp. xiii. 12-14.
[3] ii. 20; iii. 3, 6 ff., 20; xii. 8.
[4] iv. 28; v. 7; vii. 16; xi. 14; xv. 1 ff.
[5] v. 9, 29; ix. 9; xxi. 7.

make Jerusalem heaps and cast out the people
before His face.   He will give them to be tossed
among the nations for a consternation, a reproach
and a proverb, for a taunt and a curse, in all places
whither He drives them : and will send after them
the sword, the famine, and the pestilence till they
be consumed.[1]

The modern mind deems arbitrary such immediate linking of physical and political disasters with
the Wrath of God against sin.   But we have to
ponder the following.   The Prophet was convinced of the ethical necessity of that Wrath and
of its judgments on Judah—he was convinced before they came to pass and he predicted them accurately, from close observation of the political
conditions of his world and the character of his
people.   Granted these and God's essential and
operative justice, the connection was natural :
What else can I do?   It was clear that Judah both
deserved and needed punishment and equally clear
that the boiling North held the potentialities of
this, which were gradually shaping and irresistibly
approaching.   Moreover, as Jeremiah insists, and
as the history both of nations and individuals has
frequently illustrated, there is a natural sequence
of disaster upon wrong-doing.   *Be thy scourge thine
own sin!   Thy ways and thy deeds have done to thee*

---

[1] vi. 15 ; viii. 12 ; ix. 15 (xxiii. 15) ; xv. 7, 8 ; xiii. 24 ; xviii.
17 ; vi. 26 ; ix. 11 ; vii. 15 ; xxiv. 9, 10.

*these things. Is it Me they provoke, saith the Lord,
Is it not themselves to the confusion of their faces?
Wherefore have these things come upon thee?—for the
mass of thy wickedness.*[1] As St. Paul says *the
wages of sin*, not the judge's penalty on sin but
the thing it naturally earns, *is death.* Now one of
Jeremiah's most acute and convincing experiences
as the *Tester* of his people,[2] is his observation of
how all this worked out upon his own generation.
Not only were the war, the pestilence, and the
captivity, which were about to fall upon Jerusalem, directly and obviously due to the perjury and
stupid pride of her rulers; but, as he more subtly
saw, the immorality of the whole people had been
disabling them, for years before, from meeting
these or any disasters except as sheer punishment
without place for repentance. Their previous
troubles had failed to sober or humble them or
rouse them. *They would not accept correction*, he says
of them more than once.[3] To the Prophet's warnings that God will judge them, they answer carelessly or defiantly *Not He!* Instead of yielding to
the power which lies in all adversity to cleanse the
heart and brace the will they became incapable of
shame, indifferent to consequences, and so past
praying for.[4] And in this they were fortified by

[1] ii. 19; iv. 18; vii. 19; xiii. 22.
[2] vi. 27-30; pp. 132 ff.
[3] ii. 30, v. 3.
[4] ii. 25; xviii. 12; vi. 15; viii. 12; xi. 14; xiv. 11.

the specious dreams and lies of their false prophets, continued to sin, and so fell to their doom, abashed at last but unassoilable.[1] If at any time they were startled by disaster, this found them too enfeebled even for repentance by their habitual insincerity or self-indulgence; which made them incapable of truth even under pain, and of a real conversion to God.[2] All this is discovered to us by the eyes and the mouth of Jeremiah. What in it is arbitrary? The record is awful, nothing like it in literature Yet every step is real. We follow a master of observation.

But perhaps the chief glory of our Prophet is that while thus delivering, as no other prophet so fully or so ethically does, the just wrath of God upon sin, he reveals at the same time that His people's sin costs God more pain than anger. This no doubt Jeremiah learned through his own heart. As we have seen, with his whole heart he loved the people whom he was called to test and expose, and that heart was wracked and torn by thoughts of the Doom which he had to pronounce upon them. So also, he was given to feel, was the heart of their God. In the following questions there is poignant surprise; an insulted, a wounded love beats through them.

[1] v. 31 ; xiii. 25 ; xviii. 11 ff. ; xxiii. 14-17 ; xxvii. 9 ; xxviii. 15.
[2] iii. 21-25, a vain confession of sin by the people which meets only with a sterner call from God (iv. 3-4 ; see pp. 102 f., 107 f.) and was, as the subsequent years proved, ineffective ; cp. xviii. 15.

What wrong found your fathers in Me,
  That so far they broke from Me?
Have I been a desert to Israel,
  Or land of thick darkness?
Why say my folk, 'We are off,
  No more to meet Thee!'
Can a maiden forget her adorning
  Or her girdle the bride?
Yet Me have My people forgotten
  Days without number.[1]

So, too, when the deserved doom threatens, and in hate He has cast off His heritage, His love still wonders how that can be—

Is My heritage to Me a speckled wild-bird
  With the wild-birds round and against her?
    Is Israel a slave,
    Or house-born serf?
    Why he for a prey?[2]

All the desolation of Judah is on Him alone. *no man lays it to heart, upon Me is the waste.*[3] And what we have seen to be the most human touch of all, the surprise of an outraged father at feeling, beneath His wrath against a prodigal son, the instincts of the ancient love which no wrath can quench,

[1] ii. 5, 31, 32. [3] xii. 7-9; ii. 14
[2] xii. 11; cp. Gen. xlviii. 7.

> **Is** Ephraim My dearest son,
> The child of delights?
> That as oft as against him I speak
> I must think of him still![1]

That these instincts are so scattered rather increases their cumulative effect.

Thus whether upon the Wrath or upon the Love of God Jeremiah speaks home to the heart of his own, and of our own and of every generation which loves lies and lets itself be lulled by them. Sin, he says, is no fiction nor a thing to be lightly taken.[2] Time for repentance is short; doom comes quickly. Habits of evil are not carelessly parted with, but have their long and necessary consequences moral and physical. No wash of words nor worship nor sacrament can cleanse the heart or redeem from guilt. It is not the flagrant sinner whom he chiefly warns, but those who harden themselves softly. And—very firmly this—forgiveness is not easily granted by God nor cheaply gained by men; God has not only set our sins before His face but carries them on His heart. And therefore, in view both of the Just Wrath of the Most High and of His suffering Love, only repentance can avail, the repentance which is not the facile mood offered by many in atonement for their sins, but arduous,

---

[1] xxxi. 20.

[2] I shall judge thee for saying 'I am guiltless': ii. 35.

rigorous and deeply sincere in its anguish. All
of which carries our prophet, six centuries before
Christ came, very far *into the fellowship of His
sufferings.*

I have already spoken sufficiently of Jeremiah's
other original contributions to theology on the
Freedom and the Patience of the Providence of
God, and his hope that God would be to Israel
what the prophet had bravely tried to be—no
transient guest but a dweller in their midst.[1]   The
titles for God which we may assume to have first
come from himself are few, perhaps only three :
*The Fountain of Living Waters, the Hope of Israel and
the Saviour thereof in time of trouble,* and *Ḥasidh, or
Loyal-in-Love,*[2] a term elsewhere applied only to
men.   Sometimes, but not nearly so often as the
copyists of our Hebrew text have made him do,
he uses the title *Yahweh of Hosts,* doubtless in the
other prophets' sense of *the forces of history and of
the Universe* (the original meaning having been
the armies of Israel), sometimes he borrows the
deuteronomic *Yahweh thy God,* or a similar form.
But most often (as the Greek faithfully shows us)
it is simply the personal name *Yahweh* (Jehovah)
by which he addresses or describes the Deity :
significant of the long struggle between them as
individuals.

Passing now from the world of nations to the

[1] Above, pp. 186 ff., 348.   [2] ii. 13 ; xiv. 8 ; xvii. 13 ; iii. 12.

world of nature we observe how little the genuine
Oracles of Jeremiah have to tell us of the Divine
Power over this; yet the little is proclaimed with
as firm assurance as of God's control of the
history of mankind. Both worlds are His: the
happenings in the one are the sacraments, the
signs and seals, of His purposes and tempers
towards the other: the winter blossom of the
almond, of His wakefulness in a world where all
seems asleep; the sun by day and the moon and
stars by night, of His everlasting faithfulness to
His own.[1] All things in nature obey His rule
though His own people do not; it is He who
rules the stormy sea and can alone bring rain.

> Even the stork in the heavens
>   Knoweth her seasons,
> And dove, swift and swallow
>   Keep time of their coming.
> But My people—they know not
>   The Rule of the Lord.

> I have set the sand as a bound for the sea,
> An eternal decree that cannot be crossed.
> Are there makers of rain 'mong the bubbles
>   of the heathen?
> Art Thou not He? . . . all these Thou hast
>   made.[2]

[1] i. 11 f.; xxxi. 35 f.

[2] viii. 7 ; v. 22 (xxxi. 35); xiv. 22 (after the Greek); cp. iii. 3 ;
v. 24.

After all neither Nature nor the courses of
the Nations but the single human heart is the
field which Jeremiah most originally explores for
visions of the Divine Working and from which
he has brought his most distinctive contributions
to our knowledge of God.   But that leads us up
to the second part of this lecture, his teaching
about man.   Before beginning that, however, we
must include under his teaching about God, two
elements of this to which his insight into the
human heart directly led him.

First this great utterance of the Divine Omnipresence :

> I am a God who is near,
> Not a God who is far.
> Can any man hide him in secret,
> And I not see him ?
> Do I not fill heaven and earth ?—
> Rede of the Lord.[1]

These verses have been claimed as the earliest
expression in Israel of the Divine Omnipresence.[2]
Amos, however, had given utterance to the same
truth though on a different plane of life.[3]

Second, and partly in logical sequence from
the preceding, but also stimulated by thoughts
of the best of Judah[4] banished to a long exile,

---

[1] xxiii. 23 f.; above, p. 256.   [2] By Smend.
[3] Amos ix. 2 ff.   [4] See above, pp. 238-241.

Jeremiah was the first in Israel to assure his people
that the sense of God's presence, faith in His
Providence, His Grace, and Prayer to Him were
now free both of Temple and Land—as possible
on distant and alien soil, without Ark or Altar, as
they had been with these in Jerusalem.   See his
Letter to the Exiles, and recall all that lay behind
it in his predictions of the ruin of the Temple,
and abolition of the Ark, and in his rejection
of sacrifices.[1]   To Deuteronomy exile was the
people's punishment; to Jeremiah it is a fresh
opportunity of grace.

2. MAN AND THE NEW COVENANT.

In the earliest Oracles of Jeremiah nations are
the human units in religion, Israel as a whole the
object of the Divine affection and providence.
To his age worship was the business of the nation :
public reverence for symbols and institutions, and
rites in which the individual's share was largely
performed for him by official representatives.
The prophets, and Jeremiah himself at first, dealt
with the people as a moral unity from the earliest
times to their own.   The Lord had loved and
sought, redeemed and tended them as a nation.
As a nation they fell away from Him and now they
were wholly false to Him.   When Jeremiah first
urges them to return, it is of a public and general

[1] xxix. 4-13; cp. vii. 14, 21 ff ; iii. 16; and see above,
pp. 143-159.

repentance that he speaks, as Deuteronomy
had done; and when his urgency fails it is their
political disappearance which he pronounces for
doom.

But when the rotten surface of the national life
thus broke under the Prophet he fell upon the
deeper levels of the individual heart, and not only
found the native sinfulness of this to be the
explanation of the public and social corruption
but discovered also soil for the seed-bed of new
truths and new hopes. Among these there is
none more potent than that of the immediate
relation of the individual to God. Jeremiah never
lost hope of the ultimate restoration of Israel.
Nevertheless the individual aspects of religion
increase in his prophesying, and though it is
imposible to trace their growth with any accuracy
because of the want of dates to many of his Oracles,
we may be certain that as he watched under
Josiah the failure of the national movements for
reform, inspired by Deuteronomy, and under
Jehoiakim and Ṣedekiah the gradual breaking up
of the nation, and still more as his own personal
relations with the Deity grew closer, Jeremiah
thought and spoke less of the nation and more
of the individual as the object of the Divine
call and purposes.

One has travelled by night through a wooded
country, by night and on into the dawn. How
solid and indivisible the dark masses appear and

how difficult to realise as composed of innumerable single growths, each with its own roots, each by itself soaring towards heaven. But as the dawn comes up one begins to see all this. The mass breaks; first the larger, more lonely trees stand out and soon every one of the common crowd is apparent in its separate strength and beauty.

It seems to me as I travel through the Book of Jeremiah that here also is a breaking of dawn—but they are men whom it reveals. There is a stir of this even in the earliest Oracles; for the form of address to the nation which has begun with the singular *Thou* changes gradually to *You*, and not *Israel* but *ye men of Israel* are called to turn to their God.[1] As the Prophet's indictments proceed his burden ceases to be the national harlotry. He arraigns separate classes or groups,[2] and then, in increasing numbers, individuals: brother deceiving brother and friend friend; adulterers each after the wife of his neighbour; the official bully Pashhur, Jehoiakim the atrocious and petty in contrast to his sire the simple and just Josiah, the helpless and ridiculous Ṣedekiah, the bustling and self-confident Hananiah[3]—with

[1] See above, pp. 90 ff.

[2] v. 1-5; viii. 8, scribes and wise; and prophets and priests continually.

[3] ix. 4 f.; v. 7 f.; xx. 3 f.; xxii. 13-18; xxxviii. 22; xxviii. 15 f.

24

the fit word and in sharp irony Jeremiah etches
them separately, in the same vividness as the
typical figures of the harlot watching for her prey
like the Arab robber in the desert, the fowler
crouching to fling his net, the shepherds failing
to keep their scattered flocks, the prophets who
fling about their tongues and rede a rede of the Lord.[1]
Jeremiah has answered the call to him to search
for the *man*, the men beneath the nation.[2]

Then there are his readings of the heart of man
into which he more deeply thought than any
other prophet of Israel: his revelation of the
working of God in the soul of man, its Searcher,
its only Guide and Strength; his stress upon individual responsibility and guilt, and on the one
glory of man being his knowledge of God and
the duty of every man to know God for himself
and not through others; and his song of the
beauty of the personal life rooted in faith, ever-
green and yielding its fruit even in seasons of
drought. Such passages increase in the Oracles
of Jeremiah. Not ceasing to be the patriot, the
civic conscience of his people, he busies himself
more with the hearts, the habits, the sins and the
duties towards God of its individuals. Like Christ
he takes the deaf apart from the multitude and
talks to him of himself.

[1] iii. 2 ; v. 26 ; x. 21 ; xxiii. 31.
[2] v. 1.

O Lord, Who triest the righteous,
Who seest the reins and the heart.[1]

False above all is the heart,
 Sick to despair,
 Who is to know it ?
I, the Lord, searching the heart
 And trying the reins,
To give to each man as his ways,
 As the fruit of his doings.[2]

Can any man hide him in secret
And I not see him ?[3]

In those days they shall say no more: The
 fathers have eaten sour grapes and the teeth
 of the children are set on edge.   But every
 one shall die for his own iniquity, every man
 that eateth sour grapes his teeth shall be set
 on edge.[4]

Speak to all Judah all the words I have charged
 thee. . . . Peradventure they will hearken
 and turn *every man from his evil way*.[5]

He that would boast in this let him boast,
Insight and knowledge of Me.[6]

---

[1] xi. 20 ; xx. 12.   [2] xvii. 9 f.   [3] xxiii. 24.
[4] xxxi. 29 f.   [5] xxvi. 2 f.   [6] ix. 24.

Lord, I know—not to man is his way,
Not man's to walk or settle his steps.[1]

Blessed the man that trusts in the Lord
And the Lord is his trust!
He like a tree that is planted by water,
That stretches its roots to the stream ;
Unafraid at the coming of heat,
His leaf shall be green ;
Sans care in the season of drought
He fails not in yielding his fruit.[2]

The individual soul rooted in faith and draw-
ing life from the Fountain of Living Water,
independent of all disaster to the nation and
famine on earth—could not be more beautifully
drawn.

Now all this advance by Jeremiah from the idea
of the nation as the human unit in religion—
Deuteronomy's ideal and at first his own—to the
individual as the direct object of the Divine Grace
and Discipline was promoted, we have seen, by
the dire happenings of the time, the unworthy
conduct of the people, their abandonment by
God, the ruin of the State and of the national
worship—which cut off individuals from all political and religious associations, leaving to each
(in Jeremiah's repeated phrase) only *his life*, or

[1] x. 23.   [2] xvii. 7 f. ; above, p. 54.

his soul, for a prey.[1] But all these could have furthered the advance but little unless Jeremiah had felt by bitter experience his own soul searched and re-searched by God—

> But Thou, Lord, hast known me,
>   Thou seest and triest my heart towards
>   Thee—[2]

unless through doubt and struggle he himself had won into the confidence of an immediate and intimate knowledge of God.   At his call he had learned how a man could be God's before he was his mother's or his nation's—God's own and to the end answerable only to Him.   He had proved his solitary conscience under persecution.   He had known how personal convictions can over-bear the traditions of the past and the habits of one's own generation—how God can hold a single man alone to His Will against his nation and all its powers, and vindicate him at last to their faces.   In all this lay much of the vicarious service which Jeremiah achieved for his own generation; what he had won for himself was possible for each of them.   And sure it is that the personal piety which henceforth flourished in Israel as it had never flourished before, weaving its delicate tendrils about the ruins of the state, the city and the altar, and (as the Psalms show) blooming behind the shelter of the Law

[1] See above, pp. 227-229.   [2] xii. 3.

like a garden of lilies within a fence of thorns, sprang from seeds in Jeremiah's heart, and was watered by his tears and the sweat of his spiritual agonies.

We are now come to a confluence of the streams we have been tracing—the prophecy of the New Covenant. This occupies no incongruous place, following hard as it does upon that of the eating of sour grapes—individual inspiration upon individual responsibility. But we cannot off-hand accept it as Jeremiah's own; the critical questions which have been with us from the beginning embarrass us still.

The collection of Oracles to which that of the New Covenant belongs, Chs. XXX, XXXI, was not made till long after Jeremiah's time; it includes, as we have seen, several of exilic or post-exilic origin.[1] But so do other chapters of the

[1] Above, pp. 293 ff. This was rightly perceived by earlier critics of last century, Movers, De Wette, Hitzig, etc., who mostly assigned as a date the end of the exile and read the influence of the Second Isaiah upon any Jeremian material that the chapters may contain. In spite of objections by Graf their thesis was reaffirmed and expanded by Stade (*Gesch. Isr.* i. 643) and by Smend (*Lehrbuch der A.T. Religionsgeschichte,* 1893), who denied that any part of xxx, xxxi was from Jeremiah, on grounds both of alleged inconsistencies with Jeremiah's teaching, and of the representations of Judah with her people restored and her cultivation resumed. But since Smend criticism has been more discriminating; admitting post-exilic elements and consequently a late age for the whole collection but reserving for our Prophet various pas-

Book, in which nevertheless genuine prophecies
of Jeremiah are recognised by virtually all modern
critics. The context therefore offers no prejudice
against the authenticity of the prophecy of the
New Covenant, XXXI. 31-34. But the form and
the substance of this have raised doubts, so honest
and reluctant as to deserve our consideration.
Duhm starts his usual objection that the passage
is in prose and a style characteristic of the late
expanders of the Book. We may let that go, as
we have done before, as by itself inconclusive;[1]
the prophecy may not have come directly from
Jeremiah's mouth but through the memory of a
reporter of the Prophet, Baruch or another. More
deserving of consideration is the criticism which
Duhm, with great unwillingness, makes of the
terms and substance of the prophecy. He ob-
jects to the term *covenant :* a *covenant* is a legal contract and could hardly have been chosen for the
frame of his ideal by so pronounced an anti-
legalist as Jeremiah. The passage 'promises a
new Covenant—not a new Torah but only a more
inward assimilation of the Torah by the people,
and emphasises the good results which this will
have for them but betrays no demand for a higher

sages : Giesebrecht, xxxi. 2-6, 15-20, 27-34 ; Duhm, xxx. 12-15,
xxxi. 2-6, 15-22*a* ; Erbt, xxxi. 2-6, 15-17, 18-20 ; Cornill, xxxi.
2-5, 9*b*, 15-22*b*, 31-34 ; J. R. Gillies, xxxi. 2-6, 15-20, 29 f., 31*b*,
33*b*, 34 ; Peake, xxxi. 2-6, 15-22, 31-34 ; Skinner, xxxi. 2-6,
15 f., 18-20, 21 f., 29 f., 31-34.

[1] Above, pp. 36 f., 40-42, 49-52, 91.

kind of religion.   If one does not let himself be
dazzled by the phrases *new covenant* and *write it on
the heart* then the passage tells us of the relation
of the individual no more than Deuteronomy has
already regarded as possible, XXX. 11 ff., and de-
sirable, VI. 6-8 : namely, that every man should be
at home in the Law and honestly follow it.'   He
continues : 'it is impossible for me to hold any
longer to the Jeremian origin of the passage.   I
find in it only the effusion of one learned in the
Scriptures who regards as the highest ideal, that
every one of the Jewish people should know the
Law by heart.'

But in his resolve 'not to let himself be dazzled'
has not Duhm gone to the opposite extreme and
seriously under-read the whole spirit of the
passage—besides showing as usual undue ap-
prehensiveness of the presence in the text of a
legalist at work ?[1]   The choice of the term
covenant for the frame of his ideal was not unnatural to Jeremiah nor irrelevant to his experience and teaching.   Formally the term may mean
a legal contract ; but it is open to a prophet or a
poet to use any metaphor for his ideals and
transform its mere letter by the spirit he puts into
it ; and after all *covenant* is only a metaphor for a
relation which was beyond the compass of any
figure to express.   Yet it was a term classical in

---

[1] Above, pp. 40, 91, 142, 145.

Israel and most intelligible to the generation whom Jeremiah was addressing. Its associations, especially as he had recalled them,[1] had been those not of the Law but of Love. It was not a contract or bargain but an approach by God to His people, an offer of His Grace, a statement of His Will and accompanied by manifestations of His Power to redeem them. One might as well charge Jesus with legalism in adopting a term sanctioned by God Himself, and so historical, sacred and endeared to the national memory. Nor need Torah, or Law, be taken as Duhm takes it in its sense of the legal codes of Israel, but in its wider meaning of the Divine *instruction* or *revelation.* Further the epithet *New* applied to Covenant was most relevant to the Prophet's and his people's recent sense of the failure of the ancient covenant, as restated and enforced in Deuteronomy. In spite of the excitement caused by the discovery of the Book in which it was written, and the recital of its words throughout the land, the Old Covenant had failed to capture the heart of the people or to secure from them more than the formal and superstitious observance of the letter of its Torah. Was it not a natural antithesis to predict that His Torah would be set by God *in their inward parts and written on their hearts?* How else (will Duhm tell us?) than by such phrases could the Prophet

----

[1] xi. 1 ff., etc.

have described an inward and purely spiritual process ? To say as Duhm does that the phrases only mean that common men would learn the Law of God 'by heart' (auswendig), is, whoever their author may have been, to travesty his meaning. Finally, all the phrasing of the New Covenant is in harmony with the rest of the Prophet's teaching. He had spoken of God's will to give His people a new heart to know Him;[1] he had taught religion as the individual's direct knowledge of God;[2] he had won this himself from God directly without help from his parentage, his fellow-prophets or priests or any others; he had most bitterly known also how weak the word of one man is to teach his countrymen this knowledge and that it can only come by the inward operation of God Himself upon their spirits; and he had made as clear as ever prophet did that God's pardon for sin was the first, the necessary preliminary to His other gifts. Nor is the fact that the New Covenant is to be a national one alien to his teaching: Jeremiah never lost hope of his nation's survival and restoration.

Thus the passage on the New Covenant brings together all the strands of Jeremiah's experience and doctrine and hopes, shaken free from the political debris of the times, into one fair web under a pattern familiar and dear to the people.

[1] xxiv. 7.　　　　[2] ix. 24; cp. viii. 7b, etc.

The weaving, it is true, is none of the deftest, but whether this is due to the aged Jeremiah's failing fingers or to the awkwardness of a disciple, the stuff and its dyes are all his own.

Lo, days are coming—Rede of the Lord— when I will make with the House of Israel and with the House of Judah a New Covenant, not like the Covenant which I made with their fathers in the day that I took them by their hand to bring them forth from the land of Egypt, which My Covenant they brake and I rejected them[1]—Rede of the Lord. But this is My[2] Covenant which I will make with the sons[3] of Israel after those days—Rede of the Lord—I will set My Law in their inward part and on their heart will I write it, and I will be to them a God, and they shall be to Me a people. And they shall teach no more every man his neighbour and every man his brother saying, Know thou[4] the Lord! For they shall all know Me from the least even to the greatest;[5] for I will forgive their guilt and their sin will I remember no more.

[1] So Greek, Latin and Syriac; Hebrew *though I was an husband to them.*

[2] So one Greek version.   [3] So some MSS.

[4] So Greek and Latin.

[5] Hebrew adds, *Rede of the Lord.*

This is, as has been said, a prophecy of Christianity which has hardly its equal in the Old Testament.[1] It is the Covenant which Jesus Christ the Son of God accepted for Himself and all men and sealed with His own blood.

And yet not even in this prophecy of Jeremiah, in which the individual soul is made to feel that God created it not for its family nor its state nor its church but only for Himself, is there any breath of a promise for it after death. The Prophet's eyes are still sealed to that future. The soul must be content that her strength and peace and hope are with God.

[1] Giesebrecht

APPENDIX I.

MEDES AND SCYTHIANS (pp. 73, 110).

IT is very difficult, if not impossible, to give a correct account of the national and racial movements which, along with the moral conditions in Judah, called forth Jeremiah's Oracles of judgment in the years immediately following his call in 627-626 B.C. But the following facts are well founded. In or about 625 the Medes were defeated in an attack upon Assyria and their king Phraortes was killed, but at the same time Ashurbanipal died, and his weaker successor was compelled to recognize the virtual independence of Nabopolassar, the Chaldean in Babylon. Cyaxares (624-585), the son of Phraortes, soon after his succession to his father—say between 624 and 620—led a second Median assault upon Assyria and besieged Nineveh, but had to retire because of the onset from the north of the Scythians, the Ashguzai of the Assyrian monuments, probably the Ashkenaz or Ashkunza (?) of the Old Testament. And then it was not for some years that Cyaxares felt himself strong enough by his alliance with Nabopolassar for a third Median invasion of Assyria which culminated in the capture and destruction of Nineveh.

The Assyrians appear to have been in touch with

the Ashguzai for over a century and for a shorter
time probably in alliance with them; which
alliance was the cause of the Scythian advance
to the relief of Nineveh from its siege by the
Medes *circa* 624-620 (see Winckler *Die Keilinschriften u. das alte Testament,* 3rd ed., pp. 100 ff.).
About the same time must be dated the Scythian
advance through Western Asia to the borders of
Egypt, which Herodotus (I. 103-104, IV. 1) reports.   Professor N. Schmidt (*Enc. Bibl.*, art.
'Scythians') supposes that this advance was due
to the same Scythian-Assyrian alliance, in order
to preserve the Assyrian territories from the arms
of Psamtik of Egypt, who had since 639 been
besieging Ashdod; and he holds that this hypothesis explains the absence of any record of
violence by the Scythians on their southern campaign, except at Ashkelon.   This precarious
hypothesis apart, we have the facts that no Biblical chronicler records any invasion of Judah and
Benjamin by the Scythians, and yet that the
early Oracles of Jeremiah, generally attributed to
the alarms which the advance of such barbarian
hordes would excite in Judah, do closely fit the
Scythians (with a few exceptions that may be due
to the prophet's adaptation in 604 of his earlier
Oracles to the new *enemy* out of the north, the
Chaldeans).

There, are, however, modern writers who claim
that the Oracles in question were originally composed not in view of the Scythian, but of the
Chaldean invasion of Palestine.   So George
Douglas (*The Book of Jeremiah*, London, Hodder
& Stoughton, 1903), who, while assigning Jeremiah's call to 627, relegates the two visions and

all the Oracles in the first part of the book to the
years following Jehoiakim's accession in 608: cp.
Winckler (*Gesch. Israels*, I, 112 f.), F. Wilke (*A. T.
Studien R. Kittel zum* 60 *Geburtstag dargebracht*,
1913), and Sellin. This would be an easy solution
but for the fact that the Oracles, on the whole, more
closely suit a Scythian than they do a Chaldean invasion, while Jer. i. 2, 3 refers Jeremiah's prophesying to the reigns both of Josiah and Jehoiakim.
Meissner (*Deutsche Literatur Zeitung*, 1924),
Gunkel and Gressmann (Z.A.T.W., 1924, 157), take
the foe from the north to have been the Medes. But
Volz (p. 58), while placing the Oracles early, thinks
that Jeremiah is describing no definite political foe.
The Lord has told him that the foe is to break in from
the North, 'more he does not know and will not
know.' Cp. Welch, *Exp.* 1921, XXI. 139 ff.

The date of the Fall of Nineveh was accepted as
607-606 B.C. until the discovery by C. J. Gadd of a
Babylonian chronicle which assigns it to the four-
teenth year of Nabopolassar, and Gadd's argument
is that this was 612 B.C. (*Proceedings of the British
Academy*, Vol. X. 1921-23, 473 ff.; *Exp.*, 1925,
85 ff.). He reckons the reign from 626-625 B.C.; but
as remarked above, p. 175, Nabopolassar became in
that year officially not king but only viceroy. I have
therefore offered the alternative dates 612 and 607-
606 on pp. 163, n. 3, and 175. Volz. (p. XIV),
Gressmann (Z.A.T.W., 1924, 157), Welch
(Z.A.T.W., 1925, 255 ff.), and others accept 1912;
for Welch's further deductions see below p. 393.

APPENDIX II.

NECOH'S CAMPAIGN (pp. 162, 163).

In addition to the accounts in the Books of Kings and Chronicles of Pharaoh Necoh's advance into Asia in pursuance of his claim for a share of the crumbling Assyrian Empire there are two independent records : (1) Jeremiah XLVII. 1 — *and Pharaoh smote Gaza*—a headline (with other particulars) wrongly prefixed by the Hebrew text, but not by the Greek, to an Oracle upon an invasion of Philistia not from the south but from the north (see above, pp. 13, 61) ; (2) by Herodotus, II. 159, who says that ' Necoh (Nekôs) making war by land on the Syrians defeated them at Magdolos and after the battle took Kadŭtis, a great city of Syria.' Magdolos is probably Megiddo, unless it stands for Megdel, which, as well as Rumman (= Hadad-rimmon, the scene of the mourning for Josiah, Zech. XII. 11) lies near Megiddo. If, as is usually held, Kadŭtis be Gaza, Herodotus has reversed the proper order of Necoh's two actions ; but Kadŭtis also suggests *hak-Kôdesh, the holy*, an epithet of Jerusalem (*Jerusalem*, I. 270) which would suit Herodotus' order, for it was after Megiddo that Necoh became master of Jerusalem and Judah. The suggestion, though worth mentioning, is doubtful ; the epithet is late, exilic and post-exilic ; and Herodotus' phrase *took Kadŭtis* is hardly equivalent to *became paramount* there as Necoh became paramount in Jerusalem.

ADDITIONAL NOTES.

To the Preceding Pages.

These notes mainly refer to the most recent literature on Jeremiah, for which see the Bibliography on pp. xiii. ff. of this volume.

P. 5, last two sentences and footnote.—The opinion there expressed is confirmed by Volz, who says, p. XXVII, that Jeremiah 'became the proper founder of personal religion. . . . The men who subsequently led the spiritual life of Israel, the poets of Psalm lxxiii, of Job iii ff. and of Isaiah liii are pupils of the Prophets, before all pupils of Jeremiah and his personal piety.'

P. 7, n. 1.—See also Volz, p. XXVII.

Pp. 9-30.—Cf. T. H. Robinson, 'The Structure of the Book of Jeremiah,' *Exp.* 1920, VIII. pp. 17 ff., 20; and H. W. Robinson, Ch. I.

Pp. 11 ff. on the Hebrew Text and Greek Version of the Book—see Volz, *Studien z. Text des Jeremia,* pp. IX ff. and in his Commentary, pp. L f.

Chapter II, 'The Poet,' pp. 31 ff.—On this whole chapter see Volz, pp. XXXIV ff., 'Der Redner, Dichter und Schriftsteller Jeremia,' which mainly agrees with what is stated in the chapter as to Jeremiah's rank as a poet, and also (as against Duhm) as to the variety of the metres which he used and as to his use of prose as well as of metre. The following may be quoted : 'Among the classical prophets Isaiah is the greatest Orator, Jeremiah the greatest Poet' ; 'what Jeremiah speaks and writes is all present. He beholds future sufferings, xiv. 18, hears distant voices and presents [them] so

that we behold and hear them'; 'before all he is a master
of song, none of the other prophets is a lyrist to such a
degree as he is'; 'with the structure of the separate poems
and orations Jeremiah has above all paid greater care to the
strophe-construction than to the metre'; 'as "Versform"
he employs chiefly the double line, willingly also the Ḳinā,
also the double line of two beats each, more seldom the
single line (as a long line or a short line).' Among the
genuine oracles of Jeremiah Volz admits some prose passages :—i. 11-16, etc.   See also H. W. Robinson, pp. 16 ff.

P. 39, n. 1.—Volz also, p. XLII n., finds lines of only two
beats.

P. 44 n.—Volz also, p. XLII n., finds longer heavier lines
in Jeremiah's verse.

P. 45.—For the line *From the noise of the horse and the
bowmen* (Jer. iv. 29) Volz gives: Before the call 'Riders and
Archers!'

P. 47, last paragraph and p. 106.—The line (ii. 31)
O generation—you!—look at the word of the Lord is
differently rendered in the Versions. Founding on LXX
Volz reads 'ye fear not My Word.' I adhere to my interpretation of it.

P. 49—Jer. ix. 22 f. (Eng. 23 f.) is not included by Volz
among the genuine oracles of Jeremiah and he prints it as
prose.

P. 50.—Volz takes Jer. vii. 28 to refer to the Law on
Sinai and not to Deuteronomy and the reforms of Josiah.

P. 52 f. and 98 ff.—Volz (33 f.) reads and renders
Jer. iii. 1-5, 19-25, iv. 1-4 continuously as verse.

Pp. 53 f. on Jer. xvii. 5 ff.—Volz appears not to attribute
to Jeremiah xvii. 5-13.

Pp. 56 f., 334.—On 'Jeremiah and Nature,' see Elliott
Binns in the Westminster Commentary, p. 10. Volz assigns
ch. xiv. 1-15 on the Drought, etc., to Jeremiah's earliest
period, 627-625 B. C.

P. 78.—With Jer. i. 5 cp. Isaiah xlii. 6, xliv. 2, xlix. 1, 5 on The Servant of the Lord.

Pp. 79 ff.—Jer. i. 5 a prophet *to the nations*. As against those who deem that this is too wide for the Prophet's own conscience of his mission (*e.g.*, Stade, 'Der "Völkerprophet" Jeremiah,' Z.A.T.W., 1906, 97 ff., and Bruston, 'Jérémie fut-il prophète pour les Nations?' Z.A.T.W., 1907, 75 ff.) the following agree with the view which I have expressed that *nations* in the plural is authentic and not a later expansion:— Welch, 'The Call and the Commission of Jeremiah,' *Exp.*, 1921, VIII. 21, pp. 129 ff., where he supports the argument adopted above, that Jeremiah was conscious of a commission to *the nations,* by the fact that he knew the same to be true of his predecessors in Israel, Jer. xxviii. 8; Volz, who on p. XXXII says 'from the beginning onwards he feels himself a prophet for the nations, who has the commission to build and destroy kingdoms'; and Lofthouse, pp. 35, 39. On the authenticity of ch. i. see further Welch's *Jeremiah,* 37 ff.

P. 83, n. 1, on Jer. i. 10.—Volz not only omits with the LXX *to pull down* but also *to destroy* on the ground that a poet of such fine feeling as Jeremiah would set over against each other two negative and two positive expressions. But the LXX Version (followed above, p. 83) with three negative and two positive terms is even more suitable metrically.

P. 85.—The Second Vision, Welch (*Exp.,* 1921, VIII. 21, p. 139) reads נֹפֵחַ and renders: I see a caldron at boiling point, and the blower is from the north. In his *Jeremiah* he omits vv. 15 f. and connects 13 f. immediately with 17 f.

Pp. 90 ff.—His Earliest Oracles (ii. 2-iv. 4). Of these Volz takes as genuine ii. 1-3, 5-37 (placing 18 after 32 and 34 f. after 37), iii. 1-5, 19-iv. 4, iii. 6-15, 18 (in that order). He dates them between 627 and 625, to which years he also assigns iv. 5-31, xiii. 20-27, xiv. 1-xv. 3, xxiii. 9-12. Others (e.g. Welch) also run iii. 1-5 and iii. 19 ff. together. From ii Volz deletes verses 4, 5aa, 6bβ, 7. 18 on grounds both of metre, the rest of the chapter yielding regular strophes with 4 lines each, and of want of logical connection. Welch, *Jeremiah,* 77 ff., severely criticises Volz's argument; he takes iii. 6-13 as here interpolated but a genuine and early oracle of the prophet, revealing his condemnation of Josiah's reforms. Horst asserts Jeremiah appeared only after the Battle of Megiddo!

P. 94, n. 2—The Heb. addition to Jer. ii. 17, which is wanting in LXX is reasonably explained by K. Haacke, Z.A.T.W., 1901, 142, as a false dittography of the immediately following consonants which open verse 18.

Pp. 98-103.—Jer. iii-iv. 3. See Welch, 'Jeremiah and the Essence of Religion,' *Exp.,* 1921, Vol. XXI, pp. 254 ff.

P. 102.—iii. 24 f. Welch (*Exp.,* 1921, Vol. XXI, p. 264) rightly objects to the relegation of this passage to the Post-Exilic period.

P. 103.—Jer. iv. 1, 2. Volz appears to retain these verses. As against. n. 2 on this page see Welch, *Exp.,* 1921, Vol. XXI, pp. 268 f. In his *Jeremiah,* 70 ff. he gives good reasons for accepting ver. 1 but is doubtful about ver. 2.

Pp. 110 ff.—Oracles on the Scythians (iv. 5-vi. 29). As to whether these were originally written with the Scythians in view see above, Appendix I, pp. 382 f. J. M. P. Smith ('The Prophet and his Problems,' 1914, 97 f.), Binns (1919), and H. W. Robinson (1925) appear to accept the Scythians as meant. Lofthouse (1925) agrees that the foe is the Scythians and conformably with the opinion expressed in this volume (p. 110), that any expressions unsuitable to them may be due either to Jeremiah's ignorance of the race and the consequently greater freedom of his imagination or to subsequent editing (p. 58 n.), 'he does not refer his words to Jahveh, he is for the time the spectator of Jahveh's acts rather than the mouthpiece of his word' (p. 56). Volz, while denying that Jeremiah had any single and definite foe from the north in view, admits as his genuine oracles iv. 5-31 (which he dates between 627 and 625), v. 1-14, 26-28, 30 f., vi. 1-11a, 16-19, 21, 22-26, 27-30 (which he dates along with viii. 8-12 (vi. 11-15) between 625 and 622).

Welch's reasoning, *Jeremiah* 104 f., is not convincing. Nor is his argument, 117 ff., that the prophets were not stirred to prophesy by some definite political event, threatening their own nation. The rise of prophecy under Amos and Hosea contemporaneous with the Assyrian advance towards Palestine, Isaiah's defiance of Sargon and Sennacherib, the revival of prophecy with Zephaniah, Nahum, Habakkuk and Jeremiah upon the decay of Assyria and the rise of the Chaldeans, and the emergence of Second Isaiah upon the advent of Cyrus—all these show how overdone his argument is. Nor does any of the critics whom he opposes fail (as he imputes they do) to trace prophecy behind all political events to its fundamental inspiration in the God of Israel and thoughts of His character. See *e.g.* my *Twelve Prophets*, Vol. I, ch. iv., 'The Influence of Assyria on Prophecy.'— In Welch's judgment (p. 126) 'the destroyer of nations was not a historical figure, any more than the North from which he came was a point of the compass. Both were expressions of an idea.'

P. 118.—Jer. iv. 31. On this verse see G. Beer, Z.A.T.W., 1911, pp. 153 f.

P. 132.—Jer. vi. 27-30 seems dated by Volz with the rest of ch. vi. probably between 625 and 622 b. c.

P. 140.—Jeremiah sympathised with Deuteronomy. So, quoting others Volz, p. XXIX: 'In the now published Deuteronomy Jeremiah, in spite of all differences, certainly recognised a welcome ally.' Lofthouse (pp. 77 ff.): 'No wonder he welcomed the book. . . . His old message was given back to him, but with a double authority. . . . When, therefore, the covenant had been formally accepted, and was to be carried out through the country, Jeremiah was ready for an unaccustomed but very welcome rôle . . . to urge the covenant upon the people (xi. 1-11).' Gressmann (Z.A.T.W., 1925, 144) thinks that the Covenant in xi. 3 is Deuteronomy and that in verse 5 Jeremiah swore to it and could not have broken this oath. 'Jeremiah therefore was lifelong on the side of Deuteronomy.' Even Puukko, in his otherwise sceptical and grudging analysis in the essay cited below, admits (p. 153) that 'the exhortations to love, fear, and honour Jahve [in Deuteronomy] as well as the deuteronomic ideal that Israel was a people sanctified to Jahve (Deut. vii. 6) must have been sympathetic to Jeremiah.' Volz thinks Jer. iii. 1-5, 19-25, iv. 1-4 support the idea that Jeremiah's preaching prepared the way for Josiah's reforms. Horst: Jeremiah knew nothing of a genuine Deuteronomy.

Pp. 143-146.—While holding to the opinion that the *words of this Covenant* (xi. 2) refer to Deuteronomy, I must record that Volz agrees with many other critics in interpreting them of the whole Law given to Israel in the days of their wilderness wanderings. The fullest discussion of the question is that by A. F. Puukko, 'Jeremias Stellung zum Deuteronomium' (*Beiträge z. Wissenschaft vom A. T.*, Heft 13, 1913), in which, after giving a summary of various opinions during a hundred years, from the end of the 18th Century, he discusses carefully Jeremiah's relation to the personages concerned with the discovery of the Law-book in 621, and finding nothing certain in that falls back on the passages in our Book of Jeremiah which have been held to refer to Deuteronomy, but even in these finds none which reliably support Jeremiah's adhesion to Deuteronomy. In his speeches against the people's false trust in the Temple, vii, xxvi, he had in view Josiah's Law-book, but xxvi. 4 is not genuine. Marti, Wellhausen, and Steuernagel may think that Jer. viii. 8 refers to Deuteronomy, and Cornill may call it an authentic witness to Jeremiah's relation to the Law-book of 621, and indeed the only one. But this is doubtful. A written law is meant, but that it was Deuteronomy can hardly be supposed; probably it was only some clauses and distortions inserted in the Law in a selfish interest. In his speeches against the people's false trust in the Temple (vii, xxvi) Jeremiah had Josiah's Law-book in view. But xxvi is not genuine. So far Puukko. His scepticism seems to me to be over-driven.

Pp. 147, 168 ff., Jer. vii. 1-15, xxvi.—To the list in n. 1 on p. 147 of those who take the two passages are referring to one and the same Temple address by the Prophet add:

Binns ('great probability') ; Welch, *Exp.*, 1921, Vol. XXII.
46 ff.; Volz, p. 87 ('vii is expanded through xxvi, which
adds the biographic account to the address once more
given in vii; that both chapters describe the same event is
clearly evident . . . in the biographic account only the
central thoughts of the address are given; the address itself
stands in vii because it was taken up into the first Book of
the Oracles of Jeremiah which Baruch read aloud under
Jehoiakim, xxxvi. 1 ff.') ; Lofthouse (pp. 114, 215). Against
such an array of authorities I can hardly venture to maintain
the opinion I expressed above that the two chapters refer to
two distinct visits by Jeremiah to the Temple.

Pp. 151 ff., Jer. xi. 15, 16.—It may not be possible to fix
an exact date for this Oracle. But as Volz (p. 135) says, the
situation and aim are the same as in vii. 1-15, especially 10.
He takes the text as corrupt, and proposes several emendations which are not convincing, *e.g.*, asserting that *my beloved* is impossible in so severe an oracle, and proposes to
read instead a title *Concerning Judah;* further he divides
the Oracle into two, 15 with 16b *a* and the rest of 16.

Pp. 153 ff., Jer. viii. 8, 9.—As against most moderns
neither Puukko nor Volz (pp. 76 f.) thinks that this Oracle
refers to Deuteronomy. Volz takes its concern as much
more general. 'In 8b Jeremiah has in view not official
codifications of a legal kind; he thinks, *e.g.*, of judicial
decrees as Isaiah does in ch. x. 1 f. or on similar more
general interpretations.' He deletes the line *Lo, they have
spurned the Word of the Lord* as disturbing to both sense
and rhythm; and the rest of the Oracle he takes along with
vi. 11b, 12 and vi. 13-15 (= viii. 10-12) as forming a unity.
On the other hand, Gressmann (Z.A.T.W., 1925, 145-147)
thinks that the piece has to do with Deuteronomy, but takes
all of viii. 8, 9 as the words of the people under Jehoiakim,
who after the apparent failure of the Law-book of 621 to
bring victory to the people of God thus reviled it; and he
finds Jeremiah's answer to them in vi. 10-12. According to
Lofthouse (p. 86) viii. 4-13 reveal Jeremiah's disillusion-

ment with regard to Deuteronomy. Welch, *Jeremiah*, 92, taking Deuteronomy as the law of Northern Israel to which Jeremiah belonged, thinks that the priests of Jerusalem in taking it over perverted it, by prefixing xii. 1-7 to it, and it was this perversion which the prophet imputes to *the false pen of the scribes.*

Pp. 155-159, on the meaning of Jer. vii. 21-23.—Puukko (*op. cit.* above, p. 151) holds that all that these verses mean is that burnt and slain offerings did not belong to the fundamental or essential elements of the religion founded at Sinai through Moses. Volz, likewise understanding vii. 23 f. with xxxi. 31-34 of the Lawgiving on Sinai and not of the Reform under Josiah (p. XXVIII. n.), gives an explanation (p. 102) of the prophet's meaning which it is interesting to compare with the explanation I have given above on p. 158. He says, 'The grand, creative thing which Moses brought in was the moral law (the 'Berith Jahwes') ; the religion which Moses founded has its centre in the Decalogue; the knowledge which came upon him and which he communicated was that of the moral Being of God and of morality as the perfect worship of Jahwe. The generation which held to Moses lived according to this knowledge in a service of God that was without sacrifices (just as the generation of Jesus' disciples lived in complete love and even with their goods in common) ; which distinguished this original congregation of Israel from all peoples of antiquity, and constituted the foundation of Moses a new religion. Later into the service of God came again the sacrifices employed by all peoples, as in the Christian congregation all possible uses of the past and of the contemporary world again found their place.' But Binns (p. 76) falls back on the suggested translation of עֵל־דְּבַר, *for the sake of* or *on account of* burnt-offerings. Jeremiah 'was not denying the cherished belief of the people that the sacrificial system was of Divine origin, but he was trying to restore them to a worthy notion of that system,' viz. that the reality underlying all sacrifice was that God wanted the hearts of His people not their offerings. Against the translation *for the sake of,* see above, p. 156. Further, on vii. 21-23 compare Welch who says (*Exp.,* 1921, XXII. 52 ff.) Jeremiah is content to declare emphatically that it [the sacrificial system] was 'no part of the specifically Yahwistic religion and therefore could be disregarded by men who were loyal to the religion of their fathers'. It is 'condemnation of the sacrificial system in principle' as not essential to the faith, for Jahweh never commanded sacrifices; Innes Logan, *Exp.,* 1925, I. 62 ff.; J. E. McFadyen, *The Approach to the O.T.* (1926), pp. 26 f., where it is rightly pointed out that there is no shadow of probability that Jeremiah could ever have uttered the words in xxxiii. 18 which are in plain contradiction to vii. 21-23, and are indeed wanting in the LXX; and W. M. Grant, *The Bible of Jesus* (1927), p. 169, 'neither textually nor in candid exegesis can the judgment be set aside' i.e. Jeremiah's judgment. Further, see pp. 176 ff. on the attitudes of Jeremiah and Jesus to the Temple.

Pp. 162 ff.—The Battle of Megiddo, and Death of Josiah. Welch, Z.A.T.W., 1925, pp. 255 ff., accepting Gadd's inferences from the Babylonian tablet which he discovered in the British Museum, that Nineveh fell not in 606 but in 612, holds that the tablet makes it clear that Pharaoh-Necoh was advancing through Palestine on his way not to attack Assyria but to support the Assyrian Empire against the Medes and Babylonians. Dismissing the account in 2 Chronicles xxxv. 20-24 that Josiah attacked Necoh at Megiddo and was slain in battle, Welch holds that all that 2 Kings xxiii. 29 implies is that Josiah went to meet Necoh there; and he infers that Necoh, learning that Josiah was by no means as pro-Assyrian as his two predecessors had been and feeling him a danger to his plans, summoned Josiah to meet him at Megiddo, and explain his attitude. What happened at Megiddo was not a battle but a court-martial and Josiah, unable to satisfy Necoh, was immediately executed. But of this theory Volz (2nd edition, 1928, p. XV. n.) justly says that the form of the Biblical source of our information, which stands very near to the events, hardly admits of such an interpretation.

P. 165 n. 1.—With Jer. viii. 31, cp. ii. 23, xix. 5 f., 11 ff.

P. 166, Jer. xxii. 15-17.—Volz, introducing the name Ahaz, which some Greek codices have instead of Heb. *'erez, cedar,* and emending the two Heb. words *lô dan,* which end 15 and begin 16, into *Lebanon,* renders the first couplet of 15 thus: Bist du König, dass du dich misst mit Ahas in schönen Zedern des Libanon? This venturesome conjecture is very interesting. He also omits verse 16 as disturbing the metre and breaking the connection between 15 and 17.

P. 168, Jer. vii. and xxvi.—See pp. 39 f. above, and to the works given there add Horst, Z.A.T.W., 1923, pp. 133 ff.

P. 169 n.—Welch (*Exp.* Vol. XXII, 1921, 46 ff.) agrees with Skinner and others that the conditional clauses in vii and xxvi are later insertions and that Jeremiah predicted a judgment which was absolute not contingent. But Volz rightly retains the said clauses as original; see especially his remarks (p. 96) on Jeremiah's defence, xxvi. 12-14. In addition to this notice Jeremiah's express hope to Baruch, xxxvi. 3, 7, that the people on hearing the roll of his oracles read will repent and be forgiven, and also xxv. 6, and the Parable of the Potter.

Pp. 179-181, Jer. xxv. 1-14.—Volz (pp. 250 ff.) retains the reference to Nebuchadrezzar in verse 1, but rejects the last words of 3 and all 4, 6 (as an expansion), in 9 the words *Rede of Yahweh, and Nebuchadrezzar, King of Babel my servant,* and all 11, 12 (11b borrowed from xxix. 10), and alters the order of the last two verses to this, 14, 13b β, 13aba. He finds it impossible to say how much was written by Jeremiah himself and how much is due to Baruch. On Jer. xxv see Horst, Z.A.T.W., 1923, pp. 99 ff. and Welch, 113 ff.

Pp. 185-190, Jer. xviii, The Parable of the Potter.—Volz (192 ff.) takes verses 1-11 as genuine, but denies that 12 can have originally belonged to them. Welch, *Jeremiah,* 187 ff., accepts only 1-6, all that follows being due to a later writer,

who 'failed to notice that his addition clashed hopelessly
with Jeremiah's peculiar use of the figure. For the whole
point of the little later sermon turned on the possibility of
repentance. . . . Now obviously clay cannot change its
mind.' And he adds in a note, criticising Volz, 'unfortunately clay has no *sittliche Verhalten.*' But such reasoning
would clear out much of the spiritual symbolism both of the
O.T. an the N. T.

P. 191, Jer. xix.—Volz (201 f.) thinks it clear that two
events have here been mingled which have nothing to do
with each other either in time or subject. He takes as
genuine verses 2ab, 3-6, 11b, 12, 13, which deal with
Tophet. The rest is a miscellany of dire judgments, added
later.

Pp. 193-194, Jer. xxxv, The Rechabites.—See K. Budde
on 'The Nomadic Ideal in the O.T.', in *New World,* Vol.
IV, 1895, pp. 726 ff. Volz (323 ff.) accepts as Jeremiah's
virtually all except verse 15.

P. 206, Jer. ix. 23, 24.—Denied by some to Jeremiah,
e.g., Volz (*Studien,* 78, Comm. 119), 'can hardly be from
Jeremiah, the knowledge of God which it praises being not
the practical relation to God as with Jeremiah, but theo-
logical knowledge.' This is far from convincing.

P. 207, Jer. x. 1-16.—Volz (p. 122) says that Jeremiah
could hardly have dealt with Yahweh and the idols with
such prolixity as here.

P. 210, Jer. xii. 7-13.—Volz (pp. 143 f.) takes this poem
as Jeremiah's, in six strophes each of four lines in the Ķinah
metre; as is virtually done above on pp. 211 f.

P. 222 n. 1, Jer. xviii. 14.—This is read and rendered
by Volz: Weicht vom Felsen das Erdreich, der Schnee vom
Libanon? oder versiegen die Wasser des Sirjon, die
kühlenden, rauschenden?

P. 227, Jer. xlv.—In opposition to a number of leading
critics Volz (p. 371) says that there is no sufficient ground
to doubt the date set to this Oracle to Baruch, 'only,' he

adds, 'we will not press it,' and would refer it to after not the writing of the Roll in the 4th year, but the reading of the Roll in the 5th year, of Jehoiakim.

P. 236.—Volz (XX) similarly testifies to the relief experienced by Jeremiah during these years, 'six quiet years,' and to the character of those who disturbed it—prophets, the war-party they led, and the influence of foreign agents.

Pp. 238 f.—Jer. xxiv, 3 ff., is read as prose throughout by Volz (246 ff.), who judges that 5 ff. have been expanded for purposes of edification.

Pp. 240 f., 334, 340.—Except in Schmidt's statement, (*Enc. Bibl.*, 2370) that beyond the preaching of a judgment to come tending to lead men away from their evil doings (xxviii. 8, xxiii. 22) Jeremiah 'seems to have had no eschatology,' and on p. 69 of Wheeler Robinson's *The Cross of Jeremiah*, I have not noticed that any recent commentator or essayist has marked that absence from the Oracles of Jeremiah of all assurance or hope of personal immortality which is emphasised on the above pages. Yet besides what is there stated note how the prophet insists that the strength of the personal life is knowledge of and communion with the Eternal God, and how fearlessly he faced death for himself; from both of which it is not far to the hope of personal immortality.

P. 244, Jer. xxix. 8-14.—The question whether all these verses are genuine or not has given rise to very different opinions among modern critics, and in particular the definite prediction in verse 10 that the exile would last 70 years (cf. xxv. 11) has been both accepted as Jeremiah's and denied to him.

On the one hand, even Kuenen (*The Religion of Israel*, Eng. Trans., Vol. II, p. 72) admitted the genuineness of the prediction of 70 years, and more recently Driver retained all xxix. 1-13 (along with xxv. 11, but not 12-14), and Giesebrecht too (2nd ed.), with the exception of a few clauses. As I have done above, Rothstein takes vv. 8 f. as a later addition and nearly all the rest, even the prediction of 70

years, as genuine and in place. But recently Skinner, Welch
and Volz have revived the objections of some earlier
critics. Skinner reads xxv. 11 after the LXX as simply *they
shall serve among the nations 70 years,* omitting the reference to the King of Babylon, and deletes all of xxix. 8-10
(*Prophecy and Religion,* 240 f., 287.) Welch, *Jeremiah,* 172
ff., dismisses xxix. 10 on the grounds of its 'awkward form,'
and that to promise a return after 70 years 'could only turn
the men's minds away from their present tasks and opportunities.' This is not evident though Volz feels something
similar. In a well-reasoned argument Volz (pp. 268 f. n.)
deletes xxix. 10-11 as breaking the connection between
8 f. and 12, and being at least out of place, even if it were
Jeremiah's own. But, while allowing that the prediction of
a 70 years' exile must be older than Zechariah i. 12 (vii. 5),
519 B.C., and that Jeremiah believed in the return of the
banished Jews, xxiv. 6 f., xxix. 32, he thinks that the force of
these data are overborne by other considerations : the general
one that it is unlikely that Jeremiah who elsewhere always
speaks for the present and sticks to actualities should here
make an utterance without worth or reality for his contemporaries; that xxix. 32 implies that he thought the Return
near enough to be within reach of a living man unless he
were to die prematurely; and that the only natural presumption with regard to xxiv. 5 f. is that Jeremiah associated in
his vision the downfall of Jerusalem and the Return from
Exile, and believed that he would survive both. On these
grounds Volz takes the determination of the extent of the
Exile as 70 years to be the work of a later hand, probably
towards the end of the Exile, which would give time for the
quotation of it by Zechariah 20 years later in 519 B.C.

With all respect for the fairness with which Volz has
presented the reasons both against and for his conclusion,
I must, nevertheless, hold that he has failed in establishing
the latter. His inferences from xxix. 32 and xxiv. 5 are far
from convincing. Though he is right in saying that there is
no connection between xxix. 8 f. and xxix. 10 f. it is more
probable that it is not the latter which are out of place but
the former, as I have said, p. 244, n. 1, and as Rothstein (in

Kautzsch) agrees. Giesebrecht retains the whole passage. Nor need we suppose that Jeremiah meant his 70 years literally and exactly, but merely as a round number or symbol for a long period. On this see Bruston's sensible remarks, *Le Prophète Jérémie et son Temps*, pp. 174 ff., and Giesebrecht on xxix. 10.

Pp. 248 ff., Jer. xxvii-xxviii. 17.—On the date of these see H. Schmidt, Z.A.T.W., Vol. XXXIX, 1921, pp. 138 ff. He concludes that the original date in xxvii. 1 was the seventh year of Zedekiah, 591 B. C.

Pp. 273 ff., Jer. xxxiv. 8-22.—See Giesebrecht (2nd ed.) *in loco,* Horst, *op. cit.,* pp. 128 ff., and Volz *in loco,* where his common sense is evident. Puukko is not convincing when he argues (*op. cit.,* pp. 146 ff.) that we cannot conclude that in those verses Jeremiah was appealing to, or recommending, the Law-book of Josiah, the nucleus of Deuteronomy.

Pp. 276 f., Jer. xxxviii. 1-3.—Note that as against Duhm and Cornill the authenticity of verse 2 with that of xxi. 9— Jeremiah's advice to the citizens to desert the city—which I have maintained as above, is accepted by Bruston, Driver, Giesebrecht (2nd ed.), Peake, Skinner, Volz, Lofthouse, and Welch. And so with the following narrative, 4-13.

P. 284, Jer. xxxvii. 17-21, xxxviii.—As against Skinner's idea that we have in these a duplicated account of the same event, Volz takes them as relating to different events, but he puts them in a different order from that in which they stand in the text, viz. thus: xxxvii. 11-21; xxxviii. 24-28; xxxviii. 1-22.

Pp. 287-289, Jer. xxxii.—On the whole Volz agrees with most moderns as to the composition of this chapter, see p. 287, n. 1. He takes as genuine vv. 1, 7-16, 24 f., as I have done; but he adds as recoverable from the very mixed passage 26-44 these vv.: 26-29, the words *but now* in 36, 42-44. For parallels to the custom here instanced of a double copy of a deed of sale, sealed and open, see Fischer,

Z.A.T.W., 1910, pp. 136 ff.; Johns, *Bab. and Assyr. Laws, Contracts, etc.* p. 12.

Pp. 289 f., Jer. xxxiii.—With Vatke, Stade, Duhm, etc., Volz holds the whole chapter for 'unjeremianisch.' So too Welch.

P. 291, Jer. xxxix. 14.—Volz thinks this contradicts xl. 2, 4, while xxxix. 11 f. readily unites with xl. 2-4. In xl. 1-4, he finds two accounts interwoven: 1 as far as the word *Ramah,* 2b, 3 and 2a, the rest of 1, *and said to him* in 2b, 4.

Pp. 293 ff., Jer. xxx, xxxi.—Volz deems much of the previous criticism of these chapters far too drastic (p. 284) and takes as original (except for some later interpolations) xxx. 1-7; 10 f.; 12-15; 18-21a; xxxi. 2 f.; 4-6 with 9b; 7-9a; 10b-13; 15-17; 18-20; 21 f. with 27b; 31-34; 35-37. There is great difference as to the date of the original elements in these chapters—Cornill before 621 B.C.; Lofthouse (pp. 62 ff. and Append. I) 621-616; Volz early years of Zedekiah. Lofthouse (211) argues against the date I have preferred.

Pp. 304 f., Jer. xxxi. 20.—Cf. J. E. McFadyen, *op. cit.,* p. 229.

Pp. 309 f., Jer. xlii, xliii.—These chapters Volz rearranges thus: xlii. 1-18, xliii. 1-3, xlii. 19-22, xliii. 4-7, 8-13a, (except 11).

Pp. 311-316, Jer. xliv.—Of this composite chapter vv. 3-6 and 10-14 are regarded by Volz as the most distinct additions, but he adds as such 23; *to all the people* in 24, and 28a.

P. 324, Jer. xv. 10-18.—Volz also omits, as I have done, vv. 13 f. and places them with xvii. 3 ff. and omits 21.

P. 329, Jer. xviii. 21-23.—Volz agrees with me in retaining these verses as Jeremiah's, in opposition to Duhm's and Cornill's rejection of them.

P. 333, Jer. i. 17.—Cf. Wheeler Robinson, *op. cit.,* p. 51.

P. 339 f., Jer. xii. 1-6.—Verse 4 is also omitted by Volz,

save for the words, *for they say* (*in their heart*), *He sees not our ways* (sic). But I do not see why he omits verse 3.

P. 341 f., Jer. ix. 2 f.—With a few emendations Volz carries the Ḳinah rhythm through verse 3.

P. 344 ff.—On the Relation of the Prophecy of the Suffering Servant of the Lord, in Deutero.-Isaiah to Jeremiah see among other testimonies that of Wheeler Robinson, pp. 89 f.; also of Volz, pp. 3 f., 213, 215.

P. 350 ff., Jeremiah's Doctrine of God.—On this see among more recent writers Volz, p. XXVII, etc., 'The God of Jeremiah is a wholly personal, wholly human Being.'; Lofthouse, Ch. X.

P. 371, Jer. xxxi. 29 f.—As by some earlier critics this oracle, *the fathers have eaten sour grapes,* etc., is denied to Jeremiah by Volz.

Pp. 374 ff., Jer. xxxi. 31-34, The New Covenant.—As we have seen (p. 399) Volz, in opposition to Duhm and other critics, accepts the authenticity of this famous passage. He deletes from it only the words *and with the House of Judah* in verse 31, and *every man his brother* in 34, and the three instances of *Rede of the Lord.* Welch following Skinner also accepts the passage, but not without sympathy for Duhm's attitude to it.

Note that *the Covenant which I made with their fathers,* etc., in verse 32 is not Deuteronomy but that at Sinai. though, as I have said on p. 377, it was restated and enforced in Deuteronomy.

INDEX OF TEXTS.

(401)　　　26

INDEX OF NAMES AND SUBJECTS.

(407)